Mentoring and Coaching for Lawyers

Building Partnerships for Success

Consulting Editor **Rebecca Normand-Hochman**
on behalf of the International Bar Association

Consulting editor
Rebecca Normand-Hochman on behalf of the International Bar Association

Managing director
Sian O'Neill

Editorial services director
Carolyn Boyle

Production manager
Neal Honney

Group publishing director
Tony Harriss

Mentoring and Coaching for Lawyers: Building Partnerships for Success
is published by
Globe Law and Business
Globe Business Publishing Ltd
New Hibernia House
Winchester Walk
London SE1 9AG
United Kingdom
Tel +44 20 7234 0606
Fax +44 20 7234 0808
www.globelawandbusiness.com

Print and bound by Gomer Press

ISBN 9781909416413

Table of contents

Mentoring, coaching and the practice of law

Rebecca Normand-Hochman
Mentoring Collegium Limited, Institute of Mentoring

1. Introduction

It is common knowledge that artists develop their talent with mentors, that sports people achieve high performance by working closely with coaches (and that many have mentors), and that successful business managers and leaders work with coaches and mentors. So why is it that mentoring and coaching are still mainly viewed as relating to underperformance in the legal profession? Why do so few lawyers value the great talent development opportunities that mentoring and coaching offer in a profession where most of the intangible skills and knowledge are acquired outside formal training?

We know from research that, beyond individual 'Learning Styles',[1] the way we learn best is through personal experience and interacting with others. The average rates of what we remember are found to be 10% of what we read, 20% of what we hear, 30% of what we see, 70% of what is discussed with others, 80% of what we experience personally, 95% of what we teach someone else and 98% of what we teach someone else using questions (inquiry-based approach).

As a chamber music musician, I had the great privilege to have as mentor a respected senior teacher from the Royal Academy of Music in London and her assistant in Paris who both showed me the right techniques, prompted me to try new repertoires and asked me questions that enabled me to build on the initial musical talent that I had.

I have learned from my early years of practising music, and then from practising law, that talent development comes from three sources:

- motivation;
- practice; and
- strong learning partnerships (working with coaches and mentors).

One can ask oneself, what are the reasons that we sometimes learn and sometimes fail to learn? Why are some lawyers skilled at helping others to develop and grow while others are not? Why does mentoring sometimes makes an impact and is sometimes a waste of time? What competencies and conditions inspire insight and understanding?

This chapter attempts to answer these questions by first summarising what all

1 Peter Honey and Alan Mumford, *The Learning Styles Questionnaire*, 80 item version, Peter Honey Publication Limited (2006)

lawyers should know about mentoring and coaching, including their most recent evolutions, then pinning down the essential skills that lawyers need to develop to become great mentors, and finally exploring the opportunities and challenges for developing mentoring in the profession.

I have found since I started to work in mentoring and coaching for lawyers that it is very difficult to talk or write about the subject without being either technical or simply uninteresting. The objective of this project has been to present all aspects of the subject in simple terms and to constantly link it to the challenges and rewards of the practice of law. I hope that you enjoy reading this book.

2. An introduction to coaching and mentoring for lawyers

What follows is what I believe every lawyer should know about coaching and mentoring.

2.1 Why definitions matter

Very few lawyers distinguish mentoring from coaching and there are indeed reasons for that. I have heard many coaches argue that attempting to define both practices is unnecessary, but I am of the strong view that unless the person providing the coaching or mentoring and the person being coached or mentored both understand the nature of their relationship, there is some essential clarity missing which impacts on the quality of the relationship.

Having said that, it doesn't mean that there are universally agreed definitions or that there isn't a big overlap between both types of help.

The reasons for which both types of help are so often confused are numerous and include he following:

- Recent evolutions in both coaching and mentoring have made the distinction less obvious that in the past;
- The skills and techniques that mentors and coaches use are largely the same; and
- The approach to mentoring in the United States and in Europe differ.

(a) Coaching

Coaching is unlocking people's potential to maximise their own performance
– John Whitmore[2]

Coaching in its modern form is increasingly becoming a non-directive type of help, usually from someone who doesn't have the relevant experience and background. The coach explores the issues, challenges and options and helps the person find his/her own solutions.

Coaching came from the sport world. It is in the *Inner Game of Tennis*[3] that Timothy Gallwey, a Harvard educationalist and tennis expert, laid the foundations of modern coaching. The word 'inner' was referring to the player's internal state. Four decades ago, Gallwey wrote: "The opponent within one's own head is more

---

2 John Whitmore, *Coaching for Performance* (Nicholas Brealey Publishing,1992).

formidable than the one on the other side of the net." The Inner Game theory focuses on helping a person remove internal obstacles to his performance instead of providing technical input and remains the foundation of what coaching is today.

(b) Mentoring

Mentoring is off-line help by one person to another in making significant transition in knowledge, work or thinking.
– David Clutterbuck and David Megginson

Mentoring is help from someone who has the relevant background and experience. As well as listening and asking questions that raise awareness, the mentor can give specific guidance and advice based on his expertise and skills.

The term 'mentor' comes from Homer's *Odyssey* and the relationship between Mentor (an incarnation of the goddess Athena) and Odysseus's son Telemachus.

Mentoring is based on the apprenticeship model, which has always been at the heart of the legal profession. It is not so long ago that to become a lawyer, instead of attending law school, which is now a universal requirement to qualify as a lawyer, one had to be mentored by a senior member of the profession for a fixed number of years.

The Personal and Professional Development Department of Cambridge University defines 'mentoring' in a simple way:

Mentoring has been defined in many different ways but it's basically a system of semi-structured guidance whereby one person shares their knowledge, skills and experience to assist others to progress in their own lives and careers.

Mentors very often have their own mentors, and in turn their mentees might wish to 'put something back' and become mentors themselves – it's a chain for 'passing on' good practice so that the benefits can be widely spread.

Mentoring can be a short-term arrangement until the original reason for the partnership is fulfilled (or ceases), or it can last many years.

Mentoring is rather more than 'giving advice', or passing on what your experience was in a particular area or situation. It's about empowering the other person to identify their own issues and goals, and helping them to find ways of resolving or reaching them…

2.2 Coaching versus mentoring[4]

There is in practice a big overlap between coaching and mentoring, especially since mentoring, as explained later in this chapter, is becoming less directive in its modern approach.

Over the last couple of decades, business coaching has evolved to become a flourishing industry with the standards of practice and the accreditation process of coaches being continually researched and refined. Mentoring has seen a much less

3 W Timothy Gallwey, *The Inner Game of Tennis* (Random House, 1974).
4 Adapted from Ellen Van Velsor, Cynthia D McCauley, Marian N Ruderman (Eds), *The Center for Creative Leadership Handbook of Leadership Development* (Jossey-Bass, 2010).

Coaching	Mentoring
Focused on performance improvement and skills development	Focused on career guidance and development
Sets clear, performance-based goals that can be achieved in a relatively short amount of time	Explores and discovers objectives, usually over a longer period of time
In its modern form, based on asking questions that prompt the person to find his own solutions	Mentors also provide guidance based on knowledge, expertise and skills

rapid expansion in businesses and has been little researched as a subject. There are, however, signs that the most progressive companies are now increasingly using mentoring to foster excellence.

It is informative that the British Sport Federation has, alongside its coaching programme, introduced a structured approach to mentoring:

> *... to provide the high performance system with the opportunity to pollinate knowledge across a wide range of sports. In addition, this ensures that the system becomes increasingly self-sufficient, transitioning knowledge and skill rather than solely relying on the services of identified external consultants.*

2.3 Sponsoring

Another type of confusion arises around the distinction between mentoring and sponsoring.

The mentoring function has changed over time and has branched into two distinctive types of relationship. Sponsoring involves proactive, instrumental help to advance a person's career. The traditional model of mentoring based on the apprenticeship model included the sponsorship aspect, but mentoring and sponsoring are now considered as two different types of help. In the United States, most mentoring relationships have a strong element of sponsoring; but in Europe, the sponsoring aspect of mentoring is traditionally less important and often non-existent.

Sponsoring has in the last few years been on the rise, with formal large sponsorship programmes being established in some companies. Their primary objectives are usually to support women and minorities and to increase diversity.

(a) Mentoring/sponsoring and gender balance

Contrary to common belief, research now evidences that mentoring is not instrumental in helping women to access senior management and leadership roles.

Sylvia Ann Hewlett, chief executive of the Centre for Talent Innovation, describes in her latest book[5] why women need sponsors and not mentors to succeed in today's

5 Sylvia Ann Hewlett, *Forget a Mentor, Find a Sponsor* (Harvard Business Review Press, 2013).

corporate world. Ida Abbott[6] more recently also published a book on how sponsoring helps women to achieve career success. The book is particularly interesting as it explains how men play a determining role in promoting sponsorship in organisations. Avivah Wittenberg Cox[7] describes the unquestionable limits that developmental initiatives targeted at women in organisations have. In law firms, after over a decade of having introduced specific mentoring programmes for women, the number of women that are equity partners still represent less than 15% in the big international law firms.

2.4 Recent developments

The shift that occurred from a mostly directive, technical-based type of coaching to a non-directive approach in the 1970s and 1980s has also taken place in mentoring, but in a much less noticed way. Many coaches still refer to mentoring as putting in content, while a mostly non-directive approach to mentoring (also referred to as developmental mentoring) is now the widely acknowledged best practice.

(a) The US approach versus the European approach to mentoring

In the 1980s, Kathy Kram[8] in Boston and David Clutterbuck[9] in London carried out separate academic research and established the foundations of modern mentoring.

Both refer to the developmental form of mentoring, but the US practice of mentoring retains a stronger element of sponsoring than in Europe. Mentors in the United States are usually expected to open doors and use their influence to promote their protégé. Interestingly, the word 'protégé', literally meaning someone who is protected, is still used in the United States but has been replaced by the word 'mentee' in Europe.

(b) The rise of group mentoring, peer mentoring and reverse mentoring

As described in her book on mentoring,[10] Ida Abbott notes that:

> *Today, mentoring encompasses a range of different behaviors, takes many forms (from pairs, to small groups to large structured programmes), and involves mentors and mentees at all career stages. Mentees have several mentors and mentors may have several mentees – all at once or sequentially – each serving a different purpose.*

These newer forms of mentoring are discussed in Part 4 of this chapter.

3. Becoming a skilled mentor

It is often wrongly believed that senior professionals, because of the level of their skills and experience, have the requisite ability to mentor when they decide to do so.

> *Building relationships between humans is a complex process. The mistakes we make in conversations and the things we think we should have said after the conversations are*

---

6 Ida Abbott, *Sponsoring Women: What Men Need to Know* (Attorney at Work/Feldcomm, 2014).
7 Avivah Wittenberg-Cox and Alison Maitland, *Why Women Mean Business* (John Wiley & Sons, 2008).
8 Kathy Kram, *Mentoring at Work: Developmental relationships in Organizational Life* (University Press of America, 1985).
9 David Clutterbuck, *Everyone Needs a Mentor: Fostering Talent in Your Organisation* (Chartered Institute of Personnel Development, 1985).
10 Ida Abbott, *The Lawyer's Guide to Mentoring* (National Association for Law Placement, Inc, 2000).

over all reflect our own confusion about the balancing of asking and telling, and our automatic bias towards telling. The missing ingredient in most conversations is curiosity and willingness to ask questions to which we do not already know the answer.[11]

The skills and techniques involved in modern mentoring are the same as those used by coaches. They are based on questioning and listening techniques and cover a broad spectrum of topics, including setting goals, clarifying and understanding situations, helping the mentee in deciding what to do, and committing to action to ending the relationship. Most mentors in structured mentoring programmes today receive some initial information and guidance about how to mentor.

One of the most widely used tools in coaching is the GROW model established by John Whitmore.[12] GROW is also a model that provides guidance to mentors to help them structure the work with their mentee. GROW stands for:

Goals
Reality
Outcomes
Will

A practical resource that mentors can use is a set of techniques for coaching and mentoring develop by Megginson and Clutterbuck in their book on the subject.[13] The techniques include practical exercises that guide mentors in dealing with each stage of the mentoring relationship and include suggestions on aspects such as how to build self-knowledge, deal with roadblock or end the relationship.

3.1 What makes mentoring successful?

The following is a description of the three key skills that lawyers, because of the way in which they have been trained and the way they work, specifically need to pay attention to and tdevelop in order to enter into and build productive mentoring relationships.

(a) The ability to build trust and rapport

There is in mentoring, as in coaching, an element of what practitioners call 'chemistry' that is involved in the initial stage of building trust and rapport in a mentoring or coaching relationship. Before deciding to embark on a coaching journey, coaches and clients always meet for a 'chemistry meeting' so that both parties can decide whether they want to work together.

Although many mentors recognise the importance of chemistry in mentoring, this is a stage which is sometimes overlooked in formal mentoring. Some programmes even automatically assign a mentor to the mentee without much room for either party to have any say in the matching.

There is a high rate of unsuccessful or unproductive mentoring relationships in

---

11 Edgar Schein, *Humble Inquiry, the Gentle Art of Asking Instead of Telling* (Berrett Koehler Publishers Inc, 1993).

12 See note 2.

13 David Megginson and David Clutterbuck, *Techniques for Coaching and Mentoring* (Elsevier Butterworth Heinemann, 2005).

structured programmes in law firms, and one of the explanations for that is the fact that the chemistry element is not factored in sufficiently at the initial stage. When asked for the reasons why they believe that their mentoring relationship failed, many partners cite the lack of chemistry as an important factor.

It is not unusual for one or more party of a mentoring relationship to want to maintain a high wall around them. The fear of being exposed is a feeling that most of us experience in some circumstances and is a real obstacle to the development of trust.

Confidentiality and boundaries, when discussed at the outset of the relationship, enable mentors and mentees to reconcile the need for openness and rapport with the desire not to venture into personal areas.

Lawyers know confidentiality as one of the most important professional conduct behaviours that is taught in law school and it is applied in everyday practice in relation to clients, colleagues and friends. It is, unsurprisingly, a key aspect of building trust for lawyers that causes issues in some mentoring relationships. The confidentiality rules that need to be agreed between both parties depend on individual needs and contexts.

When lawyers are part of structured programmes managed by HR, there is a greater danger that confidentiality will impede on building trust between mentor and mentee. The rules around what information can end up being fed to HR need to be clearly stated in the programme guidelines. A partner recently described a difficult situation he had to deal with when he spotted clear signs of high levels of stress and depression in his mentee and felt that he had to inform HR so that his mentee could be offered some time off and support. These types of situation required the mentor to make a moral judgment as to what was right or wrong, but any confidentiality agreement should clearly state the circumstances in which both parties agree that information can be provided to a third party.

Rapport is something that lawyers often find difficult to build for a number of reasons. As described in *Managing Talent for Success*,[14] the emotional intelligence that lawyers develop with their training and their years of practice is determined by the technical and intellectually challenging nature of their work. In addition, the highly merit-based culture of many law firms tends to develop strongly individualistic professionals who find it difficult to build rapport in developmental contexts or work in collaborative configurations.

But as Daniel Goleman[15] established in his neuroscience-based research, emotional intelligence is a skill, which can be increased significantly with practice. By working to build trust and rapport with mentees over the course of their careers, some senior lawyers are stretched to develop their emotional intelligence capabilities and develop great mentoring skills.

---

14 Rebecca Normand-Hochman, *Managing Talent for Success* (Globe Law and Business Publishing, 2013).
15 Daniel Goleman, *Emotional Intelligence* (Bantam Books, 1995).

(b) ***The skill to set goals and the flexibility to adapt the goals as the mentoring relationship evolves***

No one would argue about the importance of goal setting in mentoring and coaching and a lot has been written on the subject. One of the main reasons for which coaching and mentoring relationships fail is the lack of clarity about the objectives and goals for the relationship. John Whitmore[16] explains the different types of goals that come into play in performance coaching:

- the goal for the session;
- the end goal; and
- the performance goals.

Coaches invariably start a coaching session by determining a goal for the session itself and good mentors do the same. Questions suggested by John Whitmore that mentors can ask include the following:

- What would you like to get out of this session?
- I have half an hour for this – where would you like to have got to by then?
- What would be the most helpful thing for you to take away from this session?

The distinction between end goals (the final objective) and performance goals (the performance level that you believe will provide you with a good chance of achieving the end goal) is of a sensibly different nature in mentoring relationships, where the focus in on developing and nurturing potential as a whole person and is therefore less directly linked to performance than in coaching.

However, setting the objectives for the relationship is a condition to successful mentoring, but each party must be able to flexibly adapt the objectives as the relationship evolves. The need to adapt goals in mentoring and coaching is discussed in an informative collective book on the subject, *Beyond Goals*.[17]

(c) ***The flexibility to easily move from being directive to non-directive***

Asking questions rather than telling is, unsurprisingly, a very difficult mindset that lawyers need to adopt when they mentor. Mentors cannot consider that their role is to provide advice; instead, they need to ask questions that guide the thinking process and raise awareness. To help mentors ask questions that raise awareness and self-awareness, various tools and manuals, such as the booklet put together by Clutterbuck, *Powerful Questions for Coaches and Mentors*, are found to be very insightful.

The following is a summary of the step-by-step approach to building and managing a mentoring relationship

- Holding a chemistry session.
- Agree the terms, boundaries and confidentiality rules for the relationship.
- Set the general goals for the relationship.
- Set specific goals before each session.

---

16 See note 2 above.
17 Susan David, David Clutterbuck and David Megginson, *Beyond Goals* (Gower Publishing Ltd, 2013).

- Review the relationship every three sessions to manage expectations of both parties.
- Assess whether the objectives will be met within the projected timeline.
- Wind down and ending the relationship.

3.2 The importance of ending the mentoring relationship

Some mentoring relationships fall into disuse and others are concluded deliberately.

Mentoring relationships should, whenever possible, be wound down, but this is often not an easy thing to do. Time, tensions and different personal agendas can easily make mentoring relationships drift apart. Most mentors in the big law firms will have experienced a mentoring relationship that started positively through the launch of a programme, but died over a short period of time.

As related in *Techniques for Coaching and Mentoring*,[18] this can be avoided by ensuring the following:

- a clear agreement about how and when the relationship might end;
- a willingness to revisit and change the agreement;
- a sense of two-way benefit. Mentors usually find that they gain as much as the mentees by asking for feedback on their skills and from being encouraged to seek new insights by the mentee; and
- willingness to confront issues as they occur, particularly when things are getting difficult.

3.3 When mentoring fails

As mentoring relationships are based on mutual trust, a number of problems can occur, including breach of trust, over-reliance, bad advice and an over-controlling mentor. The risks relating to mentoring problems can to a significant degree be minimised with self-awareness and careful planning. How to deal with problems if they arise needs to be agreed between the parties when they start working together.

3.4 Mentoring supervision

It was highlighted in a recent article[19] that:

> *all the coaching professional bodies in Europe and many bodies in other continents require coaches to have supervision. Few corporate buyers of coaching in Europe would hire a coach, who did not have a high level of formal qualification and regular, professional supervision. So why isn't the same expected of mentors?*

Although most mentors are not professional mentors, organisations that introduce mentoring supervision are likely to see the quality of mentoring significantly rise and will provide those being mentored with the assurance that the mentoring opportunities in the firm will be of good standard. Some companies in the United Kingdom and Denmark are already ahead of the game and it is probable that some law firms will follow in the years to come.

---

18 See note 13.

19 David Clutterbuck, "Why mentors need supervision", July 2014, available at www.davidclutterbuckpartnership.com/why-mentors-need-supervision/.

3.5 Some recommended reading

- David Clutterbuck, *Everyone Needs a Mentor: Fostering Talent in Your Organisation*, 5th edn (Chartered Institute for Personnel Development, 2014)
- Ida Abbott, *The Lawyer's Guide to Mentoring* (National Association for Law Placement, Inc, 2000).
- John Whitmore, *Coaching for Performance* (Nicholas Brealey Publishing,1992).
- Anne Scoular, *FT Guide to Business Coaching* (Financial Times/Prentice Hall, 2011).

4. Why law schools, law firms and bar associations should develop more and better mentoring initiatives

The extent to which the legal profession can tap into its talent pool to develop better-equipped professionals relies as much on developmental relationships inside the profession as on conventional training. Yet what can be observed today is the very small attention that legal institutions pay to building the essential intangible skills and knowledge of lawyers through mentoring compared to the vast amount of energy and money being spent on formal training.

In *The Fifth Discipline*,[20] Peter Senge, founder and director of the Society for Organisational Learning and senior lecturer at MIT, describes the means of creating a 'learning organisation'. The five disciplines represent approaches (theories and methods) for developing three core learning capabilities:

- fostering aspiration;
- developing reflective conversation; and
- understanding complexity.

Legal institutions still have to come a long way to become learning organisations in Senge's sense, but enabling mentoring relationships to be built and fostered in law schools, law firms and bar associations will surely be setting those who do so on the right learning journey.

4.1 Opportunities and challenges for growing legal talent

(a) In law schools

A recent roundtable organised by the International Bar Association (IBA) Law Firm Management Committee brought together a number of professors, practitioners and consultants from law schools, business schools, law firms and the Law Society to think about how those engaged in legal education and practitioners can better cooperate and advance the way law is practised today. This was a great topic for discussion and the day proved to be insightful; it led to us making some suggestions about how the IBA could play a role.

When I trained as a lawyer at what was the College of Law (now the University of Law), it was simply unthinkable to be introduced to the profession in ways others

---

20 Peter Senge, *The Fifth Discipline: the Art and Practice of the Learning Organisation*, 2nd Edn (Random House Business, 2006).

than by doing summer placements or having a close member of the family who could provide some first-hand knowledge and information about what a career in law would look like and involve.

Today, some law schools have formal mentoring programmes in place, as the importance of transitioning from law school to law firms has been recognised as one of the critical factors of success for the early stages of a career in law. The opportunity for a law student to be linked to someone who is already practising law cannot be valued enough, as many trainees start with complete ignorance about what a career in law involves.

Law firms sell outstanding professional development opportunities to future trainees at career fairs and on their websites, but the reality is that it is ultimately up to each lawyer to develop, and law firms are not so competent at providing professional development opportunities that fit individual expectations and potential. Law firms, more than other businesses, have huge difficulties creating environments that allow lawyers to develop to their best. Law students therefore need to be absolutely clear about what it takes to have a career in law and working with a mentor during their time at law school can make a significant difference for the rest of their career.

Law school mentoring programmes also allow law firms to benefit from fully informed trainees and reduce the time that it takes for them to become attuned to practising law.

(b) *In law firms*

Although most of the big law firms in the United Kingdom have introduced mentoring in the last decade, research shows that very few create the outcomes that are expected. The reasons why mentoring in law firms often fails are numerous and include:

- lack of clarity regarding the objectives for the programme;
- insufficient senior commitment support;
- insufficient training for mentors;
- no dedicated and competent programme coordinator; and
- failure to monitor or review the programme on a continuous basis.

Research also shows that informal mentoring relationships fail less than formal relationships. In an ideal professional development environment, informal mentoring would be promoted and enhanced by the firm and lawyers would be able to work with a mentor whenever they feel the need to do so. This is, however, rarely the case and this is why programmes are set up – they allow a greater number of people to get engaged in mentoring activities. As suggested by Ida Abbott,[21] there are simple measures that law firms can take to increase informal mentoring, such as:

- identifying potential mentors and mentees (and keeping a list);
- training workshops to teach lawyers mentoring skills and practices (and encourageing all lawyers to attend);

21 See note 10.

- distributing regular written material;
- promoting conferences where mentoring issues are discussed; and
- rewarding outstanding mentors.

Law firms should also take advantage of the very positive developments that mentoring has seen and not rely on mentoring programme designs and practices that are no longer considered state of the art.

While the pairing options of an experienced lawyer with a more junior lawyer remains the most common configuration, many other interesting forms of mentoring can be considered, each serving a different purpose and involving lawyers at various stages of seniority.

Group mentoring: Group mentoring enables one mentor to work with a small group of mentees. This is of particular interest in firms or departments that experience a lack of good mentors or when one particular mentor has specific skills and experience that a number of other lawyers would benefit from. One other significant benefit of group mentoring is that it builds relationships between participants and encourages teamwork and collaboration.

Peer mentoring: The learning dialogue that peer mentoring creates enables lawyers from the same level of seniority to learn from each other. Comparing notes in a specific situation, discussing challenges or ideas, listening and sharing create learning opportunities for lawyers at all levels of seniority and can be done in pairs or in small groups. Lawyers identify professional or business competencies that they are looking to develop or problems they would like to solve and, by meeting regularly to share ideas, strategies and offer encouragement and support, they learn from each other.

(c) In bar associations

Bar associations that run mentoring programmes offer their members the opportunity to accelerate their career, grow their network and take part in the work of the bar in outstanding ways. These programme are usually targeted at junior lawyers as they link newly qualified lawyers with senior lawyers. Some of these programmes are aimed at supporting specific categories of lawyer, such as minorities or lawyers with disabilities. The number of bar associations running mentoring programmes in Europe is still limited, but is much higher in the United States.

Legal mentoring has recently seen exponential growth in North America in bar associations and law courts, which are using mentoring as a way to increase professionalism and ethical standards among practitioners. The National Legal Mentoring Consortium (NLMC) has been instrumental in helping law courts and bar associations to set up mentoring programmes in the last few years and it is now estimated that one-quarter of lawyers are part of a mentoring programme in the United States. The senior management of the NLMC explained that the first programme launched took five years to take off, but then the others that followed the steps were much quicker to be launched and the process is now standardised. A particularly interesting aspect of some of these programmes is the fact that they allow law firms to take part and a lawyer can be paired with a partner from the same firm through the programme run by the bar association. This is a cost-effective way of making mentoring available to a large number of lawyers, as it minimises the running costs associated with the coordination and administrative support required.

A distinctive mentoring initiative: the IBA Law Firm Mentoring Programme

A senior-level mentoring programme is run by the IBA's Law Firm Management Committee to support the creation and development of new law firms around the world. The Law Firm Mentoring Programme links managing partners and senior partners who have law firm management experience and expertise with partners who are in the process of starting or growing a law firm. The initiative was set up in 2009 and upscaled in 2012, and now has around 140 participants from over 30 jurisdictions.

I had the privilege to restructure and lead this mentoring initiative for over two years and have encountered a number of young law firm leaders from countries such as Estonia, Brazil, Honduras, Germany, Spain, Uganda, Nigeria, India and Vietnam demonstrating often extraordinarily innovative ways to practise the business of law internationally. It is as much a productive experience for a young partner to be guided on the development of his firm by someone who has done the journey as it is humbling and informative for a senior partner to discover the objectives and specific challenges that the young partners starting a firm today have and face.

As Okhueleigbe Aikpehae, founder of a law firm in Nigeria, expressed: "I am passionate about law and I am passionate about helping my clients grow their businesses." The vision that he has for his firm in the coming years is an inspiring illustration of what practising law in today's globalised economy is.

Founding or growing a law firm today has little to do with what it was even recently; sharing and developing best practices between generations of partners across jurisdictions creates opportunities for the profession to evolve in positive ways.

5. Conclusion

Imagine a world where most lawyers would be good mentors. It could deal with many of the challenges that the legal industry faces today in relation to talent.

Interestingly, until recently it was believed that success depended on talent first and on motivation second. But in recent years, psychologists have come to believe that this is not the case. "Today, we have compelling evidence that interest precedes the development of talent. It turns out that motivation is the reason that people develop talent in the first place," says Adam Grant in his influential book *Give and Take*.[22]

The war for talent in the legal profession, as in the corporate world, requires companies and firms to attract, develop and retain more highly skilled employees than ever before. With the understanding that we now have of the motivation

22 Adam Grant, *Give and Take* (Viking: Penguin Group, 2013).

drivers and the importance that relationship building plays in individual performance and oganisational success, it is just a matter of time before mentoring and coaching becomes one of the essential tools used to develop talent in law firms. It is my firm belief that the ability of the profession to integrate the most advanced talent management practices is a guarantee that it will be able to best create value for its members, their clients and for society at large.

Mentoring senior lawyers

Heidi K Gardner
Harvard Law School

1. Introduction

Few lawyers would dispute the idea that their firm's greatest asset is its partners. Yet many experienced partners readily admit that even a decade of experience as an associate left them somewhat unprepared for their responsibilities as a newly elected partner. Meeting their business development targets, balancing producer-manager conflicts, negotiating fees with clients and origination credits with other partners, using their expanded autonomy to decide where and how to specialise their practice – all of these tasks can be significant sources of stress and risk for new partners, especially if they lack appropriate guidance. It is surprising, then, how few firms have formalised, structured mentoring programmes focused on supporting the successful transition of newly elected partners.

This chapter focuses on senior-level mentoring within law firms – that is, when a highly experienced lawyer mentors a partner-level colleague. Specifically, it examines how firms can best motivate, equip, support and hold mentors accountable, and uses mentors' and mentees' perspectives to show how senior-level mentoring can become more mutually productive.

Mentors usually start with good intentions, but it is hard to sustain a mentoring relationship unless the mentor understands what he gets out of it. Especially in law firms where partners are under increased performance pressure, partners are likely to ask, "What's in it for me?" But this conversation is rarely explicit. Section 2 focuses on the challenges for mentors to devote sufficient time, energy and attention to the task and clarifies why firms and individuals find it hard to make mentoring senior professionals a top priority. By explicating these challenges, this section aims to make these issues discussable and offers lawyers who are struggling to prioritise mentoring activities a clearer path to resolution.

Section 3 offers a case study of one firm's newly created senior-level mentoring programme, and provides insight on how that firm aligned organisational processes such as performance management, compensation and training to support the programme.

In many firms, no compensation or rewards are associated with mentoring programmes; unsurprisingly, mentoring is seen as an optional activity that people engage in when they can find time. Because the outcomes of mentoring are often intangible or indirect, both individual lawyers and their firms often struggle to understand whether their investment in mentoring actually pays out. Section 4 draws on existing empirical research and new interview data to outline the benefits that can accrue to mentors of senior-level lawyers and provides best-practice examples for ways that firms can underpin partners' mentoring efforts.

Section 5 builds on the 'how to' pieces to offer 10 straightforward lessons for firms that are interested in setting up a senior-level mentoring programme. Because mentoring involves a two-way relationship, this section also discusses ways to ensure the effectiveness of participating mentees as well as mentors.

The chapter considers mentoring that is distinct from other kinds of important relationships for senior attorneys, such as sponsorship and coaching. Specifically, a mentor has relevant expertise that is useful in advising mentees on both professional and non-work issues, but should be a confidential, objective thought partner. In contrast, a sponsor is an advocate and champion for someone else's career progression, and a coach rarely has a relevant background and instead helps someone to identify his or her own challenges, options and course of action. The ideas focus mostly on mentoring aimed at newly elected partners, but the chapter concludes by extending the ideas to suggest other opportunities for firms to increase productivity by mentoring other senior-level members of the firm such as laterally hired partners and high-ranking professional functional staff such as marketing or finance professionals. Today's legal environment demands that firms optimally use of all their knowledge resources, and a senior-level mentoring programme can be an important way to make that happen.

2. Challenges for mentors of senior-level professionals

Today's professionals face two distinct kinds of pressure that affect their willingness and ability to engage in productive mentoring relationships: the pressure to perform to exceedingly high standards, and the pressure to do so within time constraints. Later sections of this chapter cover some of the ways to mitigate these pressures.

2.1 Performance pressure

In today's hyper-competitive marketplace, professional firms and their leaders face unprecedented demands to deliver superior results. The resulting performance pressure can be a double-edged sword: although it often motivates people to ramp up their efforts, my research shows that the pressure to perform exceedingly well drives people to react in ways that are ultimately counterproductive.[1]

Mentoring in law firms is directly affected by performance pressure. Performance pressure breeds anxiety and arousal, which makes people risk averse and extremely task focused. This mindset affects not only the way lawyers under pressure allocate time for mentoring, but also the way they interact with others, including mentees.

First, anxious individuals retreat naturally to activities in their comfort zone. For many lawyers, this means focusing on intellectual rather than interpersonal tasks. Further, pressure increases people's needs to take defensible and easily justified actions, which means that lawyers will focus their time on client-related tasks rather

1 For more on the causes, consequences and handling of performance pressure, see H K Gardner, "Coming Through When It Matters Most: How Great Teams Do Their Best Work Under Pressure", (2012) 90(4) *Harvard Business Review* 82.

than non-billable ones. Performance pressure thus reduces the likelihood that lawyers engage in mentoring.

Second, the higher the pressure, the less effective lawyers are when they do engage as mentors. Most people facing performance pressure become more directive and less open to novel inputs, inhibiting their ability to hear mentees' true concerns. Indeed, senior mentees are likely to increase their mentors' stress levels by raising issues that personally and professionally challenge the mentor. For example, a partner-level mentee may raise doubts about their desire to continue the slog towards equity partner and want to explore the benefits of going in-house or joining a lower-pressure boutique firm. To discuss these options objectively, a mentor must be open-minded about the trade-offs and not see the ideas as a threat to their own identity and a challenge to the many sacrifices made along their journey to equity partner. This conversation is especially difficult for a pressured mentor who is prone to filter incoming ideas through the lens of his own experience (because that is his comfort zone and helps to lower his own anxiety). A pressured mentor is thus less likely to engage productively in conversations that raise doubts about his own choices and therefore increase his anxiety.

2.2 Billable hours

A requirement for lawyers to earn fees by billing their time to clients affects mentoring in two important ways. First, it affects their rational motivation to mentor others. Research shows that people who account for their time on time sheets see a greater time-money connection and are therefore less willing to volunteer their time. Especially for lawyers, the requirement to bill time in short increments causes them to have the opportunity costs of their time chronically salient. They begin to judge everything through the lens of productivity. Because the benefits of mentoring (discussed below in section 4) are often long term and less tangible, mentoring becomes a low priority based on its effects on extrinsic motivation.

Second, the demands of the billable hour culture affect one's intrinsic motivation to mentor. Lawyers who have learned to see time as a commodity typically get less enjoyment from activities that they would normally enjoy. For example, research shows that people who are hyper-aware of the value of their time get less pleasure from great art or classical music than others. Therefore, even if someone normally undertakes mentoring for its psychological rewards – as in, to feel connected to others or to give back to the firm – the stress of making one's billable hours target may undermine that intrinsic motivation and decrease the lawyer's participation in mentoring.[2] Understanding what value the mentor receives from the relationship, covered in section 4 below, may help a time-pressed lawyer to see the returns to time invested in mentoring.

3. Case study of one firm's partner-level mentoring programme

A T Kearney is a global management consulting firm that has made significant progress in implementing a senior-level mentoring programme. This section

2 See Pfeffer & DeVoe 2010.

describes A T Kearney's initiative, which it calls the "Adviser Programme", to distinguish it from its formal mentoring programme for associates. Many law firms might recognise the similarity to challenges they face in trying to provide appropriate mentoring support for their partners. This case study outlines the role of advisers and some of the organisational processes, such as performance management and training, that make the Adviser Programme viable. A T Kearney has also tackled the challenges of supporting pre-partner associates who need both mentors to provide off-the-record advice and sponsors to guide and champion them through the partner election process. The three-tiered system of mentors, sponsors and advisers could be readily applicable to many law firms interested in a holistic approach to support their professionals.

3.1 Challenges leading to a revamped approach at A T Kearney

The need for a more holistic approach to mentoring became clear from challenges in developing three kinds of professional within A T Kearney: associates, newly elevated partners and laterally hired partners.

(a) Associates

The career path at A T Kearney is similar to that of many law firms: associates join either right after graduate school or after some experience in a comparable firm, and spend roughly eight to 10 years climbing the ranks. Typically upon entering the firm, associates are assigned a formal mentor to help them navigate choices in their first few years. After a while, associates tend to seek informal guidance from partners who are more closely aligned to their chosen field of specialty or perhaps who just click with more them as people. Previously, as associates approached the partnership window, these more senior individuals often played a dual role of mentoring the associates and championing them for promotion. This blurring of roles meant that associates may have hesitated to initiate any conversations that made them appear less competent or committed with their mentor, who was supposed to play an advocacy role in advancing the junior's reputation with the promotion committee.

(b) Newly elevated partners

Successful associates can be promoted to partner based on their track record of client and team leadership, and their potential for continued business development. Just as in many law firms, newly elected partners at A T Kearney were historically expected to handle the job on their own without much in the way of formal support. As one partner said: "We made an implicit assumption that they knew everything they needed to know." Newly elevated partners who had questions or needed advice typically relied on their prior mentors or turned to the partner who had sponsored them in the election process.

(c) Laterally hired partners

Also like the legal sector, consulting has seen a steep rise in the mobility of partners between firms. A T Kearney also hires highly accomplished partners from the external market. Although the firm had programmes in place to help integrate lateral hires upon entry, many would have benefited from a mentor within the firm to provide ongoing advice and support after the integration period.

Recognising the importance of mentoring for both newly elected and newly joined partners, A T Kearney had made various attempts to create a formal mentoring programme for these individuals. But according to one partner: "There had been no formal incentives for mentor to do a good job, nor for mentees to use them." The best-intentioned programmes tended to fizzle out.

3.2 Advent of the Adviser Programme

To fill the demand for mentors, several experienced partners began informally counselling more junior partners. Talking to many of the juniors nearly every week, these informal mentors amassed a following of colleagues and played significant roles in their development as successful partners. But the sort of mentoring had happened only organically, and the firm needed to formalise and orchestrate it.

In 2010, A T Kearney formally initiated its Adviser Programme. Every newly elected partner and every laterally hired partner is paired with an adviser – someone who has been a partner for at least eight to 10 years. After debating whether people should be allowed to select their own partner, A T Kearney decided that a mentee can have input into the selection, but not the final choice of adviser. This approach was meant to guard against the temptation of new partners selecting powerful rainmakers or people they were close to, but who didn't have the competence or independence that a mentor needs.

The firm recognises that not all partners are capable of or interested in being advisers, and offers alternative development-focused activities that capitalise on partners' strengths.

3.3 Role of the adviser

The adviser's role is designed to be completely different from a formal reporting relationship. The adviser is supposed to provide objective, non-judgemental advice on any issues on a new partner's mind, such as, "Should I focus my practice on this or that specialty area?" or "How would you think about developing a client pitch in these circumstances?" or "What's the best way to approach Partner X who leads the type of client team I'd like to get involved with?"

To provide the best advice to a mentee, advisers need to be highly informed about the area where the mentee is working – for example, by holding frequent conversations with the mentee's practice group. One partner explained: "A good adviser needs to be a 'busy body' – constantly in dialogue to understand how others view the mentee, identify any issues and opportunities, and be proactive in helping the mentee make decisions."

A T Kearney expects advisers to engage often with mentees. One partner stated: "Frequency is expected, but we don't define it specifically. I believe it should be at least monthly – more often than that if you're both in the same office and practice." After a few years of very steady interaction, the frequency of conversations typically tends to diminish. Another partner described this transition that happened over a five-year period with one of his newly elected partner mentees: "We started talking once monthly, then once every two months, now quarterly. Plus we have another four to five interactions on specific things he might want to ask about in between structured, scheduled meetings."

The requirement that advisers have at least almost a decade of partner experience, coupled with the reality that not everyone has the capability or motivation to be an adviser, means that those who play this role often have upwards of six or eight mentees. One partner with nearly three decades of experience at A T Kearney reported having 12 to 14 formal mentees, plus another dozen informal ones. On average, advisers tend to spend about two hours per week on mentoring new partners. As one said: "It's a big investment, but if you don't have frequent enough interaction then you don't have enough insight to provide solid advice."

3.4 Organisational process to support the Adviser Programme

(a) Performance metrics and compensation

A T Kearney needed to change its performance management system both to set targets related to mentoring and to hold mentors accountable. In their former model, no penalty existed for bad mentors. Some partners had the right skills, but lacked the motivation because there was no incentive – the opportunity costs were too high to engage in a non-valued activity when they could have spent the time building their accounts.

In contrast, the present system involves an objective-setting process that includes targets related to commercial success as well as some related to firm-building activities, and a compensation system aligned with those metrics. In the process A T Kearney has redefined the meaning of 'best' partners. Now, the highest-paid partners are those who both generate revenue and help younger partners be more successful. Both parts are necessary. One partner explained: "If you can make rain, you'll be very competitively paid. But if you can do that and make someone else successful, then you'll get outsize compensation. This is fair because you're not only making your numbers, but also getting credit for indirectly helping other partners deliver more revenue to the firm."

It is important to note that the firm does not need every partner to become a senior-level mentor. Instead, they identify those partners with the strengths and desire for mentoring, and then give them very explicit objectives about making mentees successful. Those partners who are not as capable of advising have other ways to fulfil the objective of contributing to others' success. For example, partners who keep a lot of junior people staffed and teach them how to do good work will also get rewarded at the same high level as a good adviser.

Through its revised performance metrics and compensation, A T Kearney signals that the firm values mentoring enough to reward partners accordingly. One partner explained: "In a tie between two partners who are equally successful commercially, then the one who is better at developing peers will win."

(b) Formalised training and support

A T Kearney runs an 'Adviser 101' orientation in which successful advisers train others on the basics of mentoring. The objective is to make mentors highly fluent with things that will touch partners, such as understanding how to set appropriate objectives and knowing what resources exist. The programme covers topics such as what success looks like for a long-term partner and how to help someone who is starting to struggle professionally. The training programme also shares practical approaches for helping mentees to become more successful, such as attending an account review with them.

Overall, the training programme helps to guide partners towards a shared vision so that their guidance of mentees is more consistent. Previously, some advice might have been good in an abstract sense; but if it was not aligned with the firm's strategy, then following it would have been counter-productive for the mentee. At present, the firm is also designing a training programme for advisers focused on the broad theme of "What does it mean to make others better?" Participants will focus on their own leadership behaviours and styles, learning to lead through influence rather than power. The aim is to help advisers learn how to be more suggestive and less directive in their interactions with mentees. (See point 9 in the final section, below, for more on the core skills that are important for mentors).

3.5 Sponsorship programme for senior associates

Aside from the Adviser Programme for partners, A T Kearney has developed a formal sponsorship programme to address senior associates' need for support which is distinct from that provided by a mentor. The firm recognises the need for sponsorship in addition to mentoring. For example, like most professional service firms, it faces a dearth of women at partnership level and wants to ensure that its professionals have strong mentors as well as champions. Sponsorship is different from mentoring, in that sponsorship requires advocacy of a candidate, whereas mentors provide unbiased, confidential guidance that may extend far beyond the bounds of discussing an associate's promotion inside the firm.

The crucial issue is to separate the roles of the mentor versus the sponsor, so that the senior professional, the junior professional and others in the firm understand their position. Mentors should be the first to be called when others get the sense that an associate will not be promoted. If the senior is playing a mixed role of sponsor and mentor, others may be reluctant to call him and give him the honest bad news about 'his candidate.' If they understand that his objective is to help the junior correct issues or consider alternative paths, they may be more open to making a phone call that suggests, "Why not help them to move on?" The mentor needs to be, and to be seen as, an honest broker.

From the perspective of the junior, it is essential to know that it is safe to approach the mentor if he is questioning whether he can make it. In most instances, associates know before leaders that they are unlikely to get elected – maybe they are not motivated enough or maybe they are pulled towards an attractive alternative. The mentor should be the first person who can have a conversation about options: "How can you turn the situation around? What are the alternatives? Let's talk about external options for the next phase of your career." But if the partner is also supposed to play an advocacy role in championing the junior's reputation, those honest conversations get stymied. A T Kearney's creation of two distinct roles – mentor and sponsor – eliminates this tension and promotes more genuine support for senior associates.

3.6 Results so far

A T Kearney now has many dozens of partners who have benefited from the Adviser Programme. Many credit their advisers not only for contributing to their financial and client-related success, but also for making them feel more attached to the firm and satisfied as professionals.

The programme is unlikely to have succeeded had A T Kearney not aligned some of its key organisational processes to support it. The story of one partner who changed his behaviours illustrates the importance of taking a holistic organisational approach. This partner was historically a high biller with little regard for mentoring activities, who relished the prestige of being seen at the top of A T Kearney's ratings. Even if the firm had implemented a bonus for mentoring, he would have been unlikely to change his behaviour because he was already earning significant sums. Because A T Kearney implemented a multi-faceted review that requires partners to engage in both client service and people development, however, he could no longer be ranked in the elite tier with billings alone. His desire to maintain his reputation as a top player now motivates him and he is becoming a well-regarded mentor. As one leader said: "The financial incentive alone would not have been enough to make him switch behaviours and priorities. Maybe we would have made progress with that one lever, but he would not be as far along."

A T Kearney is now rolling out the Adviser Programme for lateral hires. It has reportedly become a successful marketing tool to attract them. "The message we send to the market," said one leader, "is, 'Look at the support we give you to make you successful upon joining.' And since laterals value that, we've been able to attract higher-calibre candidates."

In summary, the critical success factors for A T Kearney's Adviser Programme included the following:

- clearly defined mentoring competencies supported by bespoke training which clarifies the 'advisory' aspect of role;
- clearly articulated expectations for mentors and mentees, backed up by a performance management system adapted to hold people accountable for mentoring activities, together with alternatives for people who are not well suited as mentors;
- cultural change which emphasises the importance of developing others and creates the expectation that junior partners avail themselves of mentoring, highlighting that mentoring is not a remedial or punitive approach; and
- case studies of successful mentoring to reinforce behavioural change.

4. Benefits for senior-level mentors and best practice to underpin them

Mentoring senior-level lawyers is time and energy intensive, and as discussed in section 2, it is especially challenging for professionals facing high performance pressure or in a billable-hours environment. It is unsurprising, therefore, that many partners ask themselves: "What's in it for me?" This section focuses on the benefits of mentoring for the mentors themselves and discusses these benefits broadly in order of least to most tangible. Each subsection also includes best-practice examples for firms to support partners' mentoring efforts. The section concludes by suggesting ways that senior-level mentoring can be an important source of competitive advantage for firms that invest in formalising their programmes and making them effective.

4.1 Altruism

(a) *Results*

For some people who were beneficiaries of great mentoring, the feeling of developing others is a way to pay back. This type of involvement is truly altruistic, and for a limited number of people that motivation is itself enough to keep them involved. One partner said: "I'm head of our IP group and my client billings are well into the seven figures. But there's no way I'd be here if the former practice head hadn't taken me under her wing. I feel accountable for paying that back by bringing up the next generation."

The sense of helping to build one's institution through mentoring is an altruistic motive that kicks in for some partners who are approaching retirement. One senior explained: "I served my firm and my clients for decades, but I think my real, lasting legacy is going to be the dozens of capable lawyers I mentored."

Research suggests that altruism also has self-gratification rewards. Ghiselin's rhetoric – "Scratch an 'altruist' and watch a 'hypocrite' bleed'" – is the cynical way to look at it. But recent neuroscientific research suggests that there are positive physiological responses to altruistic acts, suggesting that humans respond to giving in similar ways that they react to other pleasurable activities.[3] In short, for some people the intrinsic rewards of mentoring – 'it feels good' – is a strong enough rationale for engaging.

(b) *Best practices*

The best firms recognise the efforts of these pro-social mentors through symbolic gestures that highlight their importance to their fellow partners. One firm, for example, bestows a chairman's award at the annual partner conference to partners who have contributed significant time and energy to mentoring over many years.

4.2 Personal gratification

(a) *Results*

Some partners consider mentoring to be important because it provides personal gratification. One said: "It's fun. The younger partners are thankful for our help, and we all need positive feedback. It's more likely to come from mentees than clients, so there's self-satisfaction from it." Mentoring can also bring reputational rewards within the firm. As seen in the case of A T Kearney discussed above, becoming a high-

---

3 M D Lieberman, *Social: Why our Brains are Wired to Connect* (Crown Publishers, New York, 2013).

profile, sought-after mentor to a wide range of up-and-coming partners allows people to transcend from being 'high performers' to being 'most admired colleagues.' One lesson for other firms is that it is essential to have a culture that admires people as 'better' when they drive performance not just through solo efforts, but also by making others better.

For some mentors, the personal benefits flow from their increased sense of cohesion in the firm. Through mentoring they enhance their connection with the colleagues whom they mentor, and they get the opportunity to deepen their own relationships with their mentees' practice heads or other colleagues with whom they interact on behalf of their mentees. "Fostering relationships among others is a form of compensation," said one partner. "At my level, it's impossible to make enough to offset the sacrifices that come with the job. You have to get some emotional gratification and for me, that joy came from mentoring."

(c) ***Best practices***

The best firms reinforce these intrinsic benefits of mentoring by finding ways to make it easier for mentors to engage. For example, one firm with an in-house dining room gives vouchers for mentoring lunches; another gives mentors gift cards to the local coffee bar to host their meetings with mentees. One firm reserves a comfortable office in the chairman's suite for mentoring meetings, and the added bonus for both mentors and mentees is the opportunity to casually bump into the firm's most senior leader before or after their meeting.

4.3 Learning

(a) ***Results***

A somewhat more tangible set of rewards for senior-level mentors comes from learning concrete tactics, tools and techniques from a younger set of partners. One prime area these days relates to the use of social media. For example, one senior partner who had authored a white paper described how his mentee coached him to use a range of online media approaches to publicise his report: "Imagine this – I thought I was going into the meeting with my mentee to show her the advantages of writing such papers, and instead she tutored me on social media!" Those who mentor newly elected partners are often similarly rewarded with access to new ideas and information, especially when their mentees are in different practice groups. "None of us can keep up with all the advancements in our own specialty, let alone others," said one partner. "But in my conversations with mentees I regularly learn about important trends in their field that keep my own work fresh and up to date." Mentoring other partners also provokes self-reflection; research shows that reviewing and thinking about one's work can boost performance,[4] but today's lawyers are so pressed for time that they are unlikely to do so unless prompted. Finally, the core clients of many senior partners are of similarly advanced age and career status;

---

4 Di Stefano, Gino, Staats and Pisano, "Learning by Thinking: How Reflection Improves Performance", HBS Working Paper Number: 14-093 (2014).

mentoring newly elected partners provides them with both contacts and ways of engaging the next generation.

(b) *Best practices*

Firms should help to foster these mentoring relationships that bridge generational, practice or geographic boundaries by offering easy-to-use tools such as videoconferencing, virtual meeting spaces and shared calendars. Depending on the technical savvy of the firm's older partners, they may also need to train mentors on using these tools.

4.4 Networking

(a) *Results*

Business development thrives on networking. My research shows that the more that partners collaborate with colleagues – that is, work on joint client matters or team up to pitch for new work – the more likely they are to get work referred to them from others in the firm. Collaborating helps lawyers to spread their reputation not only as legal experts, but also as high-integrity, helpful colleagues. This level of familiarity among partners generates trust that leads to referrals not only from direct collaborators, but also from those with whom the collaborator has spoken. The financial benefits of collaboration are significant and extend for years.[5]

Mentoring partner-level colleagues provides a similarly excellent networking opportunity. As one partner said: "As a mentor, if you meet frequently enough, then you'll be aware of the client situations that your mentee works on. By being aware, you'll be better placed to help on those clients. It generates additional opportunities. The mere fact of being exposed to opportunity gives more chances to help." Mentoring is a way of connecting people who normally work with quite different sets of colleagues – for example in different practice groups or offices. Research shows that relationship with these 'distant ties' can be especially valuable for accessing novel information and getting introduced to people who are outside one's own sphere of familiarity.[6]

(b) *Best practices*

Firms with organisational systems to support collaboration – for instance, incentive systems that reward for cross-selling, training that develops partners' capabilities for generating multi-practice work – will enhance the networking benefits for mentors and mentees.

4.5 Pipeline

(a) *Results*

One senior-level mentor recounted: "If you do it over time, you build very special

---

5 Heidi K Gardner, "Effective Teamwork and Collaboration" in R Normand-Hochman (Ed) *Managing Talent for Success: Talent Development in Law Firms* (London: Globe Business Publishing Ltd, 2013), pp 145–159.

6 Cross, 1997.

relationships. I mentored one income partner for about five years before he left for an in-house role. It was difficult decision for him and for me. But I remained his mentor and now he's one of our firm's largest clients. It's a very satisfactory relationship that provides a lot of value, including to me." Although the level of payout for a mentoring relationship may be rare, many senior-level mentors benefit from developing other partners who are capable of supporting the mentor's client service in high-quality ways. Some mentors hesitate to work directly with mentees out of caution for preserving their objectivity, but they still benefit from having a trusted set of capable mentees who provide referrals to other partners or business development opportunities, talk through legal issues and offer a sounding board for the mentor.

(b) Best practices

The best firms help mentors to maintain lasting relationships with mentees by making it straightforward for them to stay in touch – for example, by reserving ample slack time for informal meetings during annual partner retreats. Most people find that occasional opportunities for face-to-face meetings are essential for sustaining their post-mentoring relationship, and firms need to support these efforts.

This section has focused on the ways that senior-level mentors can reap significant benefits, ranging from intangible to concrete. Law firm leaders should recognise that these individual-level outcomes roll up into concrete advantages for the firm, too, even though the direct 'return on investment' may be hard to quantify. For example, people who are more emotionally connected to their firm and to their colleagues tend to be more loyal, more creative and more productive. In many instances, the cost of recruiting, hiring, and training a single lateral partner outweigh the direct expense of starting a senior-level mentoring programme. The value of increasing cross-selling within the firm almost certainly offsets the outlay for training partners to sustain productive mentoring relationships.

5. Top 10 lessons for a successful mentoring programme

Firms that take senior-level mentoring seriously treat it as a fundamental way of operating and work to embed mentoring in their culture, client service and core organisation processes such as performance management. Mentoring relies on a two-way relationship, and this section discusses ways to ensure the effectiveness of participating mentees as well as mentors. The case study of A T Kearney, above, provides important lessons, and other best practice approaches were discussed in the preceding section on the benefits of mentoring. Overall, there are 10 crucial takeaway points for law firms that are interested in setting up a senior-level mentoring programme, which are set out below.

5.1 Kicking off an initiative

Firms need high-level champions to support a mentoring initiative designed for their senior professionals. Although newly promoted partners may well recognise their own need for additional guidance and objective advice, firms may need to overcome more experienced partners' assumptions that "If I did it on my own, they'll be able to figure it out, too." The most committed and convincing champions are likely to be those partners who are already engaged in productive mentoring relationships. Firms can start by formalising those relationships and building out from that core. As with any change initiative, finding the 'hidden influencers' is essential for building commitment. In professional firms, partners often turn to high-status colleagues such as rainmakers to seek their opinions about new initiatives; gaining the buy-in from some of those individuals is crucial in helping to build momentum for a senior-level mentoring initiative.[7]

Many firms find it useful to start small, by piloting a prototype programme, then reviewing, improving and communicating its successes before the wider roll-out. As suggested below, getting the early support of high-status partners provides a big boost to the programme's credibility.

5.2 Leading the programme

Firms need a committee comprising well-regarded partners to lead the mentoring programme; the responsibility cannot be delegated to support staff alone. The committee initially needs to make decisions (or proposals to their executives) about issues covered below such as standards, accountability and training. Over time, the committee needs to review these processes to ensure that mentoring remains a high-priority activity for both mentors and mentees. After each round of partner elections, and ongoing for lateral hires, someone from the committee must work on matching these newcomers with appropriate mentors.

5.3 Selecting mentors

Not every partner is suited to be a senior-level mentor. Effective mentors need not only enough experience, but also sufficient capabilities and motivation to handle situations that are ambiguous or that challenge their own ways of working. Mentors need to be comfortable taking an approach based more on inquiry than advocacy. As one long-term mentor stated: "The more senior your mentee, the less professorial you can be as a mentor. Less 'You're going to the dentist to get drilled and this is how to be prepared,' and more 'What are your concerns and what strengths can you leverage?'" Mentors also need to commit sufficient time and energy to a task where the pay-out is hard to quantify. On the mentee side, the programme should be open to all partners who want to participate, but their ongoing involvement should hinge on their willingness to engage fully in the relationship.

5.4 Setting standards

To develop a consistent level of quality that is high enough to sustain a senior-level mentoring programme, firms must set appropriate standards for mentors and mentees. Frequency of interaction matters, although the exact amount depends on a mentee's needs. One successful mentor drew an analogy to raising his children:

---

7 H K Gardner and J S Bunderson "Informal Conversations and the Diffusion of Buy-in to Planned Organizational Change: Insights from a Professional Service Firm", Working Paper (2014) – contact author.

"When my children were small, I had to work with them every day to explain hundreds of small things that build a foundation. Now they're in their 20s and the interactions are much less frequent but the topics are much meatier. Nonetheless, we still need regular, face-to-face time in order to stay in touch properly. At all times, it's vital that they know I'm there when they need me."

A T Kearney found that monthly discussions were right for newly elected partners, and that they typically decreased to quarterly within four or five years. All partners must understand that mentors are expected to be deeply involved in their mentee's professional lives – like the 'busy bodies' mentioned at A T Kearney – in order to give them the best guidance and help them to spot opportunities. Partners should be candid with mentors and ideally proactively reach out to mentors to provide useful information about mentees. Mentees should commit to standards that make the relationship mutually productive: professionalism in setting and communicating an agenda for mentor meetings (eg, "Here are the three topics I hope to discuss in our upcoming call"), sufficient reflection before meetings to be able to discuss issues deeply, openness to feedback, reciprocity in helping their mentor to grow and develop, and so on. Standards that promote rich, open dialogue as an outcome are more helpful than prescriptive standards about inputs.

5.5 Establishing accountability

For those who commit to involvement in a senior-level mentoring programme, make it serious. When faced with performance pressure, lawyers need a reason to invest valuable time in non-client activities. The best firms will include mentoring as part of their partner appraisal process, and link valued rewards to achievement of specific mentoring-related metrics. Firms can choose to measure inputs such as number of meetings or time spent; the metrics are clear, but the trade-off is that quality is not measured, and the standards should vary depending on the needs of the mentee. A more robust and involved system measures outputs. A T Kearney, for example, uses peer feedback for those who are paired up; both the mentor and mentee rate each other's effectiveness using the firm's formal evaluation system. The mentoring committee should be responsible for flagging accountability issues and having the conversations with affected parties to understand the root causes of underperformance.

5.6 Using carrots and sticks

Accountability metrics need to have teeth. Firms that measure mentoring against agreed metrics can include it into the compensation system. But the benefits of financial rewards for mentoring are primarily symbolic: the firm can use a bonus to signal the importance of mentoring, but the money is unlikely to truly pay for the lawyer's investment. Using mentoring as a core component of one's overall performance ranking is a powerful way to demonstrate the firm's commitment. At A T Kearney, for example, partners cannot be designated in the highest performer category unless they make a substantive contribution to developing others. Leaders need to hold difficult conversations with any partners who are underperforming, and remove from the mentoring programme those who are unwilling or unable to improve. Additional non-financial, symbolic rewards for genuinely excellent mentoring are likely to carry significant weight, especially when they are publicly celebrated. One of the biggest risks, however, is rewarding the wrong partners; firms must seek mentees' views of excellent mentors or risk creating deep cynicism by praising partners who are less than ideal mentors.

5.7 Matching mentors and their partner-level mentees

A partner from the mentoring leadership committee should play a large role in helping to match newly elected or lateral partners with mentors. One important criterion is the compatibility of both individuals' experiences. As one partner said: "It has to be obvious how the mentor can add value." Although mentees should have a voice in suggesting appropriate mentors, the firm should facilitate the matching process to avoid overloading any one partner and to acknowledge the reality that new partners may lack some important perspective about what they will need in their new role and who might best provide it.

5.8 Clarifying roles

In some firms, senior-level mentors provide advice and guidance based on the issues that mentees raise. Elsewhere, firms expect senior-level mentors to take a more active role in preparing newly elected partners for their role – for example, by providing hands-on training and apprentice opportunities in business development, client relations or team leadership. Both mentors and their mentees need to know what to expect and how to engage. It is also essential to distinguish senior-level mentoring from other support roles such as that of partners who sponsor senior associates in their journey towards promotion.

5.9 Training mentors

Senior-level mentors benefit from training. All mentors should participate in some joint development activity in order to build shared mental models about the purpose of the programme and how it supports the firm's strategic objective. Standards should be reinforced, ideally by having partners roleplay both typical and tricky scenarios. In addition, some mentors need further help in learning mentoring-related skills such as holding difficult conversations, employing inquiry versus advocacy or using virtual communication tools. If mentoring training is voluntary, the risk is that the partners who need it most fail to sign up. Some of the core skills that need to be covered in the training include the following:

- clarifying objectives – with the mentee, agree what success looks like;
- planning – decide the number, frequency, location, goals and structure of meetings;
- listening and reflecting – know when to advise, question, probe, challenge or simply listen;
- holding difficult conversations – how to handle topics that make the mentor uncomfortable;
- exploring options – provide advice based on experience and expertise; and
- closing a meeting – clarify next steps, what to achieve, and how the mentor can provide support in the meantime.

5.10 Sustaining relationships

Like a marriage, a strong mentoring relationship requires ongoing commitment and occasional special events to rekindle the fire. Firms must make it as trouble free as possible for mentors and mentees to engage productively – for example, by offering simple tools such as videoconferencing, virtual meeting spaces, and shared calendars. Online firm directories must always be up to date and easily searchable by practice and office so that mentors easily can find and contact their mentees' colleagues. Firms should not wait for an annual event to celebrate excellent mentors: include a blurb in the firm's monthly newsletter about great mentoring relationships and have the managing partner write an occasional email thanking excellent mentors for their efforts. There is almost no substitute for face-to-face contact: firms must invest in regular partner retreats with ample time for mentoring meetings.

6. Conclusion

In today's hyper-competitive world, no organisations can afford to under-leverage their resources. Manufacturers frequently retool inefficient plants, airlines continually revamp routes and pricing to maximise passenger yield, and retailers use sophisticated algorithms to optimise staffing of sales associates at peak times. Why, then, should law firms not implement a fairly basic programme that has proven effective in enhancing the value of its partners?

Admittedly, multiple challenges exist in developing and implementing a senior-level mentoring programme. But this chapter provides guidance for firms to overcome these issues and create, or improve the quality of, their senior-level mentoring. Given the increased performance pressure and billable hours mandates in many firms, leaders must acknowledge that their most experienced partners have some right to question the benefit of devoting their time and energy to mentoring other partners. Especially in rapidly expanding, commercially oriented firms, the overall culture of apprenticeship and perhaps even true partnership is dissipating; no longer can leaders simply implore partners to 'do the right thing' for the collective benefit. Even if partners initially engage in senior-level mentoring, an 'altruistic' relationship is unlikely to last indefinitely.

Leaders and firms need to underpin the intrinsic benefits that senior-level mentors enjoy with some extrinsic motivators and formal structures to embed mentoring in their culture, client service and core organisation processes such as performance management. Some of the motivational tools outlined in this chapter are simple and nearly costless, such as a managing partner's one-minute email thanking a valuable senior-level mentor. Others require greater commitment and sustained support, such as training mentors on core interpersonal skills and holding them accountable for the quality of their mentoring relationships.

Overall, this chapter recommends that firms build a context and culture where high-quality senior-level mentoring thrives, rather than advocating direct financial rewards. As one senior partner commented: "I think it's important to help instil the right partner behaviours for mentoring. But at the end of the day, my gut says that this is something that people do for the love of their firm, the love of the people they work with. In a certain respect, partners need to do it in spite of other things and hope it works out. They do it because they enjoy doing it and enjoy the results. If you try to instil some concrete way to incentivise them, it then can be counterproductive." Leaders can help mentors to see the value they can get from mentoring by discussing the benefits such as learning and networking, outlined in section 4 above. In addition, selecting qualified and motivated senior-level mentors and finding other roles for lawyers with different priorities will go a long way towards making the programme successful.

This chapter has focused primarily on senior-level mentoring aimed at newly elected partners, but it is important to acknowledge that lawyers – like all other professionals – are likely to benefit from mentoring throughout their career. Senior-level mentoring is especially beneficial when lawyers change roles – for example, when they take on the leadership role of a practice or geography and need to handle profit and loss responsibility, develop strategy and resolve peer-to-peer conflicts. Likewise, laterally hired partners need significant mentoring long past their initial onboarding period; firms that develop a successful senior-level mentoring programme for laterals are more likely to get a return on the significant investment they made in recruiting talent from outside. In-house legal departments could similarly benefit from implementing senior-level mentoring programmes for their lawyers, not only to help people with the significant challenge of initially adapting from private practice, but also to guide in-house lawyers as they progress in their role as advisory partners to other employees in their organisation.

Insofar as many law firms could boost the morale and productivity of their partners through senior-level mentoring, an even greater number have an untapped opportunity to do so for other senior-level staff members, such as high-level HR or marketing professionals. These individuals add significant value to their firms and handle the infrastructure that allows lawyers to focus on legal matters. Yet these professionals often report feeling like second-class citizens, and recent research reveals that one of the biggest reasons that they feel devalued is their firm's failure to provide any sort of professional development or mentoring support.[8] Law firms that facilitate a senior-level mentoring programme among functional professionals can increase their motivation and effectiveness, thus becoming an overall higher-functioning firm.

In today's legal environment, finding ways to fully leverage the strength of a firm's partners and professional staff will be an important source of competitive advantage, and senior-level mentoring is likely to be an important part of that equation.

---

8 Gardner, Losee & Westfahl (2014) "No More Second-Class Citizens: The Value of Fully Engaging Professional Support Staff in Your Firm." Working Paper – contact author.

The chartered psychologist as coach

Robert Sharpe
Psychologist

1. Introduction

In the United Kingdom, the form of licensing for psychologists is that of chartered psychologist, a registration that I hold. What I discuss in this chapter is as applicable to any other regional registration for psychologists as it is to mine.

It's probably going to be helpful if I explain at the outset the difference between a professionally trained, licensed psychologist and a broadly based coach. Notwithstanding many apparent similarities, the difference lies in how we're trained and registered and what duties of care attach to our professional status. Because of our specialised knowledge about how people can behave – and misbehave – under a wide range of circumstances, we are expected professionally to spot things that might be systemically adverse, where non-psychologists might say, "Well, that's just the organisational culture."

For a professional psychologist, wilful blindness is simply not an option. Our role is always going to be one of special knowledge where we might be exposed to activities and behaviour (both intentions and actions) that are, essentially, wrong or bad in human terms. We may discover bad stuff, often masquerading under the sanitisation banner of 'firm's values' with unctuous reference to 'collegiality'. If that bad stuff might injure or disadvantage others, then we have no alternative but to report it appropriately. That can lead to unpopularity, especially if the bad stuff is being perpetrated by protected species such as profitable tyrants or head honchos.

If the system is endemically flawed, then coaching runs the risk of being used as a corporate sop or of coaching bad stuff into greater efficiency: "Yes, it is an inferno of unremitting stress in this company – but have three hours of coaching with Helen: she's very nice, apparently." Or: "You're not the first to say that Julian is foul after a few drinks – have a chat with that chap Andrew we've taken on for a bit of coaching." A bit of a chat with Andrew or Helen is going to be as much use as a chocolate teapot in the context of a raging alcoholic boss or an environment where leaving the office at 8:00pm brings you sneers and the label of 'lightweight'. Personally, I didn't qualify and build my practice to be a tick in the box that proves how much a modern-age sweatshop cares. I don't help to 'manage people out' and neither do I coach psychopaths, narcissists or histrionics for greater efficiency. Psychologists hold black belts in all manner of mental arts – and they are not there to be used by corporate management as excuses to do bad stuff.

Psychologists have to make judgement calls on toxicity of environment, appropriateness of management methods, corporate culture and suitability of recipients for psychological skills development. Most of us, especially with seniority, can spot a psychopathic personality disorder (PPD), narcissistic personality disorder (NPD) or histrionic personality disorder (HPD) a mile off. These are hard-wired, constitutionally determined and fundamentally unchangeable personality profiles – as impossible to alter at root as the colour of your irises. It is not our duty to enhance their efficiency through coaching. It is our duty to assist those who they are collaterally damaging to break the stranglehold they typically have over their victims. Coaches, on the other hand, may dub such people 'complex personalities' and work within an oppressive environment rather than step outside and question the systemic flaws that allow it to flourish.

It can be tough having to point the culpability finger at the top echelons. However, unless this is done, especially within law firms, which already occupy the number two position for highest incidence of workplace psychopathy (after bankers!),[1] then the 40% of lawyers who currently advise young talent not to go into the law as a career[2] can only become far greater very soon. Those 40% of disaffected lawyers know exactly how things work within the private clubs that are law firm partnerships.

At this point, readers will have split into two camps. On the one hand: "Load of rubbish – and who does he think he is anyway? He's not a lawyer." This camp miss the precise relevance of not being a lawyer and, instead, being a clinically trained observer. On the other hand: "He must have been a lawyer at some time to know exactly how it all works." This camp realises that an applied psychologist is also a participant observer of firms' tribal cultures. I guess it's "goodbye" to the first group and "let's keep talking" with the second.

With this background in mind, the rest of this chapter is occupied with illustrations of what I actually do. In a nutshell, I spend my working life fine-tuning the thought processes of professional clients whose clients are hiring them to fine-tune their thought processes. Lawyers' clients hire lawyers to impose structure and discipline on their business or personal objectives. So what do I do with the thought processes of our client lawyers?

Forty years on, I reckon that most of the time, I assist my clients in two ways. The priority is enabling them how not to let their intellectual processes get blocked with anxieties, depressive thoughts and self-doubt. That protects the downside.

Taking second place, but strategically more important, is introducing them to strengths and abilities that they have previously not had the time, inclination or self-belief to look for. That gives them options, control and self-confidence.

Professionals fall prey to innumerable random events that impair their carefully honed working lives. We psychologists and coaches aim to help prevent or clear the clutter that would possibly choke our clients' otherwise excellent performances. Mostly, I find that my lawyer clients and I are pretty similar in what we end up doing. All of us accumulate what physicists call 'noise in the system'. The hiss of a poorly

---

1 Kevin Dutton, *The Wisdom of Psychopaths: What Saints, Spies, and Serial Killers Can Teach Us About Success* (William Heinemann, 2012).

2 Catherine Baksi, "Don't choose law as a career – say 4 in 10 lawyers" The Law Society Gazette, May 6 2014.

tuned radio station can spoil the enjoyment of the symphony playing on air. The anxieties, personal dramas and self-doubts of the adviser can detract from delivering a piece of learned advice.

People ask me who clears my thinking pipelines. It gets harder the further out in the structure that you sit, but I have peer mentors too. Being a psychologist doesn't protect you from being human! I've been tricked, trapped and conflicted on the way through 40 years of professional life. I've always spotted the trick, sidestepped the trap and resolved the conflict. But not all coaches, however trained, are necessarily as robust. So, whenever you might hire in a coach or similar adviser, especially if they carry the licensing that psychologists do, try to take on a duty of care towards them – as they should towards you. Be transparent. Be unbiased. Be respectful. It takes two to tango. And try to remember that if your coaching psychologist passes along some unpalatable feedback on your systems, it may be because they are trying to help you to reduce the 40% of lawyers who would not recommend the law as a career option.

What follows is a fitting melange. Coaching is an emerging marketplace. It is as motley as it seems to be popular. Clients say it helps. No one really audits it. It is as old as time. It has acquired university and institute status. I offer the following as part of the understanding of what psychological coaching, as distinct from broad coaching, consists of.

2. Case study 1

"Robert, do you have a moment to see one of our competition partners? Jane Sheppard. She's a real asset to the firm."

"Yes, Vivienne, I've heard her name mentioned."

"Well – she's handed in her resignation and she's accepting an academic position at Dunbridge University."

"She'll be a big loss."

"Very big loss – but that's the least important part about it. We're concerned she may be making the move because of factors we (and maybe she) don't understand. Could you have a word?"

Have a word. Sensitive HR, Viv. Always picks up the non-obvious ones that most colleagues miss. Have a word. Yes, of course. Actually, two sessions of 90 minutes' worth of word. Not long at all, but long enough. Jane was mightily indignant about an initiative that the senior partner had set in motion six months previously. She and her competition partners were to be lumped in with a larger department and compared in an apples versus oranges way for compensation purposes. So why didn't she take on the senior partner?

"You don't take on the senior partner. Especially if it's Ben Griffiths!"

"Oh. Infallible, is he?"

"Well, no, of course not. Just not done."

"OK with you if we address that as the focus of our work together?"

Two sessions later, Jane had reviewed her issues, arranged her arguments – and given herself permission to seek an audience with the top man.

Two days later, directly after her full and frank encounter with Ben Griffiths, she tore up her resignation letter along with the acceptance she had received for tenure from a prominent university. Ben very quietly backed off from his divisive plan and found another restructurable target with which to concern himself. We never met again. She sent me a delightful email, though, and a couple of associates whom she reckoned needed similar encouragement. She stayed for another seven years before moving on.

3. Case Study 2

"Robert? Clive. Do you have a few minutes?"

Clive Stephenson on my private line. Clive and I had an intermittent relationship. Never any surprises. Whenever he called, it would be to discuss a hot potato. He never troubled me with good news. I guess he thought I lived such a happy life I didn't need any. Truth is, I did – still do. Always made me smile, though. Was he like it everywhere?

"Sure, Clive. What's on?"

Clive was a leading light litigator and fee rainmaker, who'd been battling for over two years in a large negligence claim. A big bank opponent, Chunky PLC, was claiming against the firm's smaller but strategically important defendant, Niche PLC. Niche knew well enough that they had dropped a ball. It was the £200 million damages that Chunky was hitting them for that was making them wince. They could live with a £50 million settlement – especially if they could stop the lawyers' clock ticking.

"Need a read. This negligence case we're on. Stepped up a couple of gears and Chunky are getting tougher. They've restructured their lead team and my opposite number's a lulu. He's playing an unusual game and I need to know what he's about."

"So you gave me a call. Thanks for the confidence! OK – run me through a scenario".

Clive and I had done this before. He knew the ropes. While he spends his life looking for facts, evidence and rational arguments, I spend mine spotting microscopic tell-tales, fleeting expressions and throwaway lines. He had to run through an encounter using my eyes and ears to pick his way through previously unnoticed diamonds and gold nuggets. Tough call, but Clive was bright. I'd taught him enough times to clear his mind, dig into the memory chest and replay a scenario without doing that judgement thing. For a lawyer, that's like asking a Tour de France cyclist to retell the race through the eyes of a landscape gardener. But Clive was bright.

"Last lead was tough, but stuck to points of law and commercial realities. This guy's a snake. I've met lots of snakes but this one seems to want to score points off me rather than our client. Always attends with a couple of juniors who don't really do much other than laugh at his jokes at our expense."

I was already 80% there. Thin slicing is second nature for a clinical psychologist. You have to be able to pick out the tiny pearls from the rest of the padding. Then you extrapolate a picture, a pattern, a bit like those anthropologists who build a complete raptor from a toe bone or a village from a few bowls. My kids used to think I could read minds when they were small. In a way, I could. Spot the type and you can predict their moves. This is the edge Clive was wanting from me.

"When he ambushes you, where does he look?"

Clive was ready. He and I both knew this was nothing to do with law.

"Always flicks his eyes to his adoring acolytes."

Gotcha. Now we can play you.

"Got yourself a narcissistic personality disorder there, Clive. NPDs, we call them. Along with the serial killer psychopaths, they're in the top three for destructiveness. The other's the histrionic but that's for another time. How often does he say, 'My view is...'?"

"How'd you kn...?"

Clive stopped himself. He knew I spot personality flaws at the same speed he spots legal loopholes. I heard him grin down the line.

"We call him 'Strutter' – he's a real peacock."

"See? You're a better psychologist than you give yourself credit for! You actually thin sliced him and knew what he was. So why do you need me?"

"Thanks for the annual appraisal services, Robert. Glad you think I'm coming along nicely. So we're there on what this bloke is – now what do I do about it?"

This was crunch time – where so many lawyers just can't play outside of the box. They talk about it all the time, put it in their mission statements, bring in gurus to teach them how to do it. It hardly ever works. If it does and the penny drops, the lawyer invariably stops being a lawyer and goes off and excels in commerce. I once taught a lawyer how to wear a string vest in his mind's eye. Behave like a truck driver (you know, normally) when his wife wanted to talk all night about the meaning of life. He imagined crashing his truck through lack of sleep. He found saying, "Yes dear, g'night," was easy, after all. Just as productive as reasoning fruitlessly for seven hours and ending in exhausted silence. Six months later, he'd left his law firm, joined a bank and was happily earning four times his previous income with weekends off. He told me later it was because I'd introduced him to alternatives and choice. Educating Rita was always a risky pursuit and his firm lost him. Now part of the 40%, I guess – but he then pushed millions in fees from the bank to his old firm, so a good outcome all round.

"Like a lot of PD antics, handling a narcissist's games is a black-white decision. If you want to use an NPD to some end, then patronise them, butter them up, flatter them and let them preen. If they're giving you grief and monstering less robust mortals, no amount of coaching or rational management will alter them. NPDs have no ability for insight or empathy. You can only get rid of them or ring fence them. End of."

"OK. Gives me a choice of one choice. How do I get rid of him?"

"NPDs are self-important, pompous and overinflated bullies. But their effectiveness is only skindeep. If they're punctured, however slightly, they deflate and have no internal reserves to fall back on. They're table tennis balls. All shell – no substance. Their only objective is to look good to others. Their terror is looking stupid. You need to take this joker out. So you make him look stupid in front of his adorers."

"How, exactly?"

Typical lawyer. Wants a foolproof script. Tough. No such thing. Lawyers do exact. Psychologists do first principles and then extemporise.

"I'll give you a mud map of the type of thing to look for and do. You spot the opportunity and provide the action. Teamwork. Key thing, though, is that when you act, you show no mercy. This is binary – it's you (and your client) or him (and his client). Half measures will have you looking stupid – not him."

"Come on ..."

(So impatient.)

"You've seen how he lays traps for you and your team? Springs surprises on you and smirks at your discomfort? OK, that's his payoff – your discomfort at his cleverness. What you're doing at present is countering each move with some logical defence. But he's already a step ahead of you. He spends his time baiting his traps while you spend yours dealing with the law. So, before your next meeting, you work on a couple of killer points that you've been holding in reserve."

"Yes, we've got several of those."

Now comes the counter-intuitive bit – the bit Clive would never have thought of. It's not in the lawyer's nature.

"Then you let your opponent begin one of his assaults ... and you don't defend ... you look crestfallen ... you let him wind up the game ... score points off you 'til he's sure he's beaten you ... then you drop in your killer point ... show he's blown his entire strategy on that issue because he's been too sure of himself."

"How will he react?"

"The same way you'd react if you were poised for action with the girl of your dreams and her mum pops in with a nice cup of tea – immediate and utter deflation. The difference is, you'd recover in about 10 minutes: an NPD won't. Ever. They have no inner reserves to recover with. They're done. Humpty Dumpty fallen off the wall."

"Are you sure?"

Lawyers, eh?

"Clive – I'm sure. But when you see the moment to thrust, you have to show no mercy. Mercifulness to an NPD is like petrol to a flame. OK?"

"OK. Thanks Robert."

Total phone time 15 minutes. Two years pass. Dinner with Clive.

"Oh, did I ever tell you the outcome of the Chunky-Niche matter, Robert?"

"No – but it must have been good because if it had been bad you'd have told me."

"Point taken! Well – Strutter went into the routine next time we met. The guys and I had chosen three killer points and tucked them up our sleeves. It happened just like you said. I acted like a limp lettuce leaf and Strutter could hardly believe his luck. He rode me ruthlessly. He was so pumped up he could have burst. Then I asked him, very quietly, if he had considered – which I knew he hadn't – my killer point. I thought he was going to be sick. He went mute. Glanced at his followers who were looking anywhere but at him. A few minutes later, they wound up the meeting and left."

"Sounds like your thrust went home."

"Yes. Didn't hear anything for five days. Then I got an email from his second-in-command. They asked if we would be prepared to drop hands on the whole matter. They just caved in. They'd been chasing £200 million. We would have been delighted to settle for £50 million. We accepted dropped hands. Robert, you saved my client a minimum of £50 million."

Sometimes the job satisfaction outweighs the need for a fee. Sometimes.

4. Case study 3

"Last week in September. Can you make it?"

Graham, global head of corporate, called to see if I would join the partner selection committee that year to comment on the process. Graham is a thoughtful and respectful leader who wanted to check out that the firm's annual ordeal by fire was both fair and effective in choosing the right new partners.

"Be delighted. You said you had 16 candidates?"

I had seen half of the annual corporate lawyer partner candidates each year for the previous four years for coaching and already had a detailed knowledge of the process. Graham had been impressed with the results and was asking if I would attend the next assessment board.

"I want you to take a look and tell us if we're measuring what we think we're measuring and whether it's a fair process".

Always collegial, Graham wanted a second pair of eyes and ears on the most crucial issue of any law firm's existence – bringing in the next partners, the stewards of the firm's future. A fascinating opportunity for me.

"Thank you for the privilege, Graham. I'll be there."

During the process, I was able to confirm the fairness and relevance of all but one of the challenges set for the candidates. The role-play scenarios were questionable. They reflected a heavy cultural bias that did not take account of regional variations in interpersonal style. That meant that some candidates could be disadvantaged in the process and I reported this to Graham and the assessment board. They agreed to modify that aspect of the task and invited me back the next year.

"The role play has changed significantly," I reported to the Board that second year. "There is now scope for cultural and geographic variation. And the candidates enjoyed the process this year, whereas they were very anxious about it last year."

Follow-up sessions with the candidates from both years confirmed that the overall process was enhanced as a result of the changes that had been made. Small alterations in the cultural and psychological detail of the legal assessment process had resulted in a more meaningful and informative partner selection experience. The lesson from this is that quite frequently we might not be measuring and assessing what we think we are measuring and assessing. Another discipline looking at a situation can often see new variables and use them to enhance an existing process.

5. Case study 4

"How on earth can we prevent this from happening again?"

Senior partner, international law firm. Jurisdictional office in widespread distress caused by the extreme excesses of its narcissistic psychopathic managing partner (its NPDs seem to pop onto my radar quite frequently). I had been involved, identified the problem as being at the top and laid out the evidence for the senior partner.

"Sadly, you'll make the mistake now and again over the years, as these individuals wear very convincing disguises. Your other problem is that you'll probably never listen to the likes of me advising against hiring them when you're salivating over their rainmaking ability!"

"I'm not feeling comfortable about what you say," replied SP, "but I know you're right. The damage he's caused to so many people…"

Duty done, that's where I left it. Seven years passed. A call comes in. Will I attend a meeting. I can't resist attending meetings that are obscure. I'm a psychologist, after all.

"Will you help us?"

I learn from the small delegation of partners who have asked me to meet them that the NPD is still ruling the roost at that office after seven years. But I'm not too surprised – they have amazing staying power and resilience (look at examples like Putin, Hitler and the staggeringly successful mass control of Kim Jong-il and now Kim Jong-un) through their ability to gain the dependency of their victims. But the toll on the rest of the 85-person office has been appalling over the years. Fragmentation is not far off and a sad part of the private clinical knowledge that I have is that suicide rates can rise under prolonged exposure to NPD regimes. I now have a formal duty of care to observe that supersedes other considerations.

"Of course. But you have to understand now that getting rid of this problem will mean that you have to take a leap of faith in the acceptance of professional advice that may seem very alien to you. NPDs do not react like normal people and you have all learned to be victims. Can you change?"

They could and did. There followed a period of coaching of the victims in the dislodging of a tyrannous NPD into which they entered with determination. Three months later, the cracks began to show and six months later the tyrant resigned. At times, the coachees despaired, as NPD appeared to rally and resist a subtle but powerful change in the atmosphere that was eroding his pathological control. Then – he was gone. Imploded and departed. The office is free, and more profitable.

What did I teach and advise the victims? That will come later in a full volume book on the subject of handling disruptive personality types. Psychological intervention is not just developing individuals. Sometimes it is helping to remove an influence that is overshadowing everyone's potential.

The lesson here, though, is not just that one bad apple can spoil the barrel. It is the revelation that just before I was asked to attend the meeting just described, a lay coach had been enlisted to work within the damaged environment to try to facilitate relations between the NPD and the rest of the office. Finding this to be an impossible task (NPDs simply cannot harmonise, by definition of their personality type), the coach had finally told all of the victims that they had simply better learn to go along with their boss and to stop being so contrary. The coach had come under the same control by the NPD as the rest of the office and taken sides with him because of an understandable but handicapping lack of diagnostic training and experience.

That was when I had got the call to the meeting.

6. Case study 5

"Robert, can you take a look at a bundle for us, please?"

Hugh, leading employment litigator. Pre-eminent breadth of vision. Nose like a bloodhound for a scam.

"Delighted, Hugh. What's the issue?"

We didn't need lengthy discussions or kilos of paperwork. We could get to the essence quickly.

"The claimant is going after our client employer for half a mill (sterling) on account of his alleged depression through work-related stress. I don't believe a word of it but he has a team of psychiatrists and a psychiatric record that appears to be solidly against us. Appreciate your view."

Twenty-four hours later, he got it. The claimant was a clear psychopath (we diagnose those from the between the lines messages as much as from interviewing them), who had cleverly set up a psychiatric injury claim over only 18 months of employment with the client employer. I told him.

"Thought it smelled bad. What do we do with it?"

"Two options. Try to refute the psychiatric evidence with your independent psychiatric evidence. You might even succeed in getting an adverse opinion. Then you'll go to tribunal and lose. Your claimant will out-act you and sympathy will lie with him. I've seen it happen too often."

"Or?"

"I'll do my best to demonstrate that he's a complex psychopath and you'll fight the case on the grounds that he is perpetrating a scam and stand a chance of winning. Or you'll get a tribunal that doesn't like hearing about the nasty world of the psychopathic 3% of our community and who rail against you for such talk and award double what he's asking for. You'll be the first ever to my knowledge who's been bold enough to fight such an action on those grounds – but it's your only option."

"How sure are you that he's a psychopath?"

Well, Hugh was a lawyer, after all!

"Oh, certain. Just proving it may be a challenge."

"I'll take instructions and revert."

Twenty-four hours later.

"Client says yes. All the way. What do you need?"

Next eight weeks were straight Raymond Chandler. Me as Philip Marlowe, which turned out to be an interesting ride. Then, from Hugh:

"They've done what?"

I had seen the claimant. He was a lulu. And good at it. Saw his girlfriend – nice lass whom he'd convinced was crazy and insisted she attend group therapy for her non-understanding of his 'reasonable' requirement that she engage in troilistic sex. He had spotted that I had spotted that he was conning. He moved into action next day.

The upmarket private psychiatric facility where he' d been admitted for the full 180 days of his medical insurance's annual benefit cover sensed danger. I was on the trail of a 'psychiatric record con trick'. Not good press for the upmarket facility. They complained strongly to my professional psychology body that I was inadequately qualified to be involved in the case. Well, they would. They were going to be revealed as liars. Makes professionals itchy when they are about to be exposed. My professional body took one look at my cred and told them to go whistle Dixie. But it was straws in the wind and Hugh had to be informed.

"Well – thought you should know."

This move by the claimant's side had come right after his lawyers had taken the time and trouble to research my entire life – just as I had done with their client's – to find transgressions. Finding none, they'd complained that I could be found at Companies House as a director of five companies. Therefore, I was a businessman, not a psychologist. Not too powerful an argument – but the snarling teeth of the angry canine were again evident.

"Look," Hugh said. "This may be going to sound a bit tough to you, but this is great news. For them to be going so much out on a limb to discredit you means they're really worried. Are you OK with this going on?"

Being boringly squeakily clean, I was delighted to be thus challenged and vetted.

"Sure am," I replied.

The claimant had a record of childhood conduct disorder, including abuse of female teachers (yes, it was that way around), rent-boy offences at the age of 11, drug dealing at 14 and more recent unpleasantnesses that, together, satisfied even the most stringent requirement of the diagnostic criteria for psychopathy. He was caught dead to rights.

"Thanks for your final report, Robert. It's with counsel, who can't wait for the Tribunal to arrive."

Day of the Tribunal. Chairman rises after the initial ritualistic procedure, saying he needs to reflect on the case for a couple of hours. Two sides settle into adjoining rooms. Door opens to reveal claimant barrister. The two barristers hold a whispered conversation.

"What are our costs so far?" asks our counsel of Hugh's team. A quick calculation revealed around £40,000.

"OK – your call," said a commercially jubilant but adversarially slightly disappointed-looking counsel. "They've just asked if we would be prepared to drop hands. His barrister has just told him that if our evidence is read out and reported, he's unlikely to work within 50 miles of London ever again. And clearly our opposing barrister has serious reservations about the character of his client. What do you want to do?"

Quick call to employer. Solicitor: "Well, we'll be just right for lunch opening time for a very good restaurant I know. Client is delighted and says no need to try to recover costs and to be sure to enjoy the celebration. We just saved them a great deal of money – as well as some probable bad press. Dropped hands it is."

Claimant was last seen sidling away from the building and back into the wild, thwarted but probably no wiser. Psychopaths never learn via insight.

We lunched till 6:00pm and then went on to celebrate.

Although this story centres around a miscreant and his undoing, there is also a very serious clinical psychology coaching component to the process. The employment law team who were involved were themselves being introduced to a very unusual alternative way of tackling a predatory opponent. Like Clive, they hadn't really appreciated that clinical profiling of the actors' personality types could be used to great advantage in attacking a complex and potentially very costly claim. In this kind of arena, especially, there is a significant overlap between psychology and law as applied practices; an overlap that demands the specialised know-how of the psychological professional in diagnosing the underlying pathology.

7. Conclusion

Often, advisers are their own worst enemy. A quick literature review reveals that some schools of thought define 'mentoring' and 'coaching' one way. Others define the terms diametrically oppositely. Then again, some advisers limit their activities to a room, chairs and a water jug. Others gird their loins and go into battle with their clients. To declare myself, if it's not yet obvious: I'm the latter type. Anthropologists would call me a participant observer. I've wandered around Ground Zero 10 days after 9/11 with New York lawyers whom I'm trauma debriefing. I've tailed a psychopathic husband who had catnapped his estranged wife's pet just to torment her and shown the distressed lady how she could level the playing field whenever she wanted, gaining secret knowledge for her. I've gone undercover to expose bullies and other social wrongdoers who are guilty of ruining quality of life for workmates. In return for such forays, I've had some of the best fun and professional satisfaction you can have. Sure, you win some, you lose some. Occasionally, I've been shot at for being the messenger. I've saved a client £50 million and they didn't even know I existed. I've kept a good man in play for four years beyond his otherwise coping power and he's produced a £70 million fee deal for his firm. They didn't know and he chose to conduct our relationship as one of just having dinner with me twice a month. It can be lonely as a participant psych – but it's never dull.

I have seen the occasional unwary coach accept mandates such as, "Coach this partner to be more 'partnerial' and in keeping with our values." The unwary will swallow such a nebulous – actually, meaningless – brief and attempt the impossible. Without definable benchmarks ('partnerial'? 'values'?), the adviser's inevitable fate is failure, since vested interest parties will evaluate outcomes according to their agendas. Such fuzzy mandates are ones that it is wise for a coach to avoid, since failure to demonstrate an improvement in some loosely defined variable will inevitably reflect poorly on the coach – and probably not benefit the coachee either.

I have also seen coaches lose their way in complex organisations by becoming the unwitting tool of a senior player who wishes to have the coach persuade subordinates to follow what may be unacceptable or inappropriate demands. Five per cent of the population will predate upon the other 95%. If the senior player is in the 5% category, then the presence of a coach who is unaware of such profiles can increase the problem rather than solve it. Coaching such aberrant personalities will either produce no results or, worse, enable the coachee to become an even more efficient predator, facilitating the tendency of psychopathy to rise upwards. This provides, of course, a very paradoxical problem. *Quis custodiet ipsos custodes?*

If this seems hard to comprehend, I would cite the case of Robert Hanssen, the most successful (until he was caught) and destructive spy ever exposed in the United States and within the FBI. The most significant aspect of his run as traitor was the ease with which he secured the position as head of the very team that was hunting the mole that the FBI believed (rightly) it had in its midst. Now that is very clever indeed, and it is little wonder that his team didn't catch him. Then consider the unlikelihood of anyone believing that a corporate head, or departmental head, or global or jurisdictional head can be a malefactor. This is the tough scenario for a professional whistle-blower apprising top management that others in top management are bad.

There are, then, red-flag warnings to the profession and these are cause for firms to be looking towards clinical psychologists for advisory input. Dutton[3] reports that the law and the judiciary have the second-highest incidence of psychopathy after banking. This, together with the 40% of lawyers who would not recommend the law as a career, has to be a serious concern for the future of the profession. In common with many other clinically qualified professionals, I invariably decline to coach, mentor or in any other way assist psychopaths, narcissists and histrionics. In my introduction, I pointed out that such profiles are not changeable. They can only be ring-fenced or excluded. To take on such individuals would be knowingly to produce more efficient psychopaths, narcissists and histrionics. That would be a little like teaching the paedophile to spot more swiftly the vulnerable in the playground – and not, I believe, the reason why I was awarded my practice certificate.

But let's end on the privileges and a high note. Somehow our clients realise they do better with us around, clearing the clutter and lubricating the machinery. And occasionally you meet with truly exceptional wisdom. I was once engaged in a wonderful purple patch by a true gentleman senior partner who paid me an annual retainer for "doing what you do best, Robert. I just want you to go around talking to our people. I know you'll pick up what needs to be done". Trusted adviser. A privilege imparted only by leaders secure in honouring their stated values to those of the same constitution.

Nothing lasts, though and I find it helps my motivation in a changing political environment to keep a rough tally of bottom-line scores. Talent retained. Client damages claimed or saved. Embarrassments averted. Internal conflict resolved. It all mounts up.

---

3 Kevin Dutton, *The Wisdom of Psychopaths: What Saints, Spies, and Serial Killers Can Teach Us About Success* (William Heinemann, 2012).

The role of bars in promoting mentoring best practices

John E Montgomery
National Legal Mentoring Consortium

Bars, because of their very numbers and worldwide presence, can play an important role in mentoring less experienced lawyers. Of all legal organisations, they have the greatest potential in the legal profession for improving the skills and competence of lawyers through mentoring programmes.

1. The growth and common purposes of bar associations

For over 2,000 years, individuals performing the role of what we would describe today as lawyers or advocates have participated in the legal systems of Western and Middle-Eastern societies. These functions were considered important enough to society that both the church and governments often regulated certain aspect of lawyering.

Bar associations, by comparison, have been relative latecomers to the legal profession. In the United States, the first bar association of any kind, the Boston Bar Association, was established in 1700, many years after lawyers were practising in the area. Statewide bar associations in the United States, now the most influential bar groups, were not organised until much later, in the mid to late 19th and early 20th century. The American Bar Association (ABA), one of the earliest countrywide bar associations and now the world's largest professional organisation, was formed in 1875 with representatives from some 20 states participating.

This pattern of bars being formed much later than lawyers practising in a particular area appears to be quite common. Similar to the US experience, the Budapest Bar Association, for example, was not formed until 1879, long after lawyers in Hungary were assisting people with their legal needs. The Australian Bar Association, like many others, was not established until the 1960s as an umbrella organisation, much like the ABA, to serve the national interests of the legal profession in Australia. New bar associations continue to be established. The Afghanistan Independent Bar Association was recently formed to support an independent legal profession in that country.

Regardless of location, or whether the bar association is specialised or general and open to all lawyers, most bars notably share common purposes. Support for the rule of law, independence of the profession, access to justice and upholding high standards of professional competence are commonly stated goals.

The promotion of high professional standards is probably the goal most shared by bar associations, regardless of location and regardless of whether the bar association is mandatory or voluntary, general or specialised. Acting on this goal, of course, is easier for mandatory membership organisations. In the United States, for example, many individual state bars are mandatory, meaning that the privilege to practise law in those states on a permanent basis is conditional on membership of the state bar association. Since 42 of the 50 states require mandatory continuing professional education and bar associations are the typical providers of such continuing education, it is relatively easy to require lawyers to regularly update their professional skills.

Worldwide, there are hundreds of bar associations. They operate in every country with a well-organised legal system. Some are mandatory, meaning that lawyers cannot practise law in the jurisdiction unless they also are members of the bar association. Many others are voluntary, open to any lawyer who chooses to join. Many, like the ABA or the Australian Bar Association, are umbrella organisations, which involve themselves with issues of national or even international significance to the legal profession. At the other end of the spectrum are local bar associations, which operate only in a limited area such as specific city or town.

The promotion of mentoring fits perfectly within most bar associations' broad goal of improving the profession and upholding high professional standards. There is a consistent body of research documenting the many benefits of mentoring, both in business and in the legal profession. Mentoring increases professional competence, reduces mistakes, transmits the values of the profession and improves satisfaction with the practice of law. Mentoring is a widely used professional development tool for corporations and businesses. Its use in the legal profession has been much less frequent.

In light of their shared goal of upholding high professional standards, bars are the best suited of all legal organisations to promote and administer mentoring programmes. First, unless they are specialised (eg, the Commercial Bar Association which represents the interests of barristers practising international commercial law; or the Federal Bar Association, for US lawyers practising in the US federal courts), they usually have a membership broadly representative of the area's lawyer population, and even if the bar association is specialised, it is usually committed to high professional standards. Second, most bar associations have an existing administrative structure with staff or volunteers working to further the association's goals. Third, bar associations have information on all members and the ability to communicate with them. Finally, at least some associations have considerable technology resources, which could be employed in administering a mentoring programme.

All these factors are important in the operation of a successful mentoring programme. In fact, one of the most crucial factors in the success of any mentoring programme is an administrative structure sufficient to support the basic mentoring process itself: recruiting mentors, matching mentors and mentees, structuring the mentoring process and monitoring progress. An inadequate administrative support structure is one of the main reasons why mentoring programmes in law firms are unsuccessful. Unwillingness to provide administrative support is often a major reason why law firms choose not to establish a formal mentoring programme. The financial cost to provide an administrative structure, even if small, is often viewed as not worth any potential benefit from mentoring.

In sum, bar associations are the obvious institutions in the legal profession to promote and administer mentoring programmes. They have broad membership with significant numbers of both new and experienced lawyers, the ability to easily communicate with members and, usually, administrative staff. Bars, while obviously concerned with costs and limited resources, have the ability and good reason to commit administrative resources to improving the professional competency of members.

2. The role of bar associations in promoting mentoring best practices in the United States: a case study

In 1995 approximately 50,000 new lawyers were being admitted annually to practise in the United States. Most were admitted to practise in a single state, although a small number were admitted to more than one state. Admission to practise in the United States is controlled by the supreme courts of the individual states. At that time, no state either required mentoring or offered it on a voluntary basis for lawyers newly admitted to practise. Of the 50,000 newly admitted lawyers in 1995, probably a small percentage received some form of mentoring, typically through their law firms. No bar association was at that time involved in mentoring.

Contrast those numbers with the situation in 2014, some 20 years later. Something of a revolution has occurred. Of the 55,000 new lawyers now admitted annually, about 25% – in the range of 12,000 to 15,000 – now receive some formal mentoring in their first year of practice. For most, this mentoring is provided through a bar association mentoring programme. Currently, approximately 20 of the 50 states have established bar or closely related supreme court mentoring programmes. These programmes operate statewide on either a mandatory or voluntary basis (about two-thirds are voluntary and one-third mandatory). At the same time as the rapid growth of mentoring by bar association in the United States, law firms and even law schools have rapidly expanded their own mentoring programmes. It is likely that bar association mentoring has triggered interest in other parts of the profession.

In total, between one-quarter and one-third of all newly admitted lawyers in the United States every year are now participating in a formal bar mentoring programme.

What has been responsible for this dramatic upsurge in mentoring new lawyers in the United States, driven primarily by bar associations? What factors contributed to bar associations taking actions? What have we learned about mentoring best practices and what is essential to the success of bar mentoring programmes?

3. The structure and responsibilities of bar associations in the United States

It is helpful to understand how bar associations in the United States are organised and function. There are hundreds of bar associations in the country. The largest umbrella organisation, the ABA, has over 400,000 members and is a voluntary association. It operates through sections, divisions and committees. Policy is set by its House of Delegates. Its objectives are familiar: supporting the rule of law, increasing access to justice, promoting high standards and improving the administration of justice. The ABA itself has not played a leading role in mentoring, leaving that role to bar associations in the individual states.

Each of the 50 states has at least one statewide bar association and some have two. In states with a single association, the bar is usually 'unified' and membership is mandatory in order to be able to practise there. South Carolina, Georgia and Utah are examples of states with a single, mandatory bar association. Other states, such as Colorado and North Carolina, have two associations and do not condition the right to practise on membership of a bar association. Statewide bar associations, mandatory or voluntary, have always played an important role in initiatives to improve the profession.

Most states also have a significant number of local bar associations. These are always voluntary, but also work to improve the profession. Virtually every major city in the country has its own local bar association, independent of the state bar associations. A few, notably in the large cities of Texas, have established their own mentoring programmes.

In the United States, all statewide bar associations and many local ones have professional staff to administer their programmes and advance their missions.

The US legal profession also has an important group of organisations usually referred to as chief justices' commissions on professionalism. They were created at the urging of the National Conference of Chief Justices (composed of the chief justices of the 50 states) to improve the professionalism of US lawyers and exist in about 15 states. Their membership usually includes bar officers and executives and other lawyers and judges. They work closely with state courts and bar associations to promote professionalism and improve the profession. In some states, most notably Ohio and South Carolina, these commissions have assumed a leading role in promoting mentoring. They always work closely with state bar associations.

4. Factors which affected bar associations promotion of mentoring

A number of factors have contributed to bar associations' and chief justices' commissions' decisions to promote mentoring programmes in their jurisdiction. In the United States, the Georgia Bar Association was the first statewide bar association to create a mandatory mentoring programme for all lawyers newly admitted to practise in Georgia. Bar leaders there became concerned in the late 1990s that many lawyers were entering practice without adequate supervision. Few firms had their own mentoring programmes. A growing percentage of new lawyers were practising solo or with a group of other inexperienced practitioners. The concern was that this situation would inevitably lead to an increase in ethical violations and damage public perception of the legal profession. The requirement that the mentoring of new lawyers – about 1,000 were being admitted every year – be made mandatory was thought to be an effective way to address the problem and at the same time improve the professional competency of the profession.

Even so, it took advocates of the programme about five years to convince the members of the bar association and the Georgia Supreme Court to adopt the programme. Many lawyers were concerned that a mandatory mentoring programme would impose unreasonable burdens and costs on more experienced lawyers. There were also liability concerns. Georgia law firms had concerns about outside lawyers mentoring their associates. There were also doubts raised that the programme could effectively handle 1,000 new lawyers annually on a continuing basis. Collectively, these were not insignificant concerns. It took about five years to work through them to get the programme adopted in 2001.

After Georgia adopted its mandatory mentoring programme, economic conditions rapidly deteriorated in the United States, ultimately leading to what was called the Great Recession. The legal profession was dramatically and adversely affected. Many firms laid off associates and virtually stopped hiring new graduates. This led to a dramatic increase in lawyers entering practice without any supervision. Large clients demanded discounts and many refused to pay for any work done by first-year associates. As firms responded by cutting costs, mentoring programmes were cut back or eliminated.

By the mid 2000s, there were compelling reasons for bar associations to consider mentoring programmes for new lawyers. The Georgia Bar Association's successful mandatory programme proved to be a valuable model and several states soon followed with their own mentoring programmes, either mandatory or voluntary.

The Georgia mentoring programme had several features that have been adopted by many other state bar association mentoring programmes:

- The programme is mandatory for every lawyer admitted to practise in Georgia. It successfully provides mentoring for about 1,000 new lawyers on an annual basis.
- The programme is administered by a small professional staff, making ample use of technology.
- New lawyers are encouraged to select their own mentors. Most, about 85%, do. Those who do not or cannot may be placed in a group mentoring programme with four to five other new lawyers. This approach takes the pressure off bar administrative staff to find mentors for every new lawyer.
- Mentors are all volunteers recruited by the programme itself. Recruitment is done online, through websites, by attendance at bar meetings and by volunteers, in addition to bar administrative staff. Mentors must all meet minimum experience and ethical standards.
- Law firms, by agreeing to meet the general requirements of the mentoring programme, can mentor their own associates. This is an extremely important element of the programme since over 80% of new lawyers start their careers as associates with firms. Since virtually all firms want to mentor their own associates, this dramatically reduces the need to recruit individual volunteer mentors.
- The mentoring programme is time limited. From start to finish, it takes one year to complete.
- Topics to be included during mentoring are specified by the programme so that everyone is aware of things that must be covered during the one-year mentoring period.
- Record keeping, such as identification of mentors and certification of

completion, is the responsibility of new lawyers. All forms must be sent to the programme administrator.

- The programme is evaluated annually. So far, over 90% of participants rate the programme as highly successful.

Two other types of bar association mentoring programme are common in the United States and are worth discussion.

5. The Ohio Voluntary Mentoring Programme

Ohio has taken a different approach to mentoring new lawyers, although an equally successful one. First, the Ohio programme is administered by the Ohio Supreme Court Commission on Professionalism, not the Ohio Bar Association. While not technically a bar association programme, it relies heavily on the Ohio Bar Association for mentors and other assistance. As a practical matter, the bar association is a very significant partner. The programme could not succeed without its participation and cooperation.

There is one significant difference between administration of the Georgia and Ohio programmes. The Ohio programme has the use of the technology resources of the Ohio Supreme Court. As a consequence, the Ohio programme makes the most use of technology of any mentoring programme in the United States.

For a variety of reasons, to do with concerns of lawyers and the size of bar, Ohio chose a voluntary approach, unlike the mandatory programme in Georgia. Ohio is a large state and admits each year about 1,500 new lawyers to practise. The state also has nine separate law schools. Because of the large number of potential participants, the mentoring programme's staff have dual recruiting responsibilities, both at the state's law schools to recruit participants and to the bar association to recruit mentors. This imposes an additional burden on the programme's administrative staff. Even so, about 85% of the new lawyers admitted each year choose to participate. This reflects on the success and perceived value of the programme and the efforts of administrative staff to market the programme. As in Georgia, the Ohio programme relies exclusively on volunteers from the state bar association to serve as mentors. Mentors must have a minimum number of years of practice and a clear ethics record.

The Ohio programme is by far the most technologically advanced statewide mentoring programme in the United States. The programme uses LinkedIn groups to allow mentors to communicate with each other about problems that arise during the course of the mentoring programmes, saving time for administrative staff. Virtually all details of the programme and required forms are accessible online, again saving considerable staff time.

Similar to the Georgia programme, the Ohio programme lasts one year. While Georgia has specific topics that must be addressed by mentors, Ohio, in addition to specifying broad general topics, has a menu of specific topics within each general topic. This allows the new lawyer and mentor to tailor a mentoring programme to the specific needs and interests of the new lawyer.

Even with this voluntary approach, about 85% of new lawyers in Ohio participate and about 95% of participants report they are highly satisfied with their experience. Ohio employs software programs to conduct annual evaluations, again minimising staff time.

6. The Texas transition to practice programme: a successful local bar association mentoring programme

Because the number of lawyers in the state of Texas exceeds 50,000 and the number of newly admitted lawyers every year exceeds 2,000, and because of a widespread belief that a statewide bar association mentoring programme is inappropriate for Texas, the Texas Bar Association has resisted establishing its own mentoring programme. Instead, the Texas Bar Association has encouraged the local bar associations of every large metropolitan area in the state to form their own mentoring programmes, and many have done so.

The Dallas Bar Association mentoring programme was one of the first local bar association mentoring programmes to be established and has been quite successful. The programme is voluntary. New members of the Dallas Bar are invited to participate and about 20% enrol each year. Like other bar programmes, volunteer mentors are used and law firms can provide mentors for their own associates.

The Dallas programme, because of its small size and more limited administrative resources, differs significantly from statewide programmes. New lawyers are mentored in groups of between four and five, with each group led by one or two mentors. Groups meet about every two months for the program's year-long duration and discuss specified topics. Between group meetings, mentors meet about once each month with individual new lawyers for more extensive discussions. Judges and experienced local lawyers are often invited to group meetings for presentations and discussions.

This programme is structured, with a one-year timeframe and topics to be covered. The group structure reduces the number of volunteer mentors needed and minimises the amount of administrative staff time required. The Dallas Bar programme has been highly successful, with over 90% participants highly satisfied. It is an excellent model for small bar associations with limited resources.

7. The current state of bar association lawyer mentoring programmes in the United States

The creation of highly successful mandatory and voluntary mentoring programmes in Georgia and Ohio clearly demonstrated that statewide mentoring can be designed and administered by bar associations. Within a decade of their establishment, almost half the states in the United States had established some form of bar association mentoring programme for new lawyers. About 15 state bar associations now offer voluntary programmes and another seven have mandatory programmes. Several offer mentor match assistance, helping new lawyers to locate a mentor but no other structure. In this last group of states, it is entirely up to the mentor and new lawyer to work out the duration and coverage of mentoring.

The number of new lawyers receiving mentoring through these bar association programmes and their impressions of the value of the programmes are impressive.

Estimates indicate that in 2014 about 12,000 to 15,000 new lawyers, about one-quarter of all lawyers admitted to practise annually in the United States – are now participating in bar association mentoring programmes. The vast majority are participating in formal, structured programmes lasting one year. Satisfaction with those programmes exceeds 90%, according to annual surveys in several states.

Several additional state bar associations are considering establishing programmes. This remarkably rapid growth of bar association mentoring programmes in the United States over the last decade has spread to other parts of the profession as well. There are approximately 200 accredited law schools in the country. In 2000 mentoring was virtually non-existent in US legal education. Now, mentoring is offered in over 50 schools and the number is growing rapidly. Like bar associations, law schools rely on volunteer mentors. Their nearly universal experience is that lawyers will eagerly volunteer as mentors. At the same time, there has been a renewed interest in mentoring by law firms and other legal organisations such as the American Inns of Court.

To serve as a clearing house for mentoring in the profession generally, the National Legal Mentoring Consortium was established in 2011. With members from bar associations, law firms, law schools, legal organisations, corporations and individual lawyers and judges, the consortium has taken a leading role in promoting mentoring in the legal profession in the United States.

Without question, the catalyst for this renewed and growing interest in mentoring in the US legal profession has been bar associations leading the way in establishing successful mentoring programmes.

8. Best practices from the experience of US bar association mentoring programmes

After a decade of experience involving the mentoring of thousands of new lawyers through bar mentoring programmes, several best practices have become clear. These best practices are based on a traditional mentoring model, one-on-one mentoring or small groups of no more than four or five new lawyers per mentor:

- At the start of a new bar mentoring programme, aggressive recruiting of volunteer mentors is absolutely essential. Ideally, recruitment efforts and strategies should be in place some six months prior to the programme's start date. While bar staff will have primary responsibility, use of a recruiting committee composed of bar leaders committed to the programme is also helpful. Publicising the programme well in advance is also important, through websites, social media if the bar association uses it email contacts and attendance at bar functions by volunteers. The experience of most US bar mentoring programmes is that a significant percentage of bar members – and potential volunteer mentors – remain unaware of the mentoring programme even six months after it has started. A communication strategy informing bar members about the programme is essential.
- If the mentoring programme is voluntary, similar recruiting efforts directed at those to be mentored are also essential. The same strategies have been found to be effective in reaching both potential mentors and potential mentees.

- During the recruitment process, all participants should be told specifically about the expectations of the programme and the time commitments involved. Surprises here should be avoided.
- The benefits of serving as a mentor – improving the profession, serving as a role model, teaching the next generation of lawyers – are a powerful recruiting tool. Mentors, once recruited, tend to volunteer again.
- Mentors and new lawyers both should be provided with information about the mentoring process. Mentors should understand that they are fulfilling multiple roles as teachers, confidants, supporters and career catalysts. They also should realise they may be dealing with confidential information and there are boundaries to the role of mentor. In some cases, mentors may be obligated to report ethical violations. New lawyers must understand that they must actively participate in their own mentoring to gain full benefits from the process and they are not in a lawyer-client relationship with their mentors. Mentors cannot directly address the legal issues of the clients of lawyers being mentored. If possible, training sessions for new mentors, lasting a few hours, are useful. In their absence, useful short publications about mentoring are readily available.
- The design of the mentoring programme is critical to its success. Clear, basic elements must be spelled out to assure uniformity of coverage of critical areas. This cannot be left to the discretion of individual mentors. In most programmes, a bar committee specifies the general topics to be covered during the mentoring process. These general topics, and sub-topics related to the general topics, must be covered by all mentors. A certification form that all required topics have been covered should be signed by both the mentor and new lawyer and submitted to the programme administrator at the end of the mentoring process.
- The programme should have a definite time period for completion of mentoring. In the United States, a one-year period for mentoring has become the standard.
- While left up to individual mentors and their protégés, monthly meetings of about two hours' duration are encouraged. Agreement in advance on the topics to be covered in each monthly session is also encouraged.
- Use of technology to facilitate meetings in the absence of face-to-face meetings is increasing and seems to be effective. However, face-to-face meetings are much preferred and should be encouraged.
- Law firms should be allowed to and encouraged to mentor their own associates. This greatly reduces the need to recruit volunteers, since most new lawyers will be employed with a firm. Usually, law firms should be required to certify that they will adhere to the bar association programme guidelines. Many firms may choose to extend or add to the requirements of the bar programme at their discretion.
- To assess effectiveness and continually improve the programme, every programme should be evaluated annually through appropriate surveys of both mentors and new lawyers. Software is available for such evaluations and

can be easily accessed through the programme's website. Most programmes require completion of the survey as a condition of completion.

- A troubleshooting process must be in place when the programme starts. Given the numbers involved, problems will inevitably arise, from mismatched mentors to ethical quandaries to failure to schedule meetings. Everyone should be aware of who to contact if questions or problems arise.
- Successful programmes usually have an influential group of 'champions' who serve as the programme's initial advocates and persuade others of the programme's value and the need to participate. These groups usually self-select and arise in the early planning stages.
- Successful programmes must be adequately staffed. Usually, two people – with adequate technology resources, and a core initial group of bar association members willing to design the programme and promote it – can successfully run a programme that handles several hundred new lawyers annually.
- The cost of administering bar mentoring programmes is relatively minimal, with about 90% of costs attributable to administrative staff. The remainder is for technology support for maintaining a website which contains the programme's requirements, all necessary forms, programme elements, a way to match mentors and new lawyers electronically and programme evaluation surveys. Most bar association mentoring programmes in the United States charge a small fee to lawyers being mentored to cover the costs of the programme.

9. Conclusion

In many ways, bar associations have led the way in reinvigorating mentoring of new lawyers in the US legal profession. They have successfully designed and now administer both mandatory and voluntary mentoring programmes, which can handle hundreds of new lawyers annually on a continuing basis. A critical element in the success of these programmes has been reliance exclusively on volunteer mentors who themselves are members of the bar association administering the programmes. Another critical element has been allowing law firms to mentor their own associates, greatly reducing the need to recruit additional mentors since the firms will supply mentors.

Mentoring is a proven, low-cost, effective way to improve the professional competence of new lawyers. Further, it fits perfectly with the commitment of most bar associations to maintain high standards.

The success of bar association mentoring programmes in the United States could relatively easily be replicated in other places. Many other bar associations throughout the world could successfully operate mentoring programmes based on their own particular culture and the characteristics of their legal system. This would be a positive development for the legal profession and increase both the competence of lawyers and their satisfaction with law practice.

External coaching and mentoring

Sally Woodward
Sherwood PSF Consulting

---

1. Purpose and scope of chapter

I believe that coaching is at last coming of age in the legal sector. By this, I mean that it is increasingly recognised as a valuable tool for accelerating individual growth and supporting the success of the firm. Ten years ago, coaching was seen as a remedial exercise and lawyers saw being offered coaching as a sign of weakness, even failure, even though many of their most successful corporate clients used executive coaches at senior levels.

Today, in some law firms the key issue is when and how best to use coaching and mentoring, and how to ensure that the investment (of money and time) pays off. However, many more firms could benefit from the experience of an increasing number of well-trained coaches who are interested in working with lawyers.

This chapter explains:

- the difference between, and relative benefits and risks of, mentoring and coaching when done by outsiders;
- how some law firms currently use external, paid mentors and coaches to help their people;
- the relative benefits and risks of using outsiders when there is a choice;
- how to choose the right help for different contexts; and
- ways to get the best value from external coaches and mentors.

It also makes some future predictions.

I use the term 'coaching' or 'coach' to describe both coaching and mentoring services and those who provide either or both, except where the distinction matters; 'client' to mean the individual coaching client; and 'firm' to mean the paying client.

I look at how law firms use coaching, although its use is growing throughout the legal services sector, at external coaches only and at coaching that is paid for (often at rates comparable to those charged by senior lawyers). Other chapters discuss the increasing use of trained internal coaches and the growth of formal and informal internal mentoring.

My focus is coaching designed to enhance clients' performance or wellbeing in their work roles, even though this often entails looking at the client as the whole person and at his behaviour elsewhere. That is, I do not deal with 'life-coaching', the primary focus of which is the life satisfaction and wellbeing of the client; or with counselling and therapy. Finally, I discuss only those meetings or other conversations formally positioned as coaching. I do not cover the use of coaching as a leadership or management style, also covered elsewhere in this book – although I do believe in the value of this, especially in law firms.

1.1 Sources

My coaching practice is mainly in firms originating in the United States or Western Europe – and coaching generally has a longer history in these countries. But the use of external coaching and mentoring is by no means restricted to these jurisdictions, or to the large or international firms.

Independent research on the use of coaching by law firms is limited – although the UK-based Legal Education and Training Group has recently commissioned a large-scale survey among both providers and clients of coaching due to publish later in 2014. Research on external coaching across all sectors confirms that it has continued to increase even during the recent recession, in developed economies at least.[1]

2. Mentoring and coaching – beyond labels to substance

Lawyers understandably find it frustrating that there is no agreed set of definitions in this whole area and one function of this book is to dispel some of the mystery. The variety of terms used reflects the current state of evolution in the coaching sector, but also the different philosophies and backgrounds of service providers. It is arguably unhelpful to seek universal labels lest these deter clients (or those who help them procure coaching) from asking important questions about a prospective coach's approach and experience. The way that a coach or mentor explains what he does and how he does it helps to ensure a good fit with the client's needs.

2.1 A shared purpose

Both coaching and mentoring share the aim of helping clients to be (or become) the best they can be – in their context. This often involves supporting some form of personal growth or development, or adaptation to change. Some outsiders who do what I term mentoring describe themselves simply as business coaches or as coaches; a few do call themselves mentors – often in order to differentiate themselves from coaches. What is the difference and does it matter?

2.2 A different approach

Anne Scoular, managing director of Meyler Cambell[2] – one of Europe's leading business coach training organisations – defines the essential difference between coaching and what she calls 'traditional mentoring' as follows: "Traditional mentoring .... puts in advice, content, information. Coaching by contrast pulls out the capacity people have within."[3]

---

1 See for example the April 2014 report by The Corporate Research Forum, available at www.crforum.co.uk/join/sample.html. See also the annual survey of coaching by Sherpa Coaching, available at www.sherpacoaching.com/executive-coaching-research.html.

2 See www.meylercampbell.com and Anne Scoular's book. *The FT Guide to Business Coaching* Prentice Hall 2011).

3 In *The FT Guide to Business Coaching* p7, (above at fn 2).

This highlights an important difference in general philosophy or method, and hints at some of the relative benefits and risks of choosing a professionally trained coach and working with someone who can properly act only as a mentor.

2.3 Coaching and mentoring contrasted

(a) *Relevant expertise and/or experience*

A paid mentor has considerable expertise and experience relevant to the specific content of the client's work role or to the organisational context of the client, and explicitly contracts to share his experience as part of the services to be provided.

For example, a newly appointed managing or senior partner of a law firm may take as a mentor a former managing or senior partner of a law or comparable professional services firm (or even a current managing partner of a comparable, but non-competing firm).

A mentor will share stories, provide tips and techniques that worked for him, and invite the client to see what might be analogous to or transferable into his own context. He may also offer specific business frameworks or processes learned in a different organisation, but which help the client structure his thinking about his own firm. Mentors see themselves as a useful sounding board for the client's ideas. Some say they offer advice, like consultants.

Academics, consultants and coaches who have never actually led or managed an organisation or team, or worked inside a law firm, will struggle to act as a mentor to lawyers, or to anyone else working in a law firm. But such people may be excellent coaches.

A coach believes that the client has within himself, or can gain access to, all the ideas, information and other resources needed to grow and learn, and to make progress towards achieving his objectives.

The core requirements for effective coaching are:

- excellent skills in questioning and listening;
- the ability to focus sustained attention on the client; and
- a belief in the client's potential.

Shared experience in the substance of the client's role or environment is not necessary to facilitate the client's thinking, though many clients say they feel more comfortable talking to someone who understands what it's like to do their job. A coach who offers such non-directive coaching may never give his own ideas or opinions, though most will do so on request and if they are confident that the client really has exhausted his own resources.

Many psychologists and therapists now offer coaching[4] to business clients, including law firms. Some business coaches are also trained in specific psychological techniques, such as cognitive behavioural coaching, and are accredited to use psychometric instruments that are regulated by psychologists, such as personality questionnaires.

---

4 The British Psychological Society set up a special group in coaching psychology 10 years ago. See www.sgcp.org.uk/.

(b) ***The nature of the relationship***

A coaching relationship is one of equals, without hierarchy in any sense. The coach brings expertise in coaching, but sees his client as being an equivalent expert about himself and his firm. An external mentor is appointed precisely because he has more relevant business experience than his client.

External mentors are different from internal mentors in this respect. Internal mentors have in-depth knowledge of the firm are invariably more senior in the firm's hierarchy, and can offer well-informed advice. Some mentors have an explicit sponsorship role in supporting their mentee's career. The relationship is more akin to that of teacher and pupil, although some firms train their mentors to use a coaching style wherever possible.

(c) ***Duration, structure and payment terms***

A coaching assignment (or programme) typically comprises a set number of individual sessions (face to face or by telephone or Skype), usually each of an agreed duration and to be completed by the end of an agreed timescale. There may be some (limited) interim contact between sessions and some flexibility in structure, such as an agreed total contact time, and of timescale. The basis of payment is usually a fixed fee for the programme (even if it is based on a charge for time or a rate per session).

An external mentoring relationship (or with a coach who is also a mentor) is often more open-ended in duration and involves an unspecified number of both *ad hoc* conversations, as and when the client wants a sounding board on an issue, and more extended scheduled sessions. The coach is paid a retainer (a fee for a period such as a year), rather than charging for time or for a specific number of sessions. A mentoring relationship may start when the lawyer is appointed to his first senior leadership role, but it may continue for many years.

Some coaching relationships also continue beyond the initially agreed objectives and programme and may look like mentoring, but the overall relationship remains a coaching one.

(d) ***A spectrum rather than a dichotomy***

In practice, most external coaches and mentors do not position themselves explicitly as one rather than the other. Anne Scoular suggests that all coaches who purport to do business coaching (being individuals with substantial business experience who also have a high level of coaching skills) should be able to move along a spectrum of styles, using a mixture of approaches as the client's needs require (see Figure 1). Some coaches may even find themselves giving some brief instruction or training – for example, in a business framework or skills relevant to a particular coaching goal. An experienced coach will know when and why to move away from pulling thinking from the client in order to put in some information of ideas of their own, but they will quickly move back to asking and listening.

Figure 1: teaching – mentoring – coaching spectrum

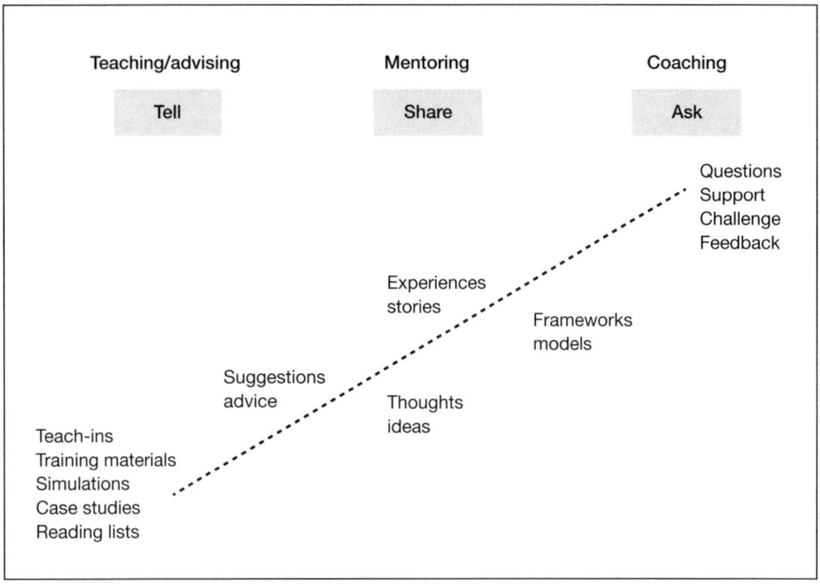

Copyright Sherwood PSF Consulting Limited, 2008

3. Do I want a mentor or a coach?

Understanding the difference between mentoring and coaching is important for both the client and the firm when choosing possible sources of external support. There are risks and opportunity costs associated with mentoring that do not exist with coaching – and vice versa.

3.1 Benefits and risks of coaching and mentoring

The biggest benefit of having a mentor is access to his experience and the credibility and empathy that come with that.

The biggest risk is that the client may treat the external mentor's experience as transferable without question, or adaptation, into his own unique context. An inexperienced mentor may even offer advice based on incomplete understanding of the situation, especially if the main source of information about it is the client himself. No external mentor will have direct experience of all issues that his client presents, or a deep understanding of his environment. This carries a risk of the client becoming overly dependent on, or unwilling to question, his mentor's views.

For example, a former managing partner of one firm might offer some strategic ideas or planning tools and help the client to explore whether these might be relevant to his firm. He should not in effect say, "This particular strategy (or process) worked for us – why not give it a try?"

The benefit of non-directive coaching flows from the fact that the client is helped to think for himself, to find solutions and identify actions to which he is fully committed. He is more likely to take the action, more ready to take responsibility for the consequences, and more likely to develop transferable confidence and skills from the experience than if someone simply tells him, or even advises him, what to do. The opportunity cost is that the results may not always be the best they could be – but that is hard to judge.

Coaching is sometimes seen to take too much time. What too much time is depends on the overall purpose of the support. Advice from a mentor may help the client to handle the immediate issue efficiently, but leave him no better able to deal with it or something similar in future. Coaching is designed to increase the client's capacity to learn and grow. Irrespective of the particular goals for the coaching assignment, many clients report that the process of being coached makes them more self-aware and better able to coach themselves when faced with new situations and challenges.

3.2 An ideal combination?

I suggest that external mentors need good coaching skills to support their role as mentors. Ideally, they should also be able to explain not simply what they did in their own organisation, but why, and why it worked (or failed). Formal business training is one basis for being able to do this. In summary, not all coaches can be mentors as well. But most mentors should be able to coach when necessary.

4. How law firms are using external mentors and coaches

There is an increasing overlap in the use of internal and external coaches – and internal coaching is discussed elsewhere in this book. What follows describes when many firms currently use outsiders even when they have a choice because there are internal coaches available. Where such internal resources do not exist or expertise is limited, firms will use outsiders whenever they regard coaching as the best way of helping the individual to pursue important performance or personal development goals.

4.1 Generic reasons for choosing an external coach

The specific coaching agenda often determines whether an internal or an external coach is appropriate, but some generic factors suggest using outsiders. Most relate to the importance of the client feeling that he controls the coaching agenda (albeit within the parameters agreed with the firm). The importance of the client making an informed choice – both of whether to engage with the coaching and in selecting the coach – has been widely demonstrated to be key to success. These generic factors which suggest using outsiders are as follows:

- Confidentiality – many professionals say they feel more comfortable talking to an outsider about personal matters that affect their performance at work, about their feelings and thoughts or about relationships with other people in the firm, especially fellow partners. Even if an internal coach can resist pressure to disclose information, his perspective on the client (and others discussed) will be changed. There may be boundaries to the confidentiality obligation, even for external coaches, and these need to be explicitly agreed as part of the contracting process.[5]

---

5 See the discussion of contracting below.

- Firm culture or organisational hierarchy – many partners say they do not feel it is 'fair' or appropriate to share their personal or business concerns with employees (even trained coaches), especially if they are junior to them. My impression is that this attitude is changing as members of Generation Y, for whom hierarchy and status seem to matter less than relevant expertise, reach partnership.
- Where the environment or key people in it are seen by the client as a barrier to progress – even if helping the client to reframe his attitude is part of the coaching agenda, the importance of gaining the client's trust and confidence makes it easier to use an outsider.
- Specialist expertise or experience – this works both ways. Sometimes the in-depth understanding of culture or context of an internal coach is invaluable. Sometimes the coaching agenda requires expertise not held by internal coaches – for example, a coach who is also experienced in business issues such as strategic analysis, has psychological training or can coach in particular skills.

4.2 Special contexts

Three areas where law firms are currently spending large parts of their coaching budget are:[6]

- transition coaching;
- leadership coaching; and
- remedial coaching.

(a) *Transition coaching*

Any significant change in role can present both technical and adaptive development challenges, however confident and competent the individual was in his previous role. Technical change means acquiring new knowledge or skills, or planning and taking action on problems to which someone already knows the answers. Adaptive change involves more than changing routine habits of behaviour; it entails adopting new perspectives and ways of thinking – changing hearts and minds as well as behaviour. The scale of the transition required depends partly on the difference in expectations between the new and former roles, and partly on individual attributes (including previous experience of change and personality traits). It also depends on how well (or not) the culture and systems support individuals in developing and using new approaches.

In law firms the main transition points for using external support are:

- becoming a partner (at least when this means a significant change of business role rather than being mainly a title to reflect seniority or expertise);
- becoming a leader (ie, taking on a significant role in leading a practice area or team with accountability for financial and business performance and for leading fellow partners (or professionals in the case of business services));

---

6 This is anecdotal evidence as there is no legal sector specific research. The CRF research referenced earlier suggests that across all sectors the first two types of coaching are increasing and the third decreasing.

- joining a new firm as a lateral hire at senior level (ie, as a partner or in a business services role);
- career transition – moving into a different role, usually outside the firm but occasionally within it; and
- maternity (and occasionally paternity) leave coaching – usually at senior level.

Research shows that even when a change in role is desired by an individual and achieves an important personal goal, there is a period of psychological disruption while he adjusts to the new requirements. Acquiring new skills and habits of working and creating new or different relationships with partners and former peers, coupled with the sense of loss from 'letting go' of things that made him successful to date (eg, the technical work), creates significant pressure and risks.

The most successful and competent individuals describe periods of feeling out of their depth and lacking confidence, which can last many months before they begin to get the measure of their new role and see some success (see Figure 2 below). In career transition, there is also the challenge of developing a whole new sense of identity. For example, if you have spent 40 years describing yourself as a tax partner at XYZ law firm, how do you now answer the question: "Who are you and what do you do?"[7]

Figure 2: Lambert transition curve

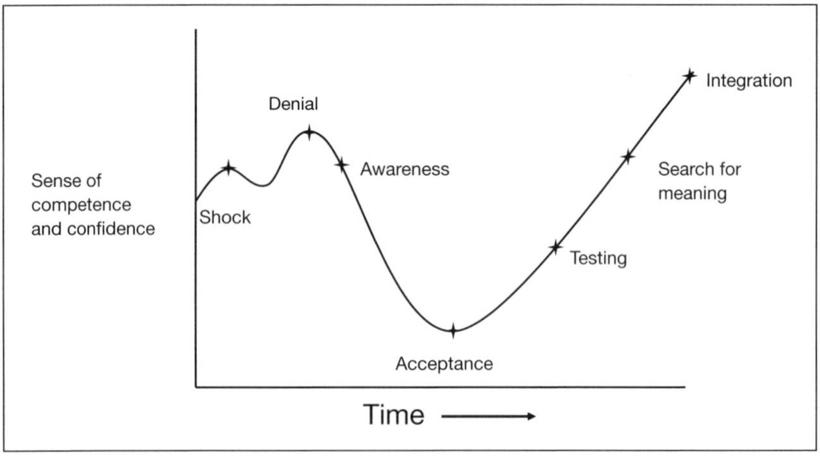

Source: Rob Lambert, unpublished paper, Cranfield University, August 1993, based on samples of executives who had recently been promoted; adapted from Adams, Hayes and Hopson, Transition: Understanding Personal Change, (1976)

These reactions are a normal and natural reaction to change and not a sign of weakness or failure, yet many lawyers nonetheless hesitate to ask for help. We need

7 See Hermione Ibarra, *Working Identity: Unconventional Strategies for Reinventing Your Career* (Harvard, 2003).

motivating and realistic development and performance goals to promote action and adaptive change, and the right mix of challenge and support to help us to recognise and overcome real or perceived barriers to progress. Skills training is helpful, but rarely enough on its own. The biggest risk is that of 'denial' – retreating to the comfort of doing those previous activities that made the client successful to date – and consequential 'plateauing'.

(b) Choice of coach and structure for transition assignments

In principle, internal coaches – with sufficient coaching skills and experience in helping people to make both technical and adaptive changes – can be successful transition coaches, especially when supported by internal mentors. As one senior partner said to me: "Why on earth would we want to use outsiders when learning to function well in the new role in our particular environment is what the coaching support is all about and for?"

In practice, much transition coaching is still being done by external coaches, partly because of lack of internal capacity or transition coaching experience and partly because clients say they feel more comfortable in talking about their challenges with an outsider who has no agenda other than to be helpful. A good combination is a limited number of external coaching sessions and support from internal mentors who have successfully been through a similar transition in the client's environment.

The structure and duration of transition assignments vary, and the time required to make a successful transition can be anything from six months to two years. Most of my transition assignments involve between four and eight coaching sessions with some interim contact, often beginning with three or four sessions held over a relatively short period. Some transition assignments are paid on a fixed-fee retainer basis for an agreed period, rather than for a set number of sessions.

4.3 Specific contexts for transition coaching

(a) Preparing for partnership

Many firms offer coaching to those on partnership track spread over a period – often a year – leading up the partnership selection process. It is often focused on developing the business and personal case for partnership, and on addressing any perceived gaps or weaknesses in skills or behaviours that may cause problems after promotion, such as the willingness or ability to delegate to and supervise juniors. This timing recognises that the incentive to develop new behaviours and the best time to experiment is before becoming a partner, rather than waiting until the gaps become more serious and the individual is facing all the other pressures of transition.

(b) Following appointment to partnership

Sometimes called 'coaching for the first 100 days', this focuses on handling adaptive and any technical challenges associated with transition and on establishing and supporting progress towards some realistic business goals for the first year as a partner. Many firms spend a large part of their external coaching budget here, and for good reason. Each new generation of partners carries many expectations, and failure is expensive for both the individual and the firms – and not simply in money terms.

Typical transition challenges include:

- learning how to manage partnership politics;
- developing new habits for managing competing demands on time, especially 'the administration'; and
- if not already addressed, learning to 'let go' of the technical legal work and to build a team.

All of this needs to be done while making the time and taking the actions needed to build a practice.

Developing a personal marketing plan is sometimes part of an external coaching agenda, though in larger firms this is increasingly handled by internal business development professionals (who ideally need coaching skills, as well being consultants and advisers). Even when armed with such a plan, many new partners welcome the challenge, support and market perspective that an external business coach provides in implementing it.

(c) Timing and structure for partnership transition coaching

In some firms all new partners are offered coaching as a matter of course. Coaching is sometimes offered on promotion to the first partnership tier in firms that have multiple tiers of partners; in others it is available only on promotion to full or senior equity partner status. I believe that the timing should depend on how substantial a change in role the promotion represents, and also the nature and scale of the transition for the individual partner.

New partner coaching assignments are usually defined as a maximum number of hours or sessions – four to six sessions or up to 12 hours is common – which the individuals can take as they choose, though the arrangement will often be expected to end within the first year. Occasionally, the firm decides on a set number of sessions to be taken at defined intervals in order to provide a clear structure for the new partner during the first challenging few months. Some firms limit the coaching to two sessions, often described as 'goal setting and action planning', especially if the culture tends to perceive coaching as remedial.

(d) Choice of coach for prospective and new partners

Pre-partnership coaching is increasingly done by internal coaches, unless there are some development goals where outside expertise is useful.

Individuals who face challenges not shared by the group as a whole are sometimes offered an external coach even if the rest have no coaching at all, or use internal coaches. Examples include coaching a new partner who had been asked to develop a whole new practice area in which the firm had no established reputation, and working with a new junior equity partner who, following the departure of a team of partners to a competitor, had been asked to take on the role of team leader as well and thus faced a double transition – from employee to partner, and into a challenging leadership role.

Many new partners welcome working with external coaches who understand the legal or professional services sector and the challenges of becoming a partner. If the primary focus of the client is on business development, he may prefer a coach who can also act as mentor. A number of coaches active in the UK legal sector have themselves been partners and built successful practices in a law firm. Provided that they are also skilled coaches, and recognise that their client is a different person, and that the client's context is different from that in which the coach succeeded, a combination of coaching and mentoring can be powerful. An alternative approach is to use an external coach and an internal partner-mentor.

What may initially present as technical challenges, such as creating a marketing plan or delegating more, often turn out to raise deeper adaptive challenges, and it is important that prospective coaches are equipped to deal with these. Experience as a law firm partner, while helpful, is not sufficient; the ability to use a range of coaching techniques and an understanding of the psychology of transition and change is even more important. Ironically, a mentor who is too ready to offer advice may hinder rather than help in such cases.

(e) Lateral hire – partners

It may seem odd to include, under the heading of transition coaching, the highly experienced partners that firms often recruit from competitors in order to fill key strategic roles. Failing to recognise that moving into a new firm – however similar the old and new firms look on paper – represents a big transition for the individual has led to much disappointment on both sides. Building a reputation and relationships in a new environment, learning about its culture and politics, and often realising that the individual's reputation may not be enough to cause previous clients to follow him, generates significant disruption to the partner's sense of confidence and competence.

Accelerating the successful integration of lateral hires is an increasing and obvious area for the use of external coaches. Firms have always been prepared to spend large sums to recruit laterals. It has always puzzled me that many then simply gave them an office and a team and apparently expected them – almost from day one – to be profitable, notwithstanding the huge contribution that situational know-how makes to our success.

There are many laterals who would benefit from coaching, but who fear to ask the firm for it lest this be interpreted as a sign of weakness. About half my lateral partner clients have paid for such coaching themselves and 'in complete confidence', which means they do not get the benefit of internal guidance and other support from the firm.

I suggest that coaching should be normal part of every 'signing-on' package for any senior lateral hire so that it is seen as a necessary and normal thing to have. For those for whom the move also represents the first partnership appointment, there is double the need – albeit one that perhaps internal coaches may be well placed to handle.

(f) Lateral hire – business services

In my experience, even fewer firms offer coaching to senior lateral hires into their business services than to their lawyer lateral hires. Yet the shock of transition can be just as great, especially if the individual is moving for the first time into a professional services environment or into a partnership structure.

I have coached people who, demonstrably successful in their corporate environment, have confessed to being perplexed by the politics of partnership and lose patience with the barriers to change they find in law firms. This is so even where bringing in fresh ideas and methods from other sectors has been a major reason for their appointment.

Some leave the law firm within their first year; and some would do so even if supported by transition coaching. A coach who can also be a mentor, a sounding board and occasionally a much-needed safety valve for frustrations can certainly accelerate their acclimatisation and help to maintain their sanity (as one client once said to me). Most business services professionals readily welcome the offer of coaching.

(g) Choice of coach and structure of coaching for laterals

The seniority and sensitivity of such assignments are the main reason for choosing an experienced external coach, although some firms complement this with internal mentoring by partners or heads of function who have themselves made a successful lateral move into the firm. This is a good way of combining the benefits of internal mentoring – since inside knowledge in this context is key to success – with the advantages that an external perspective can bring.

The number of sessions and overall duration of a coaching programme for laterals varies a lot. I usually suggest that firms offer up to six sessions, with an interim review after the first three, and that the client is left to agree the structure with their coach. The first two sessions usually focus on translating the business case for recruitment into some realistic goals for the first couple of years and on creating a plan for building the client's knowledge of the firm and his profile and network within it.

4.4 On becoming a leader

By this, I mean being appointed to a significant leadership role in the firm, such as team or group or function head, becoming senior or managing partner, or taking on another executive management role (eg, chief operating officer or equivalent).

All partners perform a leadership role in relation to their clients, matters and juniors. Some firms provide training to support them in doing so. But becoming responsible for a group of partners or business function and accountable for its strategic and financial performance targets creates many technical and adaptive challenges, especially in a partnership culture where partners often see themselves as equals and guard their personal and professional autonomy jealously. It's a major transition for most lawyers (and many business services professionals too).

(a) Choice of leadership coach and structure of the coaching

Coaching at top level is invariably done by outsiders. The ability to talk freely to someone in complete confidence, knowing that nothing that is said risks affecting the leader's internal reputation or relationships, and the benefit of having an external perspective and source of challenge, are invaluable.

A coach who can move along the coaching-mentoring-training spectrum is especially useful. Personal issues such as the setting apart from peers, or the uncertainties and risks of recommending significant strategic investments to their partners, are frequent topics for discussion. In the United Kingdom, several former leaders of law firms or professional service firms offer a combination of their stories from the front line and professional training in coaching skills. The explicit use of the label 'mentor' is most commonly found in this context.

Many lawyer leaders have not been trained in financial management or strategic analysis (although this is beginning to change). It may be important to choose a coach who can also do some 'just in time' management development or business training.

Partner leaders who have to combine their role with significant client responsibilities need coaches who can help them to handle the organisation at and psychological challenges of balancing competing demands on time and energy, none of which they feel can be met to the high standards achieved when doing client work. The pressures can be enormous and coaching to increase resilience to stress is helpful. An increasing number of coaches with a counselling or therapy background are active as leadership coaches in the legal market.

The challenge of finding the right mix of experience and skills in one person means that some law firm leaders use a variety of sources of help, formal and informal, to support their initial development and to sustain high levels of performance as a leader.

As with other transition assignments, the period over which such leadership coaching happens varies considerably. Sometimes, even if originally structured as a set number of sessions, a leader will want to keep using the coach on, say, a quarterly retainer basis – with interim contact as and when they need a sounding board for a specific issue. This does not indicate an unhealthy dependency relationship between client and coach; it reflects the continuing challenges of leading in a law firm. Many clients say that they find invaluable the discipline and certainty of a regular time and space to think about issues beyond the day job, as well as the ongoing feedback, objectivity and challenge that an experienced business coach can offer.

4.5 Career transition for partners

This is a relatively new area. Firms have for many years used external 'outplacement' consultancies for partners or other senior people whom they ask to leave because of failure to perform. Few have actively encouraged partners to start thinking about their future career and personal goals much ahead of the retirement date specified in the partnership deed.

In mature legal markets, and especially in the larger law firms, this is changing. Successful partners are choosing to leave their firms in their early 50s or even in their 40s in order to do something different or sometimes so as to have a life outside the office.

Several firms now offer coaching as part of formal succession or pre-retirement planning processes. A number of former law firm partners who have already made such a move have trained as professional coaches partly in order to target this market. However voluntary the individual's decision to move on, there are many challenges in identifying and pursuing a new working identity and set of personal and professional goals. Coaching and mentoring in this area requires a high level of empathy and skill.

Some career transition coaches also work with partners forced into involuntary career moves – for example, because market changes have made their practice unsustainable or the expectations of partners have changed in ways they cannot meet. The psychological impact of this can be immense and the boundary between coaching and therapy is often blurred. If firms offer to pay for coaching in such cases, it is vital that they help the outgoing partner to find people with sufficient expertise to avoid crossing boundaries, or who have adequate training in both coaching and counselling.

4.6 Maternity (and occasionally paternity) coaching

This is offered by some firms to staff at all levels as part of an employee assistance programme. My experience is at senior levels – working with partners or heads of department. These face business challenges such as handing over leadership responsibilities or clients as well as those of becoming a parent. The coaching usually includes one or two planning sessions before the leave starts, and two to four sessions starting just before or when the client returns to work.

The post-maternity coaching sessions address the practical and psychological issues arising from the client having yet more competing demands on her time and energy. These are often increased by a change in role or in hours of working – either permanent or temporary – and the coaching covers a wide variety of issues, including negotiating realistic business goals with relevant stakeholders and learning how to set and maintain boundaries.

In theory, any skilled coach experienced in transition coaching should be able to do this type of coaching, but most clients want someone who can mentor as well as coach – that is, someone who has experienced for themselves combining parenthood and a demanding job. However, it is important for the coach to resist the temptation to advise, rather than simply share experience or offer tentative suggestions. In this area every individual, and context, is unique. Anecdotal experience suggests that choosing someone who is trained in life or maternity coaching, but who has little experience of the business and culture of law firms, is not helpful.

5. Other contexts for external coaching

I have dealt in depth with transition coaching because this has so far been the area where most external coaching for high performers has been bought by law firms. Some firms offer coaching to their 'high fliers' or 'high potentials' as a way to support their continuing motivation and development, especially when promotion is a long way in the future. Other contexts include the following.

5.1 Leadership coaching (for experienced leaders)

During the recent recession, some experienced leaders whose firm or practice area faced a crisis as a result of the market changes took on coaches for the first time. Some had to work with their partners to agree and implement radical changes in strategy – targeting new markets or ways of getting the work done at lower cost. Many faced difficult conversations with fellow partners.

Conversely, some law firm leaders reduced expenditure on external coaching, for both themselves and their practice group leaders, just as they found themselves tackling unprecedented challenges in uncertain times, when such support was arguably more important than ever before.

In good times as well as bad, even the most experienced leader can benefit from having a coach. As clients have variously put it, a coach is an external sounding board, a conscience, a catalyst for thinking, a mirror, a safety valve and someone who ask the questions that no one else is asking. One client said: "You are the only person I always look forward to meeting, even if it does sometimes feel akin to being subjected to a benevolent Spanish inquisition."

Many leaders in other business sectors have coaches, so why should their law firm leaders see it as self-indulgent to want this too? Yet many of them tell me that they do.

I do hope that as we emerge from recession, more leaders will allow themselves the supposed luxury of a coach to help them decide where and how to take advantage of the upturn, while continuing to encourage partners to improve in the way law firms are organised and managed, and the value propositions they offer to both staff and clients.

5.2 Single issue, or performance, coaching

For senior people, some well-timed, bespoke one-on-one coaching is often more acceptable and effective than group-based training – for example, on how to handle the media, resolving conflict within a team, or creating and executing a plan to build a new type of practice. It is often helpful to find a coach who can combine coaching with both mentoring and skills training. In larger firms this type of coaching is increasingly done by the relevant business services professionals, who are also trained in goal-setting and solution-focused coaching skills.

Occasionally, coaching is offered to lawyers at any stage of their career (outside any planned transition coaching support) who have a skills gap or a behaviour that undermines otherwise good, even excellent, performance, or which might do so in future.

Examples include:

- personal impact coaching for individuals who are perceived as 'lacking in confidence' or 'gravitas' (which may sometimes be a function of personality traits that differ from those of the majority of successful people);
- a weakness in the personal organisation or prioritising skills required to handle a growing portfolio of clients or matters; or
- a tendency to over-engineer legal advice without regard to the client's (or the firm's) commercial needs to get a deal done (or to make a profit).

It is essential to be realistic about what degree of change is necessary, possible or even desirable. Such assignments usually require coaches who are skilled in supporting both technical and adaptive change.

5.3 Top team coaching

Leadership research from other sectors suggests that, in an increasingly complex world, success is rarely attributable to one or two heroic individual leaders. It derives from the decisions and behaviours of a leadership team, and the values that it exemplifies. A successful team has been said to demonstrate:

- high levels of mutual trust;
- the readiness and skills to engage in productive conflict when debating issues;
- clarity about decisions made and the actions they imply;
- the willingness to hold each other mutually accountable; and
- a cooperative mind-set that puts the organisation's interests ahead of their own (and that of their own constituencies).[8]

A few law firms are experimenting with using an external coach to observe their top teams in action, and to teach or coach them in developing the mindset and processes that will support their growth into a high-performing team. Some teams work with several coaches who complement each other and who also provide coaching to individual team members.

It is helpful to distinguish this type of coaching from traditional team building or leadership development done at off-sites, or from the facilitation roles that business consultants and leadership development experts have performed with groups and top teams in some firms for many years. What marks out this new approach is:

- the longer-term relationship;
- the presence of the external coach as observer at meetings (not to intervene, but subsequently to be able to offer feedback to the whole team); and
- a brief over time that explicitly includes helping the group to develop different ways of working together and of making decisions.

I know of a few firms whose top team are beginning to use the principles and processes of a 'thinking environment' espoused by Nancy Kline.[9]

5.4 'Remedial' coaching

Some of the earliest external coaching commissioned by law firms was overtly 'remedial' and one type of remedial coaching remains a significant area for using external coaches. This is coaching to help individuals – invariably partners or senior members in business services – to stop or to change behaviours that are seriously undermining their own performance or the morale and performance of members of their team.

Such individuals invariably have strengths such as generating high fees, which make them valuable to their firms and historically their dysfunctional behaviour

---

8 See, for example, the research of John Katzenbach in J Katzenbach and D Smith, *The Wisdom of Teams: Creating the High Performance Organization* (McGraw-Hill, 2005), and the work of Patrick Lencioni, P Lencioni, *The Five Dysfunctions of a Team: A Leadership Fable* (Jossey-Bass, 2002) and www.thetablegroup.com

9 See N Kline, *Time to Think: Listening to Ignite the Human Mind* (Cassell, 1999) and www.TimetoThink.com.

often went unchallenged. But the reputation risks and the financial costs associated with bad behaviour have become increasingly difficult to ignore. Even when the principal victim is the perpetrator himself, the opportunity costs and client-related risks of burnout merit action.

The most common areas for intervention (which sometimes overlap) are:

- bullying behaviour, or harassment or unacceptable abuse of power;
- 'control freakery' – meaning the unwillingness or inability to delegate responsibility (for anything other than administrative tasks) or the persistent use of excessive negative criticism or reworking of work delegated that takes no account of the experience of the delegee; and
- 'workaholism' – often associated with perfectionism and high levels of visible stress.

Given that most clients do not initially volunteer to be coached, the first challenge for any coach is to help the client to recognise and take responsibility for their behaviour and its negative consequences (rather than blaming others), and to find good reasons to change it. Even given the motivation, it is a big challenge to change deeply ingrained habits of behaving, and the underpinning assumptions and beliefs about oneself and others. Anecdotal evidence suggests that success rates are 50% per cent at best and relapse rates are high in the stressful environment of modern legal practice.

A major issue is the perceived cost of securing the right type of support. The typical four to six session structure over a limited period of time is rarely sufficient for this type of coaching. Initial intensive coaching may produce early results. Maintaining the new behaviour until it becomes as ingrained as the behaviour it replaces usually takes consistent support from a sponsor inside the firm, and ready access to relevant expertise – especially in testing times, and spread over years rather than months. It is unsurprising that sometimes the individual eventually leaves the firm or that occasional lapses are tolerated so long as for most of the time the worst excesses are controlled. Occasionally coaching is transformational. Choosing the right coach is key.

Successful behavioural coaches often combine a background in counselling or psychology and business coaching. Occasionally, the client's behaviour reveals underlying personality disorders (eg, obsessive compulsive disorder or narcissism), or that they are suffering some form of mental illness such as depression or anxiety that lies beyond the skills of most coaches (and even counsellors) to handle. Recognising the limits of one's competence is essential for coaches who venture into this arena. I have never known any firm to attempt to tackle this type of coaching using internal coaches.

Such cases need to be distinguished from cases of high-performing individuals who need help in creating or maintaining their physical and psychological equilibrium in a relentlessly high-performing 24/7 service environment.

5.5 Coaching for resilience and/or wellbeing

Much recent research aims to demonstrate the financial benefits of 'happiness' and how a sense of wellbeing increases the productivity of individuals at work.[10] There is concern about increasing levels of chronic stress and mental illness, especially in the legal profession. Some law firms offer support designed to increase physical and mental wellbeing and resilience to stress, including massage, yoga or other relaxation classes, nutrition advice, subsidised gym membership and mindfulness training.

Now that organisations full of hard-edged engineers such as Google overtly promote the benefits of mindfulness,[11] it has become acceptable, even desirable, in some professional services firms to provide this form of support. Much of it is done in groups, but I find that leadership coaching assignments often move into this territory, which is not surprising given the leadership challenges today.

In the United Kingdom and Europe, Michael Chaskalson[12] has been promoting the benefits of mindfulness at work, or as he prefers to call it, 'mental training'. He positions this as a way not only of building resilience to stress, but of increasing working memory capacity and the creative problem-solving and innovative thinking that this permits. Daniel Goleman[13] is an advocate of mindfulness practice for all leaders. Mindfulness is not the only approach that increases an individual's self-awareness and emotional regulation, and there are other ways to build resilience and other coping strategies to handle stress, but the research supporting the effectiveness of mindfulness is impressive; and, since lawyers like evidence-based approaches, it seems a good place to start.[14]

6. How firms get best value from external coaching

Elsewhere in this book are chapters that discuss in detail the importance of effective contracting at the start of coaching assignments and the challenges of demonstrating the effectiveness of coaching in different contexts. In my experience, more time is spent on such areas as a matter of course when procuring external coaching – perhaps because the cost is more visible, although such issues are equally relevant to the use of internal coaches.

I suggest that there is no universal approach either to contracting or to measuring the impact of coaching. The content of contracting discussions, and whom to involve, depend on context and purpose. Sometimes the impact of coaching is not directly measurable or immediately visible, or there are multiple factors involved. There are nonetheless some issues on which there can and must be clarity from the outset.

6.1 Contracting – the overall purpose and parameters for the coaching

The broad purpose of the coaching and its parameters (boundaries), if any, need to

---

10 See, for example, Shaun Achor, *The Happiness Advantage: The Seven Principles of Positive Psychology That Fuel Success and Performance at Work* (Virgin Digital, 2011); and also the work done by the i-opener institute: www.iopenerinstitute.com and its research on *The Science of Happiness at Work*.

11 See Chade-Meng Tan, *Search Inside Yourself: The Unexpected Path to Achieving Success, Happiness and World Peace* (HarperOne, 2012).

12 See Michael Chaskalson, *The Mindful Workplace: Developing Resilient Individuals and Resonant Organizations with MBSR* (Wiley-Blackwell, 2011) and also www.mindfulnessworks.co.uk.

13 Best known perhaps for popularising the concept of emotional intelligence in *Working with Emotional Intelligence* (Bantam, 1998). His most recent book is *Focus: the Hidden Driver of Excellence* (Bloomsbury, 2013).

14 See also the writing and self-help resources of Andy Puddicombe, a former Buddhist monk who recently hit the headlines for training the G10 leaders in mindfulness techniques: www.getsomeheadspace.com.

be agreed. Are there any topics off the agenda? In remedial coaching, for example, is it permissible to discuss the possibility of the client wanting to negotiate a voluntary exit from the firm? In any context, is it permissible to discuss issues outside work that affect the performance of the client in his work role? I usually request that client and coach can discuss anything that they agree has an impact on the client's work, so long as the interests of the firm and the agreed coaching agenda are kept in mind.

6.2 Contracting – performance and coaching goals

The goals for the coaching assignment itself are different from performance goals. Coaching goals should focus on skills, behaviours or other actions that are within the control of the client, even if the aim is to increase the chances of achieving results such as promotion or building a practice. In measuring the overall effectiveness of coaching, firms should try to assess whether coaching increases the success rate of individuals or reduces the time to achieve business goals, although finding suitable controls for comparison is often difficult.

In many cases of transition coaching it is enough, at the start at least, to contract that the goal of the coaching is to support the client in making a successful transition into the new role. What that means for the client often emerges as part of – indeed a result of – the coaching and the actions that result from it, such as seeking feedback or negotiating specific objectives with the practice group head.

6.3 Confidentiality

This obligation as between the individual client and coach, and any limits to it, is always an essential issue in contracting and is frequently the reason for using an external coach. Some clients will not agree to engage with coaching at all unless they receive reassurance that there will be complete confidentiality about what is said in coaching meetings and the firm can rely on the coach to work within the agreed parameters for the coaching.

Many coaches accept no limits on the confidentiality of individual clients once the coaching contract is agreed and will report back only on the fact that the coaching has happened. Some will agree to specific limits, usually relating to situations where it appears that the client may need professional medical help or where the client reveals some conduct which could or has already put the firm or its clients at significant risk in some way.

Clearly, the coach must keep information he receives about the firm and its business confidential, and some firms ask external coaches to sign a non-disclosure agreement. Many professional coaches ask for exceptions for disclosure to professional supervisors (who are in any case under equivalent duties to their coach clients).

6.4 Three or four-way stakeholder meetings

In many cases, realistic goals for the coaching assignment and the way in which progress towards them can be observed (even if not measured) are best agreed when setting up the coaching. This frequently requires input from those in a position to see the client in action. It is always helpful to know expectations about the results and constraints on action that the client needs to meet or respect. Involving the head of department or other internal sponsors is the best way to clarify these, as well as, or occasionally instead of, getting input from the person who is actually procuring the coaching. Such conversations should normally include both coach and client to ensure they each hear what the other does. They are especially helpful in the following situations.

(a) ***New partner (or pre-partnership) coaching (and also ideally for lateral hires at senior level)***

The practice group or function head responsible for agreeing relevant business objectives can clarify the business context relating to promotion (or recruitment), including any strategic goals or constraints, and agree what resources and help will and will not be available to support the client. A line manager or internal sponsor might want to share perceptions about perceived strengths and areas for development for the individual. Others involved in HR or talent management may have data arising from development or assessment processes undertaken in preparing for promotion.

(b) ***Remedial coaching***

Creating a shared understanding of precisely what behaviour needs to change and what an acceptable outcome is for the firm is essential. This should involve someone senior – maybe the senior or managing partner. These assignments can fail from the outset because the task of contracting is delegated to someone in the HR department and no one from the senior leadership team is willing, or has the mandate, to make clear to the client the seriousness of the situation and the consequences of the client not changing his behaviour.

(c) ***Leadership coaching***

Three or four-way stakeholder meetings are not invariably necessary or helpful – at least not for initial contracting. The business context and related goals are usually already clear and known to the client – although if they are not, then obviously some input from a relevant source, such as the board or managing partner, is needed.

Sometimes, the purpose of the coaching is to help the client to articulate both business and related personal development goals, and the main purpose of involving a more senior partner is to affirm support and observe progress.

Obtaining or giving feedback to the leader is often an essential part of the coaching, in which case meetings with relevant sources (with or without the individual client present) may be needed. This is part of data gathering to inform the coaching, rather than part of the initial contracting as such.

Where an experienced leader wants to use an external coach or mentor as a sounding board or for other support, the purpose of the coaching may be to help the client to reconnect with or create some new stretching personal goals, or to address unforeseen opportunities or challenges in the business as they arise. It may not be possible to agree specific goals for the coaching assignment or retainer, or do more than to agree with the board or other relevant stakeholder the overall context and budget.

Multi-party stakeholder meetings are often, but not always, necessary or helpful at the outset. They may become so at some later point in the assignment – for example, to get some reaction to or support for some development or business goals that have emerged from the coaching.

In all cases the choice of 'stakeholder' must take account of the reasons that have brought the client to coaching in the first place.

7. Choosing the right external coach (and/or mentor)

I have considered some relevant factors in specific contexts. For an excellent source of general advice in this context and an overview of the type of people who are currently serving the business coaching market, including law firms, see Anne Scoular's "Ten tough questions to ask a prospective coach", reproduced below, and also Chapter 2 in her book, referenced earlier. The overriding factors are that the client makes his own choice of coach, albeit perhaps from a selected pool, and that someone with knowledge of coaching check that the experience and experience of the prospective coaches is fit for purpose.

Ten tough questions to ask a prospective coaching provider[15]

1. What style of coaching do you use and why?
   How do you distinguish between coaching, counselling and mentoring?
2. Where were you trained?
   How many of your associates have formal training in coaching and where were you/they accredited?
   What other relevant formal qualifications do you/your associates have?
   What professional memberships do you/your associates have?
   What ongoing professional development do you/your associates undertake?
3. Tell me about your breadth of experience
4. Tell me about a coaching "success story"
   When has your coaching failed?
5. How do you monitor the individual and organisational impact of your coaching performance?
   How do you evaluate your coaching?
   What reporting methods do you use?
6. What support and monitoring systems do you have for yourself?
   Who coaches you/your associates?
   Who supervises you/your associates?
7. Tell me in what situation you would not coach
   Are there any individuals you would not coach, and how do you identify them?
8. Tell me about your availability to a coaching client
   Where does your coaching occur?
9. Who can I speak to about your coaching?
10. May I ask what led you to choose to work as a coach?

(Reprinted courtesy of Meyler Campbell – leading providers of business coaching training, See www.meylercampbell.com)

15 Reproduced from p36 The FT Guide to Business Coaching, 2011, FT/Prentice Hall

If someone presents himself specifically as a professional mentor (rather than as a business coach who can also provide some mentoring), it is useful to ask what methods he uses and experience he brings over and above having learnt to do his job, in its context, and having a wealth of stories to share as a result. Such experience may indeed be valuable for a client who knows when and how to filter and adapt it into a different time and culture. It is different from what an experienced coach can provide.

8. Future trends?

Here are some closing thoughts and predictions:

- Interest in coaching will continue to grow among lawyers – especially with regard to how it can help already high performers to sustain their motivation and success and develop new approaches to match the opportunities and challenges law firms face.
- More law firms will train leaders and others to use coaching as a day-to-day leadership style – to understand when to tell and when to ask (ie, when to give directions or advice, and when to coach an individual to work out his own route to achieve the task). Business services professionals will benefit from adding coaching skills to their skills as internal consultants.
- More law firms will invest in encouraging training internal mentors to support junior lawyers and others 'just in time', and at key points in their career and development. No amount of external coaching is a substitute for the wisdom and experience of internal mentors who have a genuine interest in and concern for the growth and development of their mentees.
- More law firms will recognise and invest in providing a group of properly trained internal coaches to do much of the high-performance coaching that is currently done by outsiders, but does not require specialist expertise or experience beyond a high level of coaching skills and understanding of context. Some will also employ coaches with specialist psychological or counselling expertise.
- There will remain an important role for experienced external coaches, and external mentors (especially those who also have coaching skills), for senior leaders and top team coaching. They bring a broader perspective, reduce the risks of 'group think' and can alleviate the leader's sense of isolation.
- Accrediting bodies will continue to evolve to monitor the quality of providers of initial training and continuing education, and to set professional standards for individual member coaches. There is room for a number of these, representing different methods and contexts for business coaching and for coaching psychology. It is also important that independent research continues to test the underlying methods and impact of coaching and mentoring.
- I hope that external coaches (and mentors) will work more closely with procurers of coaching in law firms, and with internal coaches, to provide a judicious combination of internal and external support for the wellbeing and high performance of lawyers and others throughout their career, and on into

the next phase of their life and career outside the firm. This will be especially important in meeting the aspirations of Generation Y.

- An integrated approach to talent management will include coaching alongside many other means of developing potential. Learning the hard way takes too long and is too risky for many individuals and their firms, however well it may have served previous generations.

The greatest benefit of good coaching – internal or external, irrespective of its goals – is that it raises self-awareness, stimulates independent thinking and encourages and equips clients to take responsibility for continuous learning. The biggest obstacle to its success is the fear of asking for or accepting help, in case it is seen as a sign of vulnerability or failure. I hope that this book helps to change this perception.

Coaching needs of lawyers at various stages of their careers

Christopher Bockmann
Executive coaching and organisational consulting

---

1. Introduction

Helping individual lawyers to diagnose the nature of their needs is a key step in identifying the type of support they might benefit from. This chapter aims to provide greater perspective on the needs of lawyers as they evolve during their career. Career phases will alternate between stable and transitional periods. Individual lawyers can benefit from coaching and mentoring, particularly during these transitional periods, by providing a safe environment, perspective and tools to facilitate coping with professional and personal challenges. Career and professional development support in law firms has traditionally been concentrated at associate level rather than at partner level – the peak of achievement in the profession. The need for coaching and mentoring is being increasingly felt at partner level, with the broadening range of contributions being expected notably in business development and firm management. Partner succession is also becoming an increasingly new area of attention and is addressed when talking about needs of senior partners.

Career stages are influenced by professional factors such as changes in formal roles and in seniority. During those stages a lawyer may face a number of professional or even personal challenges, such as having to renegotiate relationships, coping with anxieties linked to acquiring new skills and greater responsibilities. These challenges will surface irrespective of the size of firm, as they are inherent to a lawyer's career progression. Careers are also impacted by less identifiable personal factors. These will typically affect levels of career motivation, ambition and choices. Both professional and personal factors will be explored in this chapter.

Addressing these needs with coaching is essential as they influence behaviours that will help a lawyer to become a better professional and may therefore enhance career satisfaction and progression.

2. Associate career stages

The career of an associate will be shaped by the nature of the work, requiring an ever-broadening range of skills. Some law firms decide to formalise these stages to provide a sense of career path and progression, and may apply a selection process to move from one step to another. Professional development needs are at their most pressing in the run-up to a potential promotion and in the first months following promotion. This is therefore an effective moment to resort to coaching. As the associate grows in responsibilities, so do the challenges in terms of professional development.

In the career of an associate there is a gradual shift from an early emphasis on developing a broad legal grounding to a wider range of skills, primarily client and people related. The technical development is naturally maintained throughout the career of the lawyer, but from a developmental perspective it will diminish in importance over time.

When looking at possible coaching and mentoring needs, stages of development (needs) of an associate can be broadly grouped under the following categories:

- individual contributor/junior associate;
- case/matter manager/senior associate; and
- counsel/partner candidate.

2.1 Junior associate

"Need to fit in and get up to speed as quickly as possible."

The first years of an associate are principally about developing legal, research and drafting skills applied to a business environment. The priority is to enable the associate to become operational as a business lawyer as efficiently and swiftly as possible. The emphasis is primarily on the acquisition and fine-tuning of professional and technical skills. This development process is achieved through practice and is often referred to as the apprentice model. In many ways, informal mentoring characterises this apprentice model, in which there is a virtuous loop of practice-feedback-learning-application. The custom of a more junior lawyer sharing an office with a more senior one is in many ways also a form of informal mentoring – helping the younger associate to move up the learning curve. This helps the junior associate to gain exposure to how legal expertise is applied in practical client work. The reflective dialogue created in mentoring will help the young associate in reframing, probing, generating hypotheses and designing new approaches to adopt in applying legal expertise to client matters. Many junior associates regularly share how much they learn by just listening to a more senior lawyer working on the phone. At this career stage, a junior associate will need to practise and develop the skills of managing communications with more senior lawyers, balancing the wish to express the numerous concerns and doubts at this early stage of the career in a way that does not feel detrimental from a career progression perspective. This ability to be assertive in a constructive manner will grow in importance with the career.

There is also a parallel exercise of integration into the workplace environment, where mentoring can play an important role. This may even take the form of buddying. The objective of such an integration exercise is to help the individual lawyer to understand the values of the firm he joined, standards of behaviour and work ethics – all critical to ensure a long-term future for the new recruit.

Mini-case study[1]

Onur, a fresh graduate from law school, got a good offer from a Dutch firm with plans to expand into Turkey (his country of origin). In addition to doing the typical work of a young associate, after two years he would also get invited by

1 Names and details have been changed for confidentiality purposes.

partners at his firm to important client meetings and events focusing on Turkey. Onur realised that his outgoing manners, combined with what could be perceived as special treatment by the partners, was gradually pulling him away from his peers. He found it increasingly difficult to integrate with his peers, even at times feeling rejected. Through coaching, Onur learned to be more in tune with his peers, pay more attention to how he communicated and listen differently to others.

2.2 Senior associate

"I will only be able to take on more responsibility if I let go of my urge to control and therefore delegate more."

The key evolution as a lawyer moves from junior to senior associate is a wider scope in responsibilities in managing matters, the teams involved and dealing with clients. These are gradual changes and formal promotion, when in place, confirms a potential that has already emerged with the associate. A senior associate will also start to feel pressure from both below (juniors) and above (partners) and will be expected to know everything on a matter.

This is the first significant career transition for a lawyer because it requires a shift towards greater management-type of activity and represents a departure from what has been one of the main sources of professional progression so far – technical competence. It will engage the lawyer in a regular exercise of self-awareness. This exercise in self-awareness and consequent fine-tuning will remain a vital ability throughout the rest of the lawyer's career.

(a) People management

The senior associate needs to balance supervising and taking responsibility for work done by more juniors without an excessive form of micro-management. It requires the senior associate to pass on tasks to more junior lawyers, guiding them in their own learning path, accepting that the work may be done differently and in the short term will be more time consuming than doing the work oneself. This process means shifting from a position of individual to a team contributor. The performance of senior associates will also be assessed on their ability to get the team working together and not just their own competence. The skills that a lawyer needs to acquire at this stage will also provide the first foundation for performance management skills.

It is important to stress the sense of loss of control for the senior associate in the exercise of delegation. Accepting to let go of tasks in order to engage in new ones represents a significant challenge and will remain with the lawyer as he grows into the career and in responsibilities. In an environment where setting ambitious targets for billable hours is often the norm, delegation may pose a dual threat – fewer recorded hours for the senior associate and possibly a budget over-spend of recorded hours for the junior associate trying to get to grips with stretching tasks.

The senior associate's development needs will revolve around how to provide feedback, reflecting on and understanding different motivational drivers in a team and linking those to setting targets. All of this requires the senior associate to develop greater emotional intelligence – an ability to recognise and guide one's emotions and those of others. These are areas where coaching can really provide value.

Development needs of a greater business nature may also appear in relation to supervision – for example, developing a greater sense of financial implications in managing a matter and in particular the allocation of work between junior associates and trainees. This is likely to be best supported through mentoring, being more a skills-based need than a behavioural-based one.

Mini-case

Alice was technically one of best lawyers in her team and her accelerated recruitment was a testament to it. She found it challenging to delegate, and when she did, it became a real source of tension with juniors. This was becoming a real problem when Alice was sometimes also rude to clients that she felt were not technically competent. Coaching helped her to appreciate the diversity of skills and personal traits in the team of juniors she was working with. In the process, she understood that she was replicating – unfairly – her level of expectations onto junior associates. She was able to build a healthier basis for her relationship with juniors.

(b) Client management

"How can I pay more attention to what my client really needs?"

At senior associate stage (or at times earlier), lawyers need to develop an understanding of how to manage and meet clients' expectations and gradually start to learn how to grow a relationship with a client. Such an ability requires the lawyer to form – through listening and questioning skills – a highly individualised picture of what a client needs and how the legal service should be provided to meet its needs most effectively. In other words, it implies developing a greater commercial awareness of the client's situation. Lawyers will also need to handle challenging client conversations. As such, client management relies on similar aptitudes of emotional intelligence used in managing people.

Developing the relationship beyond the (regular) transactions requires developing a greater commercial understanding of the client's business drivers beyond the provision of a technical/legal solution. Mentoring can be helpful in providing shared experiences and best practice.

(c) Coaching and mentoring support for senior associates

Law firms can support (senior) associates' needs in several ways. A personal awareness of the need is a prerequisite for any subsequent developmental work to be effective. Regular performance reviews fed by valuable 360 feedback will often help in highlighting specific needs that a lawyer may have. Coaching can provide value at this stage, but from a cost perspective a formal training programme could be more financially effective, leaving coaching for individuals needing more specific and tailored support. These training programmes can adopt an approach of co-development among participating lawyers, inspired from coaching principles. For firms not having the critical scale to develop a training programme or offer individual coaching, mentoring can offer an alternative. Mentoring may help through regular reviews and post-mortem analysis of matters and cases. The mentor can offer advice and share personal experience and best practice with the associate(s).

2.3 Counsel

The practice of having a counsel level between senior associate and partner is not widespread in law firms. Insofar as there would be specific coaching and mentoring needs at this stage of a lawyer's career, they are unlikely to be of a fundamentally different nature from needs that a senior associate may have in order to prepare for partner track.

If any specific needs occur, they are more likely to find their origins in career choices or satisfaction/disappointment with the counsel position.

2.4 Partner candidate

As discussed earlier, coaching needs can be more pronounced in preparation for and just after important career stages. Preparing for partnership, the most significant career stage in a lawyer's career, is one of those critical moments. This moment is defined from the stage when partners believe that a senior associate is on track and therefore needs further support to provide him with the best chance of success. This could, therefore, cover several years. Ideally, the earlier this is engaged, the better the results from a development point of view.

This transition translates into different types of needs:

- First is the need to reaffirm the expectations outlined above for senior associates around people and client management skills, as well as a greater sense of commercial awareness. Coaching, and tailoring its approach to the individual, may be particularly effective at this stage to address areas that may not have been sufficiently developed through the traditional methods of on-the-job learning and formal training. The possible reward of partnership can also be a real incentive to address a need that might have been put aside for a while. For such a situation, coaching has the additional advantage of providing a safe yet external perspective to the lawyer.
- By this stage, a senior associate is expected to have developed one or more areas of specialism feeding the business case being prepared by the practice for the partner candidate. This will also entail an in-depth understanding of the market potential in the sector(s) in which the lawyer applies his specialism. Mentoring could be a rich source of support and guidance in developing such specialism and sectorial focus. Indeed, the mentor may also provide a useful introduction to relevant networks outside the firm to strengthen this focus.

3. Partner career stages[2]

Partners careers are not structured in the same way as that of associates, yet phases of development can be identified over the whole career of a partner. These changes rarely coincide with the date of appointment – the first signs will probably appear before. The partner will find it more difficult to deal with needs felt after the appointment. With one exception, on-boarding, these phases are influenced by the nature of contributions and level of responsibilities in client relationships and in firm management, whether formal or informal. These phases will engage primarily the leadership and entrepreneurial qualities of the lawyer.

3.1 On-boarding

"As a new partner I feel the clock has been reset and because I am now a partner I am expected to deal with the situation on my own."

On-boarding for recently elected partners can represent a challenging transition.

The essential challenge met by a recently promoted partner is a paradoxical combination. The partner will feel tremendous personal satisfaction at having achieved the highest form of recognition at his firm – joining the partnership – yet it is also a form of professional 'reset'. The newly elected partner will also rapidly realise that what has been a major contributor to his professional success so far may be insufficient to grow and meet the new expectations as a partner. Many partners have shared the challenges of having the clocks put back to zero again, going from a high-performing senior associate held in high regard by partners to the most inexperienced member of the partner group who needs to demonstrate the validity of the decision in making him a partner.

At this particular stage, the need revolves principally around reassurance on the normality of the ambiguous feelings of satisfaction and anxiety. Mentors can respond well to such needs.

3.2 Junior partner

Junior partners are primarily concerned with being on track and meeting their firm's expectation of being a partner. Legal expertise, transactional skills, client management skills and hard work have already become part of the assets of the lawyer and have contributed to making partner.

One of the difficulties for a junior partner lies in the fact that firms seldom express explicitly what is expected of their young partners. The culture of law firms is characterised by a socialised process whereby expectations are not formulated explicitly; rather, they get revealed over time, a process that is faithful to the apprentice model of learning. As a senior associate, some leadership and entrepreneurial qualities may have been developed, but the need becomes much

---

2 This section draws on an Europe-wide study conducted in law firms on partners' careers highlighting new trends in partners' careers and identifying key phases of career transitions of partners. The study was conducted by Christopher Bockmann between July and December 2013 across international law firms with a combined revenue of €2.5 billion. The study included a survey of more than 270 partners on career aspirations and challenges, as well as some 60 interviews of partners across Europe.

more acute as a junior partner. At this stage of their career, junior partners face several professional challenges that can be grouped as follows.

(a) Business generation

There are two elements to business generation: developing clients and increasing market visibility by developing new services and products.

A partner needs to grow legitimacy with clients, develop further commercial sense, move from being a key contact in a client relationship managed by a partner to developing a partner badge and becoming the principal client contact on his own account. This is in fact key to the partner's future. Though senior associates are encouraged to develop sectors of specialisation, it is only as partners that they tend to have real autonomy in doing so, within the bounds of the firm's strategy. The firm strategy matters because gaining new clients is one thing, but alignment with the firm's strategy (eg, sector, size, type of legal needs, risk of commercial conflicts) can represent a further barrier to winning new clients. New partners therefore also need to look at expanding relationship with existing clients at their firm. Relationships with fellow partners will be critical in that context. Depending on how much this was encouraged when the lawyer was an associate, it may require going much more beyond the lawyer's comfort zone and accepting a continuous process of trial and error, which will be an additional source of stress.

Raising market visibility requires increasing investment time, placing pressure on effective billing time (see more under "Balancing producing and managing" below). The challenge resides in balancing the short-term need to generate billable hours and the long-term goal to raise overall level (rate) of billable hours through greater added value, visibility and innovation in legal advice. Peer pressure may force the relatively inexperienced partner to go either way. Resisting this peer pressure may provoke misunderstandings or trigger unhealthy reactions.

Mini-case study

Ralf, who recently made partner, sought support because of difficulties in generating new business, in particular by trying to capitalise on the client relationships of his (more senior) fellow partners. The coaching conversations, in fact, shed light on his independent way of working. His silence was often interpreted as a lack of interest or even negative judgement by his peers. Coaching helped him to share more and express his inner thoughts and therefore contribute to building more balanced relationships. By having closer working relationships, he also learned to ask for help.

(b) The changing nature of relationships

The junior partner goes through a phase in which relationships need to be re-contracted with former peers – senior associates – with whom a new form of legitimacy and authority needs to be established. Credibility also needs to be built with the new peers – partners. As the balance of those relationships shifts, the new partner needs to demonstrate greater empathy to understand the possible reactions of others and exercise greater assertiveness with subtlety. One of the more complex relationships to manage is with the partner(s) who sponsored the senior associate for partnership. These partners were more than likely the most important source of work for the senior associate. The junior partner may still depend in the early years on this work referral, but some of the sponsoring partners will want to see the new partner start developing his own book of business. Some of those sponsoring partners may even start refraining from passing on work because of implicit fear of competition. This last point matters because it can be a source of confusion.

Mini-case study
Sofia recently made partner and felt this was a great mark of recognition for her work. The good relationship she had with two of her previous fellow senior associates turned sour when she was put forward for partnership. As a consequence, she would end up doing the work herself, adding to her overall level of stress. Coaching helped her to understand some of the obstacles in those relationships. She understood she had to gradually become more assertive, something she was finding difficult generally. She was concerned about the possible impact of being too assertive. She learned to be more explicit about her expectations, discussing upfront and openly any perceived difficulties. Also, she gradually addressed the issue by accepting that she could have constructive professional relationships without feeling the need to be liked or even be friends with former senior associates.

The nature of the relationship with clients is also changing. The young partners will realise that as a partner, they have ultimate responsibility for the client relationship and will need to address any performance or communication issues that may originate in the team. Clients go to partners for advice, but also for criticism on the performance on a matter. The most strenuous moments of a young partner's early career are likely to be around coping with this challenging and the fear of losing a client.

(c) ***Balancing producing and managing***
" I have now five jobs but only one is billable – please help!"

In addition to building up one's practice, the junior partner will get exposed to a number of new areas of responsibility and will need to balance producing and billing matters with carefully managing the investment time (business development, team and financial management). As Lorsch and Mathias pointed out in the *Harvard Business Review* (1987), this balance is skewed towards producing by the identity of a lawyer – advising clients and applying legal expertise is what initially drew the individual to the profession. Depending on the opportunities provided as a senior associate, a partner may be more or less familiar with some of those areas of responsibilities. Although the junior partner will have learnt to delegate earlier on, becoming partner places renewed emphasis on the ability to free up time (delegate and prioritise) for investment-type activities. So from a professional point of view, this means further letting go of control, yet bearing the risk of negligence. It becomes even more important for the partner to accept and strengthen the ability to succeed through others.

Good financial management is a key enabler in finding the right balance between managing and producing. It is a time-consuming activity (pitching fee quotes at the right levels, scoping and leveraging a matter appropriately, timely billing and ensuring optimal recovery). Although many partners do not find much motivation in these aspects of their practice, the right pricing and making effective use of leverage enable them to grow their practice.

The complexity for the young partner is that all three needs set out above are interlinked: it is only by freeing up more time (delegating) that the partner will be able to engage in greater business development, which in turn will help to generate a pipeline of work for his team and reinforce/validate the changes in relationships. Re-positioning oneself is what will contribute to greater support from associates and fellow partners who might be more pre-disposed to share clients and matters/cases.

(d) Coaching and mentoring support for senior associates

In-house mentoring, a form of proactive guidance and sponsorship/encouragement, can be effective for developing business generation skills. Sharing of best practice can also be effective in balancing producing and managing. Coaching is most impactful in addressing the changes in relationships and looking at barriers to free up more time. It does so through an exercise of reflection to build a clearer picture of repetitive patterns of behaviour that undermine developmental change and understanding the triggers for those behaviours. Coaching may also help the partner to come to terms with and therefore more easily accept the new pressures of the role.

3.3 Seasoned partner

At this stage, which is probably the longest phase of all, partners will have developed a personal reputation in the market, but also within the firm. In firms working on large matters, the partner may shift from working less on transactions to greater management of transactions and client relationships run by more junior partners. Professional developmental challenges will mainly arise from a role change such as taking on management responsibilities. In some law firms and practice areas, partners may also be expected to make a broader contribution to the firm's reputation and external brand. A short note will also be made on needs arising from challenging partner group dynamics.

(a) Management roles

"In a management role, it is challenging to both be part of the partnership and 'above' it, to steer it."

A possible significant evolution for a seasoned partner is when taking on executive responsibilities (practice, office level or wider geographic ones). This tends to be more complex in partnership than in other types of organisation, by virtue of the nature of partnerships. These roles yield limited formal powers and are not always held in high regard by peers/fellow owners of the business. As a consequence, partners taking these roles need to make a particular effort to use and further develop leadership qualities – an ability to articulate, embody and realise a story of possibilities that connects meaningfully with those over whom influence is exercised. It is above all an informal form of authority.

From a development need point of view, a seasoned partner may find the challenge of management roles particularly difficult as it calls upon a different skill set from being a successful lawyer. It is true that having an impressive portfolio of clients and deals/cases will often be a prerequisite for a management role, although that is now less true than it used to be. Such success in the practice and the confidence that comes with it may also reduce a partner's ability to listen, a key ability in a management role. Partners are particularly prone to such behaviour because they have a status that equates with professional achievement, and as partners they are likely to be more isolated from external feedback that may provide perspective.

Partners taking management roles are likely to face three imperatives in extending their informal authority:

- Engage and stimulate useful conflict. This implies being able to overcome either any personal conflict-avoiding or conflict-prone tendencies and facing the tension in a productive manner. This is an essential element in any management role in order to address critical business issues and challenge organisational inertia. This quality is about separating personal aggressiveness from having a robust dialogue necessary to question policies, structure and behaviours in place. This quality is also about accepting that consensus is not sought for its own sake, but rather applied on a project/initiative basis.
- Manage a different timeframe. The cycles of strategy formulation, execution and impact which are key in any executive role tend to be much longer than legal practice related. This can be a source of frustration and even impatience in how the executive role is lived. Working on a basis extending beyond the time span of a mandate, ensuring that results are sustainable in the long run, will also provide a new dimension for the partner. Partners craving short-term results to feel satisfied and fulfilled are likely to be frustrated.
- Expand one's network of people. This requires working with a broad range of people of different personality, values and ambition. This ability to overcome personal differences for the sake of a greater goal can also be described as developing political skills. As a consequence, one's professional agenda is much less self-contained – for example, to one's own practice – but needs to include a wider range of interests.

Mini-case study

Wang had been asked to take a global management role for her practice, which had performance issues. Her managing partner knew she was the right person to turn it around. Her tough talking style was appreciated by clients and had worked well during the chaotic and rapid development of her own practice. In her new role, she found it difficult to get the support of people who now spanned many countries and often had conflicting agendas. With a coach, she learned to flex her style. She learnt also to co-construct in the early stage of her initiatives, building alliances rather than running the show alone as she used to. Coaching also helped her to realise that in fact management was a good experience, but not something she wanted to do for a long time: it was not something that made her professionally fulfilled. She also realised that this frustration was the source of her sometimes abrasive style.

Another significant change in taking a management role is the shift in the source of professional satisfaction from an external one – clients who show their appreciation through the fees they pay and their feedback – to an internal one, where the prime source of appreciation is from the peer group of partners. In taking those roles, partners move away from the day-to-day activity and the frequency of client contact is likely to change and possibly diminish. Partnerships sometimes have difficulties in evaluating and appreciating the different type of contribution involved in taking a management role. Coaching may provide support insofar as taking management roles may affect a partner's self-image and therefore confidence.

(b) External reputation

Having reached a stage of maturity, firms may encourage or even expect their partners to help raise the overall visibility and reputation of their firm. This may imply participating in a range of activity such as industry-wide bodies – regulatory or judicial – some of which have broad (innovative) implications for the community, business and beyond. The complication with this development resides possibly in having to take a stance at the risk of exposing oneself. This can be uncomfortable for a profession that is concerned with managing risks and compliance within an existing legal.

(c) Partner group dynamics

Partners in management roles are likely to feel more confronted with the challenges of dealing with tense or even conflicting group dynamics among partners, although this could in effect happen at any career stage of a partner. The nature of partnerships can also affect team dynamics. Tensions arise between autonomous members running a practice who need to cross-sell a 'hard-earned' client or share the credit for a high-profile matter. Compensation models, contribution or seniority-based, will have a significant influence on partner team dynamics. Tensions will be present in particular if the practice type and behaviours of the partners are not sufficiently coherent – for example, balancing the entrepreneurial type with collaborative ones – (hunters and gatherers in the words of David Maister, a leading analyst of professional service firms).[3]

These tensions may in fact only be the symptoms of underlying issues affecting the relationship between partners. A group of partners is likely to have many

---

3 In *Managing the Professional Service Firm* (1997).

different agendas with some shared themes, but sometimes these agendas may not necessarily have anything to do with the primary task of the group – developing a practice or an office. In fact it could be personal issues such as the need to seek attention, to feel secure or to have a high level of autonomy. These personal and sometimes implicit issues are just as likely to account for partners' behaviour in a group as the professional and primary tasks, and will affect core elements of the group such as level of trust.

(d) Coaching and mentoring support for junior partners

Coaching can be valuable in these cases because it can provide a framework for partners who may feel isolated in their role and find it difficult to express some vulnerability and therefore desire for help. Coaching can also help to assess the impact of personal issues on the professional realm. Taking on a management role can be a lonely task – one is expected to make choices, consider long-term objectives and execute sometimes unpopular decisions.

With regard to group dynamics, group coaching can be impactful for several reasons:

- It can reinforce behaviours beyond the intervention, as the group will have undergone a reflection journey together;
- People are more willing to be open to learn and experiment by realising that others face similar challenges;
- It provides insights on how group members can complement each other and reinforce perspectives;
- It makes the group dynamics more functional – for example, better at listening, at expressing the unsaid; and
- It contributes to a more intuitive alignment among the partners in a group.

3.4 Senior partner

Senior partners are those who have reached full professional maturity. Their role is likely to concentrate on managing senior client relationships, enhancing the firm's reputation in the market, enriching the partnership and mentoring other partners. As very experienced professionals, none of these challenges is likely to provoke a need for support.

Where a need may arise is in relation to stepping down from a management role or passing down over other major responsibilities, such as client relationships – in other words, preparing for one's own succession. The challenge lies in the fact that these changes mean that the partner may start contemplating the concluding years of his career at their firm. This career phase may occur at the same time as the personal transition into late adulthood (addressed below). This transition is further accentuated where the partner is a founder of the firm or has played a significant role in its development.

The nature of the challenge in this career stage is twofold:

- stepping down and the prospect of leaving behind a role and all that comes with it (eg, status, identification with a role of power). There is a real issue for partners stepping down from a management role, as the challenges of rebuilding a practice after several years of having concentrated a significant time on management are numerous. In the future, as working life extends for health and financial reasons and firms need to explore ways to capitalise on the experience of their most senior partners, the of-counsel type of role may become a more regular feature at law firms. These roles may have an important part to play in the transmission of expertise, networks and client relationships; and

- stepping out. This relates to options for continued professional fulfilment beyond the firm. In the past decade, stepping out for senior partners was primarily towards retirement, in itself anxiety provoking. Increasingly, this will change towards continued professional activity, albeit at a lesser rhythm and maybe in the form of a portfolio of activities. This could be seen as a post career.

The two are intrinsically linked: the more attractive the options in stepping out, the easier it will be to step down. Many factors facilitate the transition: a sense of having left a legacy and completed a lifetime's work, having been a good steward – leaving one's firm better than it was found – and having found a trusted implicit heir.

Mini-case study

Felix made a major contribution to the development of his office, first through the development of a real estate practice and then as a managing partner. In many ways, he was a natural managing partner: he enjoyed it and was acknowledged by all as being good at it. After nearly eight years, Felix decided to go on a sabbatical and took advantage of this to explore other professional opportunities, in particular in the non-profit sector. He was not convinced. Conveniently, his identified successor left for the competition so he stayed on. Felix worked with a coach to understand where he wanted to go next and realised in fact that until that was clear and matured, he was unlikely to leave his role as managing partner. The coach helped him to reconnect with some of his earlier personal passion that was set aside as he became a successful lawyer – the music industry. He embarked on developing a transition plan to identify ways to put his experience at the service of young musicians.

(a) Coaching support for senior partners

Coaching may help senior partners in several ways:

- to come to terms with the transition. For a partner taking an of-counsel type of role, this means accepting a (reduced) role which has a different status and recognition in the firm, reconciling oneself with the need to work longer than planned. For some partners this transition may be more clearly associated with the final years at their firm;
- to gain clarity on the key and possibly evolving personal ambition that will continue beyond the role and being a partner at that firm. Reconnecting with one's personal aspiration may facilitate developing a range of options for moving beyond one's firm; and

- to better understand any awkward dynamics and changing patterns in power relationships that may take place in a succession process between an incumbent leader and potential successor.

4. Personal lifecycles in a career

It is important to review other triggers for making use of coaching. These triggers are not linked to formal changes in roles, but rather originate in personal lifecycles and individual drivers, yet have a clear spill-over effect into the professional realm.

The nature of the triggers for these cycles will vary. Some may be associated with the various development cycles of adulthood, while others will find their origins in the high-pressured environment or be associated with some traits linked to the profession. Those development needs may not be necessarily age-related and therefore may affect a lawyer at any time in his career. These cycles may differ in cause, but may have common characteristics – for example, feelings of doubt, anxiety, sadness or weakened motivation. The effects can be felt professionally, affecting performance but also in private life by disturbing relationships.

Although some of these cycles and syndromes may occur at any times in a lawyer's career, they are more likely to affect partners because of greater pressure, a longer career as a partner (as opposed to an associate). Moreover, as there are no real formal career stages, some of those cycles may feel more pronounced in the absence of career milestones.

4.1 Personal drivers in a career

All lawyers will see their careers affected at some point by personal developmental cycles. The signs of these cycles could be reflected, for example, in a special drive to achieve a career objective, a dip in motivation or even a more profound questioning of one's career choices. While the origin may be personal, it will impact professional activities as well and therefore could bring about a development need and support from a coach.

To better understand these cycles, a career model has been developed by L Mainiero and S Sullivan[4] which identifies three stages in the pursuit of professional goals: authenticity, balance and challenge. According to the authors, one of these quests will weigh more depending on life stage and, interestingly, will vary according to gender.

For women and men, the first phase of career progression is driven by challenge, often measured in greater level of responsibility, status and compensation. Gender differences occur at the second stage of career progression: for men, authenticity – being aligned with one's true goals – comes first; whereas, for women, balance takes precedence in an attempt to better integrate professional and private lives. In the final stage, women will then prioritise authenticity and men balance. Even if some may not recognise the gender differences, the shift in core priorities (challenge/authenticity/balance) reflect broad stages of psychological development in adulthood (see below). Those shifts can take place around certain events or even

4 In *Using the Kaleidoscope Career Model to Understand the Changing Patterns of Women's* (2008).

be provoked by them, such as parenthood or a professional setback such as a delayed or refused promotion.

The event triggering a need could also be a personal disappointment with the realisation that professional success is not being experienced in a meaningful way – for instance, a lawyer who after several years at a firm reconsiders his professional choice and options (eg, moving to an in-house role), or a young partner realising an imbalance between the perceived aura of partnership and the reality of the role. This is sometimes called the 'emptiness syndrome', to reflect the gap between the efforts to reach an important professional goal, projected success and the actual feeling once the goal is reached.

Two principal stages of psychological development of adulthood have potentially clear repercussions on professional activity and therefore could engender a developmental need: the mid-life and late-adulthood transitions.

4.2 The midlife transition

"I have had a successful career as a partner, but what now?"

In the words of L Mainiero and S Sullivan, "The first half of life is about compulsion, second half is about choices."

Many professionals will pass through one or more mid-life transitions – in fact, the kaleidoscope careers could suggest at least three phases. Those transitions can be gradual or abrupt and a professional may be more or less conscious of the transition. In some cases transition may be provoked by the individual (loss of professional fulfilment, confidence) or induced by external factors (eg, absence of promotion to partner, market slowdown). This period highlights the importance of engaging in meaningful activity for a professional, whether in his relationship to society (making a contribution), clients (adding value), his team (sense of belonging), but also to himself (feeling empowered). Maister highlighted the importance in engaging in meaningful work for professionals such as lawyers.

Mid-life transitions are characterised by a feeling of a reduced congruence between chosen professional goals and ambition (eg, wanting to be a lawyer, a partner or a litigator) and achieved goals. There can be several possible sources of disappointment – maybe the lawyer has been unable to achieve the goal, or sufficient satisfaction. The lawyer may have succeeded in achieving the ambition, but realises it does not bring the hoped-for personal fulfilment and therefore is characterised by a certain form of disillusionment.

The mid-life transition, sometimes several months long, will have an impact on the mental presence, relationships and ultimately performance of the lawyer. It will typically lead to two outcomes: either recommitment to the initially chosen professional goals and ambition, maybe with some fine-tuning (eg, taking a management role in one's firm or developing a new line of business) or a reassessment leading to more profound choices (changing type of organisation or changing profession). US psychologist Bob Kegan[5] calls this the stage when adults

---

5 In *In over our heads: the mental demands of modern life* (1994).

move into self-authoring mode, in which an adult will develop an internal compass, be able to formulate his own sets of judgement rather than being dependent on an inherited frame of mind and ambitions (eg, family, professional peers, significant others or pressure of a perceived role such as partner).

It is important to stress that it is normal for all professionals to have these periods at various moments in their career. It may be that in some cases it is helpful to bring these questions to light with the help of a coach to gain perspective on underlying causes rather than just understand symptoms at the surface. Clarity can then support building strategies that bring greater alignment between personal drivers and professional context.

4.3 Late adulthood transition

Professionals reaching the concluding phase of their careers may feel the need for a broader contribution, having achieved their set goals to a certain level of satisfaction. Developmental psychologist Erik Erikson refers to this period as one of generativity:[6] striving to make a mark and create something that will outlast them, whether at their firm or in society more generally, as a source of motivation and reward. This desire to contribute is what leads lawyers at this stage to take on greater mentoring roles and encourage their firms to take an active role in corporate social responsibility.

The prelude to this second transition may manifest itself through similar symptoms (motivational or behavioural) as the earlier mid-life transition.

5. Other professional crisis and syndromes

5.1 Disillusionment with partnership

A partner may face a number of disillusions linked to the evolution of the profession and the role of the partner. Partners may feel alienated by increasing detachment from key decisions in the firm, loss of control over client relationships or a weakening sense of entrepreneurialism. This could also simply be caused by too large a gap between the perception and reality of what is associated with partnership. It is likely that such disillusions will be combined with one of the mid-life or late-adulthood transitions.

5.2 Bathsheba syndrome

With professional success can come a certain amount of complacency, partially reinforced by status, level of financial reward and access to information, people and resources. A secondary effect identified by Ludwig and Longenecker[7] is a temptation of thrill-seeking activities and possible transgression of firm values and even ethical norms. "Power corrupts", goes the popular saying. The Bathsheba syndrome is named after the wife of King David of Israel (1000 BC). The king was a visionary, highly appreciated by his people and wealthy. He could not resist seeking the forbidden – having an affair with the wife of his best army officer. He asked his

---

6 In *Childhood and society* (1950)
7 In "The Bathsheba syndrome", *Journal of Business Ethics* (1994)

commander to send him unsupported to a lethal battlefield. His officer died, the king lost his best soldier, his commander rebelled against him and internal strife in his kingdom grew when this was discovered. He lost the child he had with Bathsheba. It is as if some form of providential punishment for his actions had fallen upon him. The authors suggest a number of lessons against such self-destructive behaviour:

- It can happen to anyone – King David was not unethical at the outset;
- A balanced life (including private/professional) reduces the likelihood of such slippage;
- Avoid complacency by maintaining focus on the primary task; and
- Surround oneself by people at work and in private who either challenge or comfort when either is needed.

This last point is particularly important for senior partners who may feel alone in handling the challenges of their roles.

Coaching can provide a safe space for a partner to be both supported and guided in their reflections and yet be challenged on some assumptions that may be the source of dissatisfaction.

5.3 The summit syndrome

This syndrome is linked to the notion of reaching a plateau in one's career. For Pascale and Parsons,[8] this is a "vulnerable time for over-achievers … after the novel demands of the current position have been conquered and before the next job begins". Some partners may experience after many years a feeling of boredom in keeping on with the same type of work, even if the law evolves and new client relationships are developed. The negative impact on performance, health and private life can be significant. The authors suggest a number of symptoms as one approaches, reaches and descends from the plateau. Internal symptoms will include discontent, doubt about personal impact and cynicism. From the outside, the person is likely to see a dip in performance and, worse, may start hiding this dip from the organisation. Distractions may start to dilute focus through various coping mechanisms such as engaging in obsessive behaviours (eg, hobbies, food), in dangerous sports or in substance abuse, and others not so different from the Bathsheba syndrome.

5.4 Burnout

The pressure of the legal profession is high and periods of physical and mental tiredness are common. Lawyers will learn over time to manage these pressures; there is in fact a form of natural selection in which endurance grows over time. However, in some cases, the challenges may be more profound and lead to burnout. Burnout is characterised by a number of signs, both physical (loss of/excessive appetite, sleep, fitness) and mental (mood swings, helplessness, feeling alone).

Coaching will help in breaking down the challenges, reality checking, reconnecting with personal desires and regaining control over one's life.

---

8 In "Crisis at the summit", *Harvard Business Review* (2007).

5.5 Impostor syndrome

The term 'insecure over-achievers' (in fact, the two are linked) is sometimes used to describe lawyers. A partner working for a large firm once said that a lawyer, and especially a partner, may feel insecure when considering the hourly fees objectively. Were the partner to provide the same legal service outside the firm, would the same rate be accepted? In other words, is there real value for the fees charged? The impostor syndrome is more about perceptions and fear than an effective weakness in professional capability. The impostor lives in fear of being discovered one day and that his role and success are seen as fraudulent. As a consequence these individuals can be particularly reluctant to receive feedback on performance and sensitive to criticism, which in some cases is necessary to continue progressing professionally.

6. Conclusion

Development needs have multiple origins and feed lifelong learning. They are therefore also a real opportunity in personal growth. Growing self-awareness over time is key to the ability to recognise these needs and how they affect professional and private behaviour. Such an ability is also critical in understanding the sources of professional satisfaction and growth, an essential ingredient for the high performance that the law firm environment requires. When there is no role change, any need for coaching is likely to have its origins in a gap in alignment between one's sense of purpose and fulfilment and the professional activity one engages in. The meaning of being a partner is also evolving, with the increase in size of firms, market changes and demands of the role. Re-contracting on a new basis, incorporating all these changes, may also address some structural causes of coaching needs. Positioning coaching in particular as a support for development, helping it to move away from a perception of being a remedial method reserved for under-performers, will contribute to raising the acceptance of coaching in law firms. Lawyers may have a coach, but because of the perception of coaching and how it is used and proposed by firms, there is a trend not to share widely about its application and therefore where it can add value.

Coaching is intended to help the lawyer with a specific need. In addition, the exercise and practice of self-awareness support the lawyer in becoming more autonomous and better prepared to face future challenges. The value and power of coaching in particular derive from the fact that it attempts to bring greater coherence between the professional and the private – an essential foundation for the overall personal wellbeing and therefore improved and sustainable performance.

Summary of possible coaching needs of lawyers

	Coaching
	Reflective and experimental approach, with a particular focus on behavioural and motivational drivers of an individual
By career stage	
Junior associate	
Senior associates	• Supervising and delegating • Communicating with and managing a client on a matter
Partner candidate	
Recently elected partner	
Junior partner	• Changing nature of relationship with former peers (associate) and new peers (partner) • Freeing up time to cope with additional partner responsibilities and to develop one's practice • Coping with new sources of pressure (client, people and financial responsibilities)
Seasoned partner	• Addressing challenges linked to taking on a management role: developing an informal authority, handling increased criticism, overcoming conflict-prone or conflict-avoiding behaviour, reinforcing the ability to work with and draw on wide range of personality profiles • Managing complex partner group dynamics and the gap between behaviours and expressed thoughts • Reinforcing the ability to take a stand and expose oneself in contributing to a firm's external reputation
Senior partner	• Coming to terms with succession planning, stepping down or stepping out of one's firm • Developing options for continued professional activity beyond the firm

By life stage or issue	Characteristics	Coaching support
Mid-life transition and late-adulthood transition	• Loss of motivation • Reduced meaningfulness of work • Career disappointment or even disillusion • Increased apathy or aggression in the workplace or outside • Relationship difficulties	• Identifying the root cause of the professional challenge, not just the symptom (eg, behavioural change), challenging assumptions and constructed beliefs, raising self-awareness • Understanding or reconnecting with the source of professional satisfaction • Helping in clarifying core interests • Facilitating the acknowledgment of a change in career priorities • Revisiting career choices and reconfirming, realigning or reorienting those choices • Breaking down the challenge into manageable components, separating perception from actual situations, regaining control • Accepting and overcoming a transition period and providing tools for becoming more autonomous in managing future professional challenges
Bathsheba syndrome	• Power corrupts an individual into self-destructive behaviour	
Summit syndrome	• Overcoming boredom syndrome of over-achievers leading to dysfunctional coping mechanisms (eg, obsessive behaviour, dangerous sports, substance abuse)	
Burnout	• Physical and mental signs of over-stretch	
Impostor syndrome	• Professional anxieties and insecurity	

Coaching and mentoring as a key leadership development tool across legal generations

Nigel Spencer
Reed Smith LLP
Jon Stokes
Stokes & Jolly Ltd; Saïd Business School, Oxford University

1. Introduction

The value of coaching in the legal sector has been recognised increasingly in the last five to eight years and has been embraced with greater frequency, especially for those in senior leadership roles.[1] Leadership situations where coaching is used especially frequently include those where senior lawyers are making different types of transition, and it is a tool recognised as delivering important value and support for leaders during these periods of role and/or career change. Such transitions might include promotion; joining a new firm; entering a new role as an office, industry sector or practice group leader; or return from a long-term secondment or period of absence (including maternity leave); and preparing for change at the end of a career.

As these topics are relatively well known and often discussed, the focus in this chapter is placed instead on other, less well-examined issues such as the design and structure of learning programmes, in particular those where coaching can enhance leadership development and deliver even more value for firms and their clients. In offering these observations, our perspectives are those of two individuals who, over the last 10 years, have often worked together as a team where one of us has been the in-house adviser leading a learning and development function (Spencer) and the other an external consultant and coach (Stokes), responsible together for the design and delivery of leadership development programmes for partners. Our objectives for these programmes have usually been to create lasting behavioural change at an individual level, and coaching has been an obvious tool to utilise in pursuit of these aims. In this chapter we explain what we have learnt from implementing these approaches and where we feel that there has been additional value created from doing so.

The chapter is split into two main sections.

1 T J Delong, J J Gabarro, and R J Lees, *When professionals have to lead: a new model for high performance* (Harvard, 2007), 158–59; J Stokes and, R Jolly "Executive and Leadership Coaching" in E Cox, T Bachkirova and D A Clutterbuck (eds), *The Complete Handbook of Coaching* (London/California, 2010), 245–56; A Scoular *The Financial Times Guide to Business Coaching* (Harlow, 2011). Another indication of the increasing focus on coaching in the sector is the growth of accredited coaching programmes in the last decade, such as the Meyler Campbell Business Coach Programme (attended by many focusing on coaching in the legal sector), the School of Coaching and, in the United States, the Georgetown University Leadership Coaching Programme.

The first section looks at the ways in which coaching can enhance senior leadership development programmes, in two ways:

- through the style of learning adopted on programmes and in making such programmes more 'experiential' in their content; and
- how the implementation of coaching activity in longer development programmes can enhance the overall structure of the programmes and add significant value by ensuring greater effectiveness in the transfer of learning back to the office, together with the alignment of an individual's objectives to those of the firm.

The second part of the chapter then looks at the opposite end of the legal career path: the graduate population. Our case study in this part will highlight how an innovative approach to coaching and mentoring has proved to be a useful tool to begin the leadership development 'journey' of lawyers at an early career stage. In particular, the study highlights how this plays well with the desires of Generation Y/Millennials who are seeking immediate opportunities to contribute and high levels of involvement in the workplace.

2. How coaching can enhance senior leadership development programmes

2.1 The context of leadership development in law firms: our approach to address the inherent challenges

Before describing the programmes, it is important to set out the context and challenges which, from a learning perspective, were some of our main drivers for utilising coaching in the way described here. There are two main points to emphasise here. First, as noted elsewhere in this volume, lawyers live in an incredibly 'time poor' environment, especially those who perform senior roles in their firms. The challenges they face in balancing their focus of activity are often summarised as the well-known producer-manager challenge,[2] whereby it is impossible for them to leave behind the production element of their role and concentrate solely on management or leadership. Leadership therefore becomes a part-time activity for all but a very few people in any firm, with the issue of credibility (and therefore their position in the firm's hierarchy) being driven largely through the client relationships held by any individual, and their consequent revenues.

In addition to the paucity of time available for individuals to focus on their leadership role, a further challenge in designing any interventions for the senior legal population is that the partners' individual business units (even within a single firm) often face unique challenges and can have very different business models. Therefore, to gain recognition from participants of a programme's value, its learning needs to be readily applicable to each partner's unique challenges in his office or practice group. In other words, the leadership development sessions must be highly tailored,

---

2 J W Lorsch and P Mathias "When professionals have to manage", *Harvard Business Review* (July–August 1987), 78–83; T J Delong, J J Gabarro, and R J Lees, *When professionals have to lead: a new model for high performance* (Harvard, 2007), 7 and 1342. Note that the complexity and challenge of this 'juggling' have become even greater in recent years.

and utilising one-to-one coaching in programmes is an obvious way to achieve this tailored feel for the senior lawyer cohorts.

Given these environmental challenges, our approach to leadership development for senior leaders where one is seeking to create sustained, individual behavioural change has two elements, which are described in more detail below: designing sessions to have highly experiential coaching content, and structuring programmes so that coaching acts as a thread to link different modules over a whole programme.

2.2 Embedding coaching techniques in experiential leadership development programmes for senior lawyers

With regard to the style of leadership development interventions, that we have found most effective in developing skills and creating behavioural change, highly experiential programmes (learning by doing) have the greatest lasting impact.[3] We are both of the view, expressed by other psychologists, that behavioural change needs to happen at three levels: thinking, feeling and behaving. As lawyers have a strong preference for the first of these three elements, there is a strong need for leadership development with lawyers to give opportunities to 'act themselves into a new way of thinking'. Change will not happen by 'thinking themselves into a new way of acting' and, therefore, the creative use of experiential inputs (and experts) where participants practise, in real time, new behaviours and receive feedback from both expert coaches and each other give most benefit.

Our experience in law firm partner groups is that this approach is especially valuable for those who are relatively new to partnership at law firms, for whom some aspects of the manager role may be relatively (or completely) new. The skills needed for these new aspects of their roles – ranging from how to inspire or lead a team of people (or one's clients) to other important areas such as 'difficult conversations' to drive up team performance – become increasingly important, and require guidance and practice.

Such topics lend themselves particularly to coaching inputs and expertise from worlds such as the theatre, as the skills actors require to connect with an audience are highly transferable to the business context of how to connect with one's team and clients. We have used these techniques in partner programmes for many years and found that the most effective design on such programmes is if one engages the senior lawyers for as much time as possible on coaching-style exercises. Examples which work particularly well are 'goldfish bowls' (where a member of the group practises a skill and receives immediate feedback from their audience of the coach and their colleagues) or small group work where partners work with a coach to draw out learning from real-time practice of skills and situations they will face soon in their office – ideally next week!

There is another key benefit to this type of experiential activity on learning programmes: it builds high levels of trust between members of the senior leader group,

3 We are aware that the programme design described here differs significantly from some other leadership development methodologies which use case study and debate as the key course content (eg, the leadership programmes at Harvard Business/Law Schools). Both approaches can achieve important objectives. For example, the Harvard approach is an excellent way to explore issues, challenge approaches and ideas of the individuals, and to hear from peers in a group how they approach potential challenges and reach solutions. Our proposal presented here is that, where one is seeking skills development and lasting behavioural change, the experiential methodology has greatest impact.

which is a challenge for all law firms in what can be a relatively individualised profession. The act of repeated giving and receiving of feedback and constructive peer critique through coaching-focused activities (plus careful selection of who attends) therefore adds a significant business benefit, as partners who know each other well and trust each other will be much more likely to refer clients to each other. These types of learning experience enhance business referral levels across firms and strengthen the 'glue' of the personal ties which, ultimately, hold firms together at a senior level. Learning programmes, when used in this way, are therefore part of a managing partner's strategic toolkit for creating networks and linking together different elements of their businesses.

2.3 'Stretching' learning episodes using coaching approaches

In addition to enhancing the use of coaching within offsite leadership development programmes, another beneficial element to include in multi-session curricula is the use of coaching to build links between modules of a longer programme. Coaching after groups of senior leaders have attended offsite education programmes is particularly under-used and has two main benefits, which address some of the environmental challenges outlined above.[4]

First, such coaching input keeps the learning from programmes 'front of mind' when the senior lawyers return to busy day jobs after a leadership programme. Second, it allows the senior attendees to tailor and apply the learning effectively from such offsite programmes to their individual challenges. The latter is particularly important because learning transfer from classroom to the office is known to be one of the biggest challenges in executive education; investing in one-to-one follow-up coaching sessions with individual leaders after programme modules mitigates these challenges as far as possible and is therefore key to ensuring that value is created from the programmes themselves.

In diagrammatic form, when designing multi-phase leadership programmes, the model we have often tried to create is set out opposite. Originally (Figure 1), there may be leadership programmes in place consisting of more than one event, but initially these events are not linked. Depending on the precise objectives for the learning intervention, the programmes have been developed to a situation (Figure 2) where the events are woven together with a series of coaching interventions and feedback loops.

One important element illustrated in Figure 2 is that the coaching input is not just an extension of the relationship between the coaches with whom the senior lawyers interacted on the programmes themselves. Instead, to follow best practice, the coaching also engages the line manager in the process for 'contracting' purposes and includes follow-up to review and measure progress. This latter engagement with the line manager is key for driving implementation of development objectives created on programmes and, importantly, for aligning them with those of the group or office from which the attendee comes.

---

4 This element of coaching is now being built into many executive coaching programmes at major business schools (including MBA and EMBA programmes) to ensure an ongoing thread of reflection and goal-setting for personal skills development. Examples include the programmes run at Oxford University's Saïd Business School and the Judge Business School in Cambridge, where significant programmes of coaching have been developed.

Figure 1: 'Stretching' the learning episodes for our leaders

Figure 2: 'Stretching' the learning episodes for our leaders

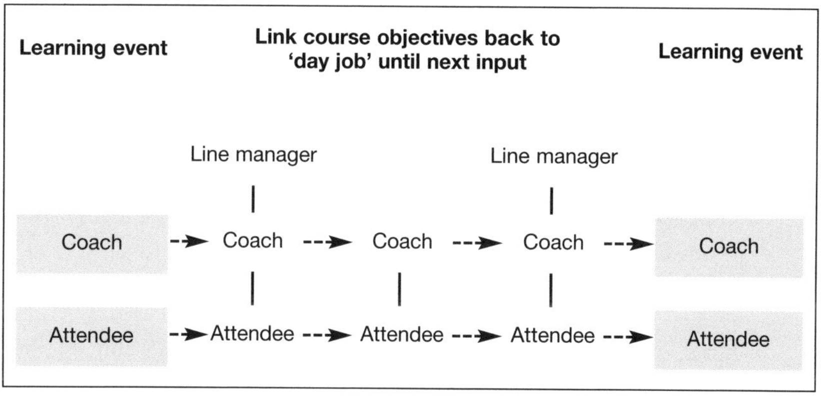

In terms of the benefits of this approach, as one managing partner once put it, the coaching follow-up work after programmes helps to "open the black box" of what happens on leadership development programmes to maximise the benefit for the firm. With careful management, one can respect confidentiality of any feedback (including 360 feedback) discussed on programmes between participants and the programme coaches, but still allow the individuals to disclose overall themes which they would like to work on with their line managers. These line managers – often more senior partners who are group, department or office heads – take part in a three-way meeting with the attendee and the coach with whom the attendee has built up trust on a programme (Figure 2). This approach ensures the alignment of the lawyers' objectives with those expected by their practice groups/offices for the leadership roles they hold on client or office teams. In addition, coaching addresses many of the challenges raised above by assisting the transfer of the learning back to the office and tailoring the learning to be effective for the individual partners who attend leadership programmes, thereby enhancing significantly the return on investment from such programmes.

Finally, another related benefit of implementing such three-way meetings after programmes with the line managers of senior lawyers is that it is one way of reaching very senior individuals who may not have attended programmes themselves, experienced coaching and/or be confident to voice its benefits to senior peers in the firm. Without this buy-in from the most senior leaders, coaching will not be seen as a mainline leadership development activity or of importance.

It is more straightforward to obtain this support if an influential figure such as the managing partner of a firm tells fellow partners that he or she has personally found coaching useful. In this situation, our experience is that one immediately sees a change in the attitude of the firm towards coaching as the most immediate culture change in a partnership comes from the top.

If the latter is not an option, however, the three-way meetings with line managers gain heightened importance and value as a bottom-up way of culture creation within the partner group. In other words, because leadership development programmes are often aimed (for appropriate reasons) at the middle or lower strata of a firm's partner cohort, growing a culture where leadership coaching becomes the mainstream can be achieved by 'lighting small fires' of such positive coaching experiences among as many different levels of the partnership as possible. The three-way meetings are a way of achieving this latter goal, and situations have often arisen where some partners (the 'line managers' of Figure 2) have never experienced coaching previously, but will make contact with the learning and development team after three-way meetings, extremely impressed with the coach's approach and interested in pursuing coaching either for themselves or for other partners. In this way, another 'small fire' of coaching activity has been lit in the firm at a different (very senior) level, and it is an interest that can be nurtured through time to create other streams of coaching inputs – ones where a high level of impact on the leadership of the firm is highly likely to result.

3. Early career stage leadership development opportunities for graduates with creative mentoring and coaching programmes

In addition to the more traditional focus of leadership development coaching at the senior stages of the legal career path described above, there are significant benefits which coaching and mentoring can bring to support leadership development at the opposite end of the legal career path – namely, for new graduates. The examples described here are case studies of work done at an international law firm (Reed Smith), and show the value created by allowing the leadership development journey of individuals to begin much earlier than has traditionally been the case, supported by creative mentoring and coaching interventions. The case studies also highlight how these interventions have significant value not just for firms themselves, but also for their clients.

This focus at a graduate level on 'leadership' may seem counter-intuitive and prompts questions. For example, should one begin leadership development activities with legal graduates or wait until the more usual mid-career level to begin such work?[5] Also, if one does try to develop leadership skills among this group, is it equally possible to create opportunities for the graduates to then practise and implement the leadership-related learning in a sector which is seen as traditional and hierarchical?

Third, can coaching and mentoring interventions assist in this leadership development process so early in the career path?

Despite these questions and challenges, we both believe that leadership can occur at any level in an organisation; it is not a function of role, but of attitude and character. Furthermore, two phenomena are beginning to drive significant change in the legal sector, and these encouraged us to explore the possibilities for early career stage leadership development with coaching and mentoring as a methodology.

First to consider is the issue of value delivery for a firm's clients and the so-called 'more-for-less' challenge.[6] In summary, the changes in the legal services market since the credit crunch have forced firms to consider even more than before how they can deliver enhanced value in their client service delivery. Of all the stages of the career path which this drive for efficiency affects, Richard Susskind picks out the junior phase as one where challenges will grow in the coming years, with clients seeking value and cost efficiency from alternative sourcing of commoditised legal tasks previously done by these junior team members.[7] Developing a broader skills base in this generation – not just of commercial skills from the MBAs and business masters courses put in place in recent years,[8] but also leadership skills – therefore seems one way to mitigate these challenges and allow junior lawyers to continue to deliver value.

Second, there is the arrival of Generation Y/Millennials into the workplace and the engagement challenge which comes with groups who have significantly different career aspirations from their predecessors. Research indicates that among the top drivers of engagement for these generations are aspects such as:

- engagement in real, meaningful activities as soon as possible in the workplace;
- a desire to be exposed to senior management, customers and clients;
- a preference to work in teams; and
- the desire for knowledge and learning which they can use to build their career.[9]

Another often-cited perspective of this generation is that they will not stay in a single firm or business for the duration of their career; they expect to change role two

---

5 N Spencer, K Best, and D Woods "The changed economy of legal knowledge: response through a radical change to the legal trainee career path" [online]. *HRM in the Knowledge Economy: British Academy of Management* HRM Special Interest Group Workshop (2011), available at: www.royalholloway.ac.uk/management/events/bam-workshop/home.aspx; in particular, see Figure 1 for the time when traditionally the leadership aspect of a lawyer's role has begun to develop.

6 R Susskind, *Tomorrow's lawyers: an introduction to your future* (Oxford, 2013).

7 *Ibid*, 29–38.

8 N Spencer "Lessons for the future" [online]. *Legal Week* (19 March 2009), available at: www.legalweek.com/legal-week/analysis/1163544/training-education-lessons-future.; N Spencer, K Best, D Woods "The changed economy of legal knowledge: response through a radical change to the legal trainee career path" [online], *HRM in the Knowledge Economy: British Academy of Management HRM Special Interest Group Workshop* (2011), available at: www.royalholloway.ac.uk/management/events/bam-workshop/ home.aspx; L Manning, "Reed Smith launches combined MA and LPC" [online], *The Lawyer 2B* (April 2 2012), available at: http://l2b.thelawyer.com/reed-smith-launches-combined-ma-and-lpc/1012051.

9 These aspects also arise regularly when speaking with current students and graduates at university open days, with questions such as the learning opportunities in any firm featuring highly on the students' agendas.

or three times, or even more. The challenge to law firms is to innovate in their learning and career management strategies to deliver on these different demands.[10]

3.1 Hierarchy and leadership in the legal sector

With these clear needs for change in the traditional learning and development strategies for legal graduates, creating leadership roles for this population seemed a way to address both the client value challenge and the Generation Y/Millennial demands. However, the perceived nature of the legal sector as a traditional and hierarchical industry appeared to present an immediate challenge to such an approach. It is often said that leadership is a "non-hierarchical concept", more about creation of followers than positional power;[11] but could this be true for graduates in the legal sector?

To understand how one can truly empower junior lawyers, it is useful to reflect briefly on what creates hierarchy, especially in law firms. By identifying these elements, it is then possible to see how leadership opportunities for junior team members can be created and how they can be fitted to the environmental context, in particular utilising coaching and mentoring initiatives.

In the *Oxford English Dictionary*, the definition of 'hierarchy' is "a system in which members of an organisation or society are ranked according to relative status or authority". In terms of how this "status or authority" is created in a law firm, this is more complex that it first appears because the constituent elements are not solely driven through seniority or experience. There could be said to be three key aspects.

Clearly, one element of status is the level of technical expertise, perhaps unsurprisingly in a classic knowledge business, although this is an element of social status and hierarchy which anthropologists would tell us has changed little since prehistory.[12]

Another factor, again in common with studies of social hierarchies in many periods of history, is either personal membership of exclusive, senior networks (eg, leadership committees), and/or the ability of individuals to be linked into these networks. There is a significant body of research to indicate that career success correlates closely with people who have the strongest personal networks and – especially – those individuals who act as bridge-points between different networks.[13] This issue of access to senior level networks has received increasing focus in professional service firms in recent years, including from the perspective of how one can improve gender balance in leadership roles in firms.[14]

---

10 N Spencer and K Best "Turning the so-called 'Generation whine' into 'Generation shine': utilising graduates to optimise strategic organisational success", *International Talent Professionals Council – Understanding Talent: Generation* Y [conference presentation] (February 2014).

11 R G Goffee and G Jones, *Why should anyone be led by you? What it takes to be an authentic leader* (Harvard, 2006).

12 J C Barrett, *Fragments from antiquity: an archaeology of social life in Britain, 2900–1200BC* (Oxford, 1994); J Robb *The early Mediterranean village: agency, material culture and social change in Neolithic Italy* (Cambridge, 2007).

13 M S Granovetter "The strength of weak ties", *American Journal of Sociology* 78 (1978),1360–80.

14 One recent focus of the work of the '30% Club', founded to increase the ratio of women on FTSE-100 boards to 30% by the end of 2015, has been increasing the level of senior sponsorship of women to increase their penetration to the higher levels of organisations within which they work.

Perhaps most importantly, however, it has been observed in many studies of partnerships that possibly the strongest corollary for status, credibility and influence is with those partners of any firm who are responsible for key client relationships and significant income generation. It is from this element above all that invisible hierarchies exist among apparently egalitarian groups of owner-managers who are often equal owners of the firm, that people become key network holders in a firm and often will gain sufficient influence to be voted into leadership roles (as such roles are rarely within the gift of a single senior sponsor, votes need to be sought across the body of equity partners).

Following from this brief analysis about hierarchy creation and maintenance in a partnership, if one were to begin leadership development at the very early stage of the career pipeline and aim to enhance the standing of junior lawyers, there would seem to be four elements to include in any such programmes to maximise the chances of success:

- Provide access to knowledge – ideally knowledge which is not possessed further up the organisation;
- Ensure access to networks and the ability to build these as broadly as possible across the organisation;
- Establish a focus on linking the early-stage leadership development activity to the firm's clients – creating opportunities for the individuals to develop and lead their own client-facing projects; and
- Persuade senior members of the firm (or clients) to become involved as sponsors of programmes or even to attend themselves.

Over the last few years, law firm Reed Smith has focused on developing leadership activities at the early career stage, implementing many of these aspects and allowing us to test this hypothesis through practice and case study. The practical examples set out below are structured around each of the four elements of hierarchy and status outlined above, highlighting in particular how coaching and mentoring has proved important in each stage and been a useful leadership development technique. The aim is to emphasise two points: first, that coaching and mentoring is a useful development tool early in the career path if used creatively – playing well with a number of engagement areas for Generation Y/Millennials mentioned above; and second, that leadership development activities can be started effectively from early in lawyers' careers, engaging and stretching them, and adding significant value to clients as a consequence.

3.2 'Pupils into teachers': reverse mentoring as a leadership development activity for early career stage lawyers

The opportunity to test the validity of some of these issues came with a recent initiative at Reed Smith where the firm innovated in the education delivered in the early career path, evolving the mandatory, post-university Legal Practice Course into a full business masters programme. The aims of this programme, which added MBA learning and a client placement into the year before students joined the firm as trainee solicitors, focused largely on the strategic need to create a different type of skill-set in junior lawyers given the increasing client demands for more commercial advisers.[15] By turning junior lawyers entering the firm into more rounded advisers with both legal and business knowledge, the strategic aim was that this innovation would deliver enhanced client service and, in turn, help to create competitive advantage over other firms which had yet to implement such broader learning.[16] In addition, the course was structured to deliver as much added value for clients as possible through the free offering of young graduates to work on topical business (not legal) research projects in-house for a month.[17]

The opportunity and value of a reverse mentoring initiative arose because, with the implementation of the new graduate business masters programme, the new core business knowledge (which ultimately the firm wanted all those in the firm to have) existed only through formal education in one generation within the firm – namely its graduates, who had not yet entered as trainee solicitors (see Figure 3).[18]

Figure 3: New core knowledge in graduate team

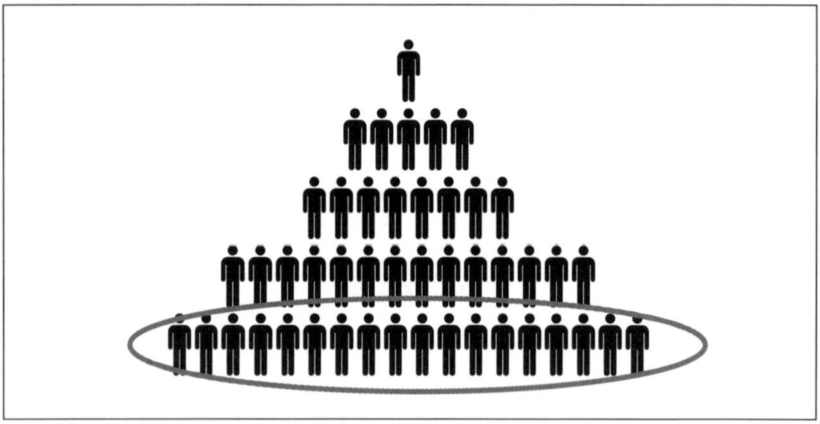

The aim of the mentoring initiative, therefore, was to spread this knowledge upward in the firm, across the traditional hierarchies. In doing so, this was, in effect,

15 N Spencer, K Best and D Woods "The changed economy of legal knowledge: response through a radical change to the legal trainee career path" [online], *HRM in the Knowledge Economy: British Academy of Management HRM Special Interest Group Workshop* (2011), available at: www.royalholloway.ac.uk/management/events/bam-workshop/home.aspx.

16 Other firms (including the Magic Circle) are now adopting this same course; see R Simmons "A&O turns to BPP to launch business-focused LPC and MA" [online], *The Lawyer 2B* (December 16 2013), available at: http://l2b.thelawyer.com/ao-turns-to-bpp-to-launch-business-focused-lpc-and-ma/3013842.article.

17 The firm was recognised for this innovation and enhanced client service in numerous awards over 2013–14, winning The Peer Awards for Innovation and Learning Excellence, 'People Development/Coaching' category, The Personnel Today award for 'Innovation in Recruitment', The Managing Partners' Forum 'Practice Management Award for Leadership Development' and the Association of Graduate Recruiters 'Best Induction Programme' award.

18 In UK legal firms, graduates are recruited whilst still at university, and then are sponsored through their mandatory post-university legal training by their recruiting firms before entering the firm as trainee solicitors. In this case, therefore, the graduates studying the new business masters course had not yet entered the firm as trainees, but were in their final, pre-joining year studying the course at BPP University College's Law and Business Schools in London.

creating a practical leadership development opportunity for the graduates, reversing their role (and hierarchical position) in the firm and asking them to swap the pupil hat they might normally wear at this career stage for a teacher hat instead.

The sessions were structured as group mentoring sessions. The graduates were asked to work in teams of four and to mentor knowledge of core business models from the new masters course to more senior members of the firm (eg, Porter's Five Forces and other similar business or strategy analysis models). At each session (about 45 to 50 minutes in length), the graduates prepared the same business model, but each team (sitting at a different table) applied the model to a client from different industry sectors from the firm's core focus areas: shipping, energy and natural resources, media and technology, financial services and life sciences. After the graduates had explained the model, and applied it to an example client in the relevant sector, the more senior mentees then reflected back how they saw the model applying to clients they were already working with and ways in which this could enhance client conversations.

One of the aspects which made the mentoring sessions work particularly well was that there was learning in both directions: the more senior mentees learnt business analysis models which they had not covered in formal education previously, and the graduate mentors also learnt more about activity in the firm's core clients. As one more senior mentee put it well, the structure of the learning sessions allowed a meeting of theory and practice.

3.3 Benefits and the inversion of traditional hierarchies

There were a number of other benefits from the approach adopted related to the drivers of status and engagement outlined above.

First, the activity established significant new networks for the graduates in advance of joining the firm, thereby serving as an excellent induction and on-boarding activity for them in the year before they joined. This is important because effective on-boarding is a challenge for law firms given the length of time between recruitment of graduates (in second or third year of their university degree) and their first day in the firm as a trainee lawyer, some two to three years later. This mentoring initiative, allowed the graduates to build cross-generational networks with those already in the firm and, importantly, to interact in these situations with them as a teacher, not as a pupil; the hierarchy was inverted and their confidence was boosted as a result.

The graduates' empowerment and engagement was also drawn from another element of status mentioned above and always highlighted by anthropologists – namely access to knowledge not possessed by other social groups in the organisation. The mentoring sessions allowed the graduates to bring new knowledge into the organisation, but also to learn from others in the sessions about the firm's client base and sectors (which would ultimately ensure that they delivered more value upon joining).

Third, from a purely return on investment perspective, there was a great advantage in allowing the graduates attending the first course to share this knowledge across the firm rather than running courses for those at other levels of the firm too. Interestingly, the firm found that the knowledge tended to spread virally from the senior mentees who attended sessions to others with whom they worked, so it utilised the firm's informal networks to share the knowledge more widely even than those who attended the reverse mentoring sessions.

Finally, as one of the graduates said, putting the graduates in a position where they had to teach more senior people forced them to consolidate knowledge effectively, and the reciprocal learning which they gained in the sessions from senior colleagues enhanced their speed to capability when they joined the firm.

3.4 Mentoring and coaching for graduates during client placements

A final area of status and hierarchy discussed above was that which arises from access to client relationships. This area was built into the masters programme as an opportunity was created for the graduates to gain such relationships (and therefore status and confidence) through a client placement as a MBA-style 'business intelligence project'. The projects ran for four weeks at a client in the summer of the masters course and required the graduates to lead a project directly with senior client stakeholders (a team leadership role which they would probably not have otherwise played for a number of years).

The process for establishing the projects was that clients were asked whether they would like extra support from graduates on any strategic business research or in-house commercial projects.[19] Replies were often enthusiastic and, after initial mentoring from partners in the firm who managed the client relationships, senior client executives acted as mentors throughout the projects until completion.

Returning to some of the themes discussed above, the projects achieved a number of aims. Above all, perhaps, it gave empirical evidence to clients that Reed Smith was developing its future junior lawyers to be broader businessmen/women; they carried out projects ranging from future product development to competitor and sector analysis or the impact of regulation on a company's business model and revenue streams. In running the projects, the graduates also developed their own network of relationships at the clients which they maintained after they joined the firm.[20] The skill-set they demonstrated also therefore helps to mitigate Susskind's challenge of the value they can deliver as junior lawyers, as their expertise and client-facing experience was not merely legal service delivery (which could potentially be commoditised), but more akin to graduate training in business consultancy.

3.5 The experience of leadership development from the graduates' perspective

Perhaps the easiest way to show the impact on the initiatives put in place is to hear one graduate's experience and consider how this expresses the objectives outlined above of giving them a real-world task to do, building networks externally, with

19 This activity delivers on another imperative of Susskind's future legal service model – reaching trusted adviser and partner status in one's client relationships. In this case the firm was partnering with clients on their future business planning, beyond engagement on solely their legal issues (R Susskind, *Tomorrow's lawyers: an introduction to your future* (Oxford, 2013), 15–22).

20 In terms of the graduates' status in the firm's hierarchy, one point to note is that many of the networks and relationships they created at clients went beyond those already in existence for more senior people in the firm, given that the process of creating the projects often meant the graduates were cross-referred within client organisations to commercial and business units running their specific projects.

access to a firm's clients and, above all, putting them in a leadership role where they had to learn by doing. Once again, this was experiential leadership development, as it had been for the senior leaders described in the first half of this chapter.

> *The client project was the best learning experience I can remember having taken part in, for several reasons. This was the first project I've undertaken that is genuinely important in the grand scheme of things. Whereas throughout the academic stages of my education work really only needed to be good enough to get the requisite grade, this project had to be excellent. I feel that this has prepared me for my training contract more than anything to date.*
>
> *Just as important, the project was a real-world task of genuine use to the client. Not only did this make the problem more engaging, it forced us to focus entirely on the client's needs. In all prior educational projects, it was possible to take the discussion in different directions or focus on tangential issues. In this case, with respect to any research we were considering adding to the report, we were forced to constantly think, "is this relevant to the client's specific problem?" This taught us to be disciplined and prioritise relevance to the end user over other considerations. On the flipside, there were issues that the client had not raised at all in their assignment, which we found were very relevant. We had to be imaginative and willing to depart from the assignment where it was necessary to deliver the most useful report.*
>
> *It was also useful in developing client relationship management skills. We kept in constant contact with the key stakeholders in the project, ensuring the scope and direction of the project was in line with their needs. We also had to manage differences and conflicts of opinion between individuals within the client. This taught us to ensure that everyone was heard (and perceiving themselves to have been heard) and their input valued, while not letting them unduly affect our recommendations.*
>
> (Reed Smith 2012–13 MA/LPC Student)

3.6 Conclusions and recommendations

The examples given in this short chapter indicate the possibilities that exist for coaching and mentoring at different stages of the legal career path. For senior lawyers, experiential learning and structuring programmes with a high degree of coaching inputs can build momentum for individual behavioural change and also engage line managers in leadership development, despite the time-poor environment in which they live. For graduates, creative uses of mentoring and coaching can map well with the behavioural drivers of Generation Y/Millennials, plus deliver on the increasing demands of clients for enhanced value creation from the junior team members of law firms.

Our experience over 10 years of the key ingredients for effective coaching and mentoring interventions as part of leadership development in law firms could be summarised, therefore, as follows:

- Obtain senior level buy-in.
- For skills development and behavioural change, make programmes experiential (learning by doing), and focus on developing skills and behaviours on programmes for challenges or situations which can be immediately applied back in the office.

- Ensure that development programmes have follow-up and metrics to stretch the learning episodes for executives living in a time-poor environment (thereby maximising the likelihood of behavioural change).
- Use coaching as a way to embed learning after programmes and assist with learning transfer.
- For alignment of personal and organisational objectives, link in line managers of attendees in the follow-up coaching activity (including in three-way contracting meetings).
- Involve junior lawyers early on in high-profile (and ideally client-facing) leadership development activity to add value to client relationships and deliver on the motivational drivers of Generation Y/Millennials.

Mentoring and coaching to leverage the learning from formal training

Sally Sanderson
Profex Consulting

What do you expect when a team member returns from a day or half-day at a training event? We know both from experience and from research[1] that much of what is learned in formal training is never applied on the job.

Law firms spend a huge amount on formal training each year. Seminars, workshops and conferences are used to share best practice and to short cut learning from experience. Many firms have a curriculum of formal training that provides development at the time new responsibilities are taken on – for example, when starting to supervise, to manage client accounts, to make presentations or to pitch for new business. A survey by Moeller PFS Group in association with the Legal Education and Training Group in the United Kingdom found that 20% of its member firms had development budgets of over £1 million, with only 32% of member firms with budgets of less than £330,000 in 2013.[2] On top of these budgets, firms are investing participant time. If firms want to maximise a return on this time and money invested, more needs to be done before and after a training event to ensure the learning isn't lost. This is where coaching and mentoring have a role to play.

Part 1 of this chapter looks at how coaching and mentoring can assist the transfer of learning and is based on case studies in law firms. Part two is a practical section providing coaching questions to use in six different situations.

1. How coaching and mentoring can assist the transfer of learning

1.1 Before and after conversations

I have been running workshop for lawyers for over 20 years. I often ask my participants about the conversation they had with their supervising partner before attending. Common responses include the following:

- Make sure you check your BlackBerry.
- Have a nice time (if travel is involved).
- Come back to the office at the end of the day.
- How will I get hold of you?
- Why do you need to attend?

---

1 As much as two thirds of new learning is never applied in the form of work behaviour: H M Hutchins, *In the trainer's voice: A study of training transfer practices*, (2009) 22 Performance Improvement Quarterly, 69–93.

2 Henry Marsden & Steven Maslin, *Law Firm Partner Development: A Maturing Activity* (November 2013).

Based on these comments or questions, how is the participant likely to feel? Focused? Energised? Ready to learn? Expected to demonstrate an improvement in his performance on return? It is extremely rare for anyone to have had a proper discussion focusing on what the wants or need to get out of a development programme.

What happens after the event? The story is often much the same:

- Where were you yesterday?
- How did it go?
- What did you learn?
- Good, now get on with your work.

One of the keys to improving the return on investment in training is to improve the quality of these conversations by asking partners to coach or mentor team members on the following occasions:

- when setting development objectives and selecting courses;
- before the course, providing focus on what needs to be learned and what is most relevant to that individual – clarifying expectations;
- after the event, focusing on what has been learned and how it will immediately be applied; and
- three months later, reviewing progress, providing feedback, assessing level of mastery and planning or how to build on what has been learned.

These aren't difficult conversations to have and they don't need to be lengthy. However, done well, they could transform the pace of development of less experienced lawyers.

By way of example, let's consider what happened on a half-day supervision skills course I ran recently for nine lawyers. At the start, the participants were asked to say what they expected from the workshop. Most found this difficult to articulate in anything other than very general terms. Three were attending because they had just started supervising trainees, one because she had been told to delegate more, one because he was fed up re-doing delegated work and two because it was part of their firm's approach to risk management. The remaining two were there just to get some tips.

During the course, their more specific and varied learning needs emerged. These included:

- a tendency towards micro-management;
- reluctance to delegate stretching tasks;
- sitting on instructions until it was too late to delegate effectively;
- dumping – for example, forwarding emails with a 'Please deal';
- failure to check understanding;
- insufficient briefing, especially on context;
- taking back work as soon as things went wrong;
- excessive review; and
- failure to give feedback promptly or at all.

Their partners or mentors probably could have raised the participants' awareness of their own specific needs before they attended the course and so primed them to learn. This would have been particularly helpful for the participant who complained that he had to re-do everything – he could not see that his style was likely to be intimidating and that his attitude (he claimed everyone he delegated to was either stupid or lazy) was part of the problem. Some feedback from his supervising partner or mentor would have been less easy to ignore than that of a trainer tactfully trying to address the problem in a public forum.

Ideally, their partners would have had a 10-minute discussion covering:

- the importance of delegation for them and their team;
- specific challenges when delegating the types of tasks in their practice area;
- clarifying what the lawyer wants and needs to focus on/learn; and
- the partner's expectations for changes in behaviour on return to work.

The course was rated highly, but as the participants left, I knew that I was sending them back into a vacuum to try out their new delegation skills. Most were enthusiastic and had specific actions they were going to take, but would anyone encourage them or review their progress? I was particularly concerned for:

- two participants who were overwhelmed by how much they would need to do/change;
- one participant who thought she wouldn't have a chance to delegate in the foreseeable future as she was the most junior in the team; and
- another participant who was keen to delegate, but thought his partner wouldn't allow it because of fee recovery concerns.

Coaching or mentoring on their return would both challenge and support them in addressing these issues. It can take a while to develop new habits and for old habits to die, so further discussions would keep the lawyer focused on experimenting and improving his delegation style. This could easily be achieved by the partner spending five minutes after the lawyer has delegated a significant piece of work, helping the lawyer to review what went well, what was done differently and whether it had had a positive impact on quality, service, profitability and the development of the delegatee.

1.2 Limitations of relying solely on formal training

In the last 20 years, training in law firms has progressed from what was predominately lecture based. Gone are the days when lawyers, just because they are bright, were expected to pick up skills by being told what to do. We know that typically we retain only a small percentage of what we hear. For skills training particularly, we also know that recall is only part of what needs to happen: people must be able to apply new skills to the job – effectively and in a range of situations. We need these new skills to become ingrained, a habit, so that the lawyer doesn't have to think consciously about applying them. To do this, a learner needs to go through the four stages of the learning cycle.

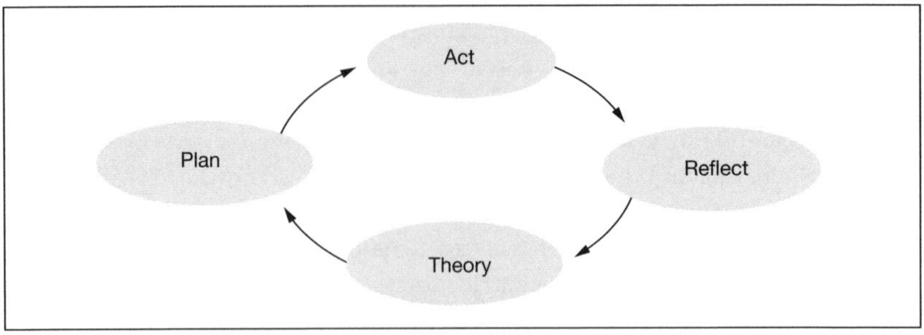

Adapted from David Kolb, Experiential Learning: Experience As The Source Of Learning And Development, *(Financial Times/Prentice Hall, 1983).*

When trainers design courses, they take this learning cycle into account by providing time for:

- practice – to have an experience, (eg, through exercises, case studies, role plays);
- reflection – review that experience and work experience through discussion or diagnostic questionnaires;
- theory – what can be generalised from the experience as rules, best practice or theories; and
- planning – actions to take on return to work.

Trainers also plan for a range of other factors which we know assist with the transfer of learning:

- ensuring that the content is perceived to be relevant to the job;
- planning and communicating clear learning outcomes to participants and their managers;
- varying activities to suit different learning styles;
- maintaining high energy and focus (eg, through interaction, pace and breaks);
- demonstrating or modelling best practice and desirable behaviours;
- providing reference materials to assist recall;
- creating opportunities to practise immediately after the event; and
- identifying the optimum size of the group.

However, as it is so difficult and expensive for lawyers to take time away from client work, training design is often compromised. Law firms attempt to deliver training in an hour that would typically be delivered over a whole day elsewhere. For example, in the legal sector we are often asked to develop leadership skills in a day, whereas elsewhere it would be covered on a week-long course or through a modular programme of several one or two-day workshops. Rarely is there sufficient time for lawyers to complete the learning cycle fully during a course and there is certainly never enough time to embed the learning through repetition of this cycle. Embedding the learning requires hardwiring the change into the brain so that we think or behave in the new way.

In *Your Brain at Work*, David Rock explains that managers need to help facilitate self-directed neuroplasticity. This is when an individual's brain creates new neural pathways or connections, which are necessary for the hardwiring of new skills. Using the findings of neuroscience, he suggests:

> *There appears to be three key components to this kind of change. First you need to create a safe environment so that any threat response is minimized. Second you need to help others focus their attention in just the right ways to create just the right new connections. Finally to keep any new circuits alive, you have to get people coming back to pay attention to their new circuits over and again.*[3]

A well-designed training programme can assist with the first two components, but the partner needs to assist with the third through coaching or mentoring conversations. "If you want a specific new map to stay in place, it's important to reactivate that map regularly."[4]

If lawyers are left to complete the learning cycle and this repetition on their own, there is a high risk that this will not happen. In their busy world, lawyers prioritise the needs of clients over their own, including their own learning. Returning from formal training, they go back to doing things as they have always done – not because they necessarily plan to do so, but because it takes too much time and effort to try out new things.

1.3 Experiments in helping the learner to transfer the learning

Recognising this trait, learning and development (L&D) teams in law firms have experimented with ways of forcing the lawyer to complete the learning cycle and to embed the learning. In some firms this even goes so far as the L&D team writing up the lawyer's development plan for them. More common approaches are:

- follow-up assignments where new skills have to be used;
- individual coaching with the programme trainer to create an action plan;
- individual coaching with the programme trainer to review implementation;
- individual coaching with members of the L&D team; and
- review workshops six weeks to three months after a programme.

A top 100 UK firm has planned its academy around facilitating this transfer of learning from the classroom to the job using project work. Each programme is designed in three phases:

- Phase 1 – know-how taught via a workshop facilitated by an expert;
- Phase 2 – a work-related project to which the know-how has to be applied when back at the desk; and
- Phase 3 – workshop review of what has been achieved in the project work and how to extend the learning going forward – facilitated by the expert who led phase 1.

The approach has been successful. At the end of his first academy programme, one lawyer commented: "I realised that after Phase 1, I couldn't just close the file and

---

3 David Rock, *Your Brain at Work* (Harper Collins, 2009), p 227.
4 David Rock, *ibid* p 233.

forget about it!" Faculty have been cheered by what has been achieved: many success stories have been told in Phase 3 workshops. For example, one senior associate on a Developing Others programme found that the workshop gave her "the strategy for dealing with it [a team member's underperformance], the tools and language", but the project made her practise the skills and develop good habits. She now coaches the team member every three months, since "things have shifted", consciously using more "positive language". The team member is grateful as this has "helped her", and is also grateful for the senior associate "taking the time to deal with it". Through repetition of practising these coaching skills, the senior associate's own learning is getting hard-wired.

At partner level, Phase 2 has sometimes been supplemented by one-to-one coaching with the expert to assist with planning the project. One partner, leading for the first time and whose project was to plan a first team meeting on strategy, commented that this had helped with "streamlining my thoughts…helped me to prepare…and plan how to approach the team members…It gave me the confidence to run the meeting." She had had feedback that "people were happy with the way the meeting had gone". Her view was that it was the combination of the group workshop with the coaching that was invaluable: "If I had just gone to the course, I think the course would have been helpful but wouldn't have got me to the point where I can do this."

The aim has always been to involve the supervising partner in supporting the Phase 2 project work. In practice, this doesn't happen enough and on several occasions the lawyer's partner has been unaware of what has happened – the learning has been invisible or below the partner's radar. Even the partner who had experienced the value of being coached when working on her project didn't support her own team members in their follow-up work. "I know I should have done it," she said, but there wasn't time. The firm is working on how to provide more coaching or mentoring within the team in Phase 2.

In other law firms, many of the initiatives to force follow-up work or review have not achieved as much as hoped. L&D teams report that lawyers often cancel their individual sessions or don't attend the follow-up – the suspicion is that they are too embarrassed to admit they haven't implemented the actions they signed up to at the end of the course and so cancel. Clearly in the short term there isn't sufficient incentive for the lawyer to prioritise this application of their learning. This is why the partner needs to be involved: to cue the consequences of not applying the learning.

1.4 Case study: Clifford Chance LLP – the need to get partners involved

A recent piece of independent research by Dan Leatherdale[5] identified lack of accountability as a major factor affecting the implementation of follow-up actions and the transfer of learning. His findings show that the role of the partner is crucial

5 *"I know I should go to the gym because it's good for me, but that doesn't mean I do it": Environmental factors and issues of accountability in the transfer of training* (MSc Organisational Behaviour, Birkbeck College, University of London, Submitted September 2013).

in bridging the gap – forcing the learner to complete the learning cycle and embed the learning before it is lost.

For the research, a magic circle firm gave access to some of its participants who had attended one of its in-house programmes. The Firm's Academy provides courses for around 5,000 employees a year. It is a very professional, well-run academy with bespoke courses tailored to the needs of lawyers at each stage of their career. It enjoys a strong reputation within the firm – the average evaluation score at the end of a course for content, presentation and relevance is 4.6 out of 5. The firm's investment in the academy is massive and it is regarded as strategically important for the recruitment, development and retention of talented people in the firm.

Leatherdale interviewed European participants six weeks after they attended the leadership skills course. The course comprises two pre-course tasks, 7.5 hours of training over two days, supplemented by a 15-minute confidential one-to-one coaching session in the evening between the two half-day workshops. The aim of the pre-course and the coaching is to help each lawyer plan how to apply the skills and tools to his own leadership situation, including how to adapt his personal leadership style based on psychometric feedback.

This programme has been running for several years and three months after the workshop lawyers are asked to comment on what they have achieved. The following two examples demonstrate that lawyers can complete the learning cycle on their own and learning can be transferred to the job:

> *I have been genuinely impressed with the outcomes from the changes in my approach to leadership. … I certainly feel more confident in leading this way and I know my boss has noticed that these projects are making faster progress than before. [London participant]*
>
> *"I had an informal review with my trainee soon after I attended the leadership skills course. The review was very helpful and everyone in my team thought my trainee developed very well after we had the review. She followed my advice and became much more proactive and responsible. Since the informal review, I also gave regular feedback to my trainee to ensure that she was fully aware of how she could improve her performance. I felt like I made good use of the leadership skills that I picked up during the course. (Hong Kong participant)*

However, after three months, not every participant attending the programme reports back with a success story. Leatherdale's research provides some useful insights. Although the lawyers described the course as "very useful", "very interesting, very, very helpful", and "an eye-opener", only some of the 13 participants interviewed could report improvements or achievements. Others had not made progress with their action plan even though they had left the course feeling enthusiastic and determined to do so. What happened was illustrated by one participant:

> *We talked about an action plan that was tailored … to my career and my specific situation … and I said, 'Yeah, well that's something I could really do that could really have a positive effect on my career.' But then, when I returned to work, I went back into the usual daily routine [and] unfortunately, I think, it hasn't had much of an effect on my daily practice.*

Lawyers at any firm can often blame a culture where the client comes first and hours are long for why they don't make sufficient progress with post-course actions. However, at Clifford Chance, one lawyer commented:

Of course, I can always say it was workload and things were distracting me ... but at the end of the day, I'm used to working under pressure. It's also a matter of priority setting.[6]

This is why the role of the partner as coach or mentor is so critical – for making the returning lawyer prioritise his own learning, ensuring that actions are implemented and the learning is extended further. Having a conversation after a course would signal to the returning lawyer that they are expected to do things differently:

I immediately receive negative feedback if I don't manage to live up to deadlines or expectations – whereas I don't receive immediate negative feedback if I don't implement the content of the academy course.[7]

At its simplest level, a coaching or mentoring conversation can make a lawyer feel more accountable for the investment that has been made in his or her development:

Interviewees felt that informal assessment in the shape of follow-up conversations would support transfer via enhanced accountability, because 'if you know there's a meeting coming up, and you're going to have to explain and demonstrate, you're sort of forced to do it' .... Another interviewee agreed it would help 'halt the slide' to have someone 'embarrass you into admitting that you haven't done half the things that you initially said you were going to do – because you might then actually do them'.[8]

Coaching would also reinforce what has been learned and be an opportunity for the returning lawyer to tap into the partner's experience:

We associates heavily depend on the instructions we receive from the partner. Because of that, it would be helpful if you could really discuss such things with the partners and discuss how to implement that into daily work life.[9]

It is not just immediately after the course that coaching could make a difference. It is also later. Has the training made a difference to how work is done? Has the learning been extended to a range of new situations? A coaching or mentoring conversation six weeks to three months later would ensure this extension of learning is taking place. Another good opportunity for this is during an annual performance review. One interviewee's experience of his review shows that this opportunity can be missed: "I go there and say, 'Yes, I attended my class', and the partner says, 'Fine.'"[10] Ideally, his performance review would include a discussion on what has been achieved through application of the new skills and how to build on it in the year ahead.

These findings all point to the crucial role the partner plays in ensuring that the learning is not lost. Overall, the research found inconsistency between partners in their approach to supporting a lawyer's learning. It is possible that younger partners

---

6 Leatherdale, *ibid.*
7 Leatherdale, *ibid.*
8 Leatherdale, *ibid.*
9 Leatherdale, *ibid.*
10 Leatherdale, *ibid.*

who have personally benefited from academy programmes are the most supportive and in the best position to link specific training provision to a lawyer's development goals – thus increasing pre-training motivation and laying the foundations for accountability.

The firm has embraced the findings and the recommendations have triggered several initiatives, including:

- asking participants to email their follow-up actions to the partner so that the participant feels more accountable and the partner can monitor and support the lawyer as learning is implemented;
- making partners more aware of the content of courses so that they know what to expect and can have better conversations pre and post-training; and
- in partner training, emphasising the role of the partner in bridging the gap between classroom and practice.

1.5 Case study: Ashurst LLP – forcing coaching and mentoring conversations

Why aren't partners initiating these pre and post-course conversations? In addition to the busyness of firms and the culture that clients come first, other barriers can get in the way:

- Some partners believe that by investing in an L&D function, they have delegated all their responsibilities for training and development and so don't need to make time for this.
- Many partners have limited experience of formal skills training, since a decade ago there was very little provision and many firms have focused their budgets on associate development. A partner, used to being the expert, can feel at a disadvantage if the associate has learned something that the partner has not had access to or, even worse, found out that the partner's approach isn't considered best practice. Of course, this is exactly where a post-course conversation could increase the return on investment in training if the partner were to use it to enhance his own approach. Done well, a coaching conversation means both parties have the opportunity to learn.
- Often it isn't clear who should have the pre and post-course conversation with the lawyer since it is common for a lawyer to work for more than one partner, especially in large teams. Each partner may assume that someone else has had time to discuss how to apply the learning.

Ashurst LLP last year created its new emerging leaders programme for a select group of top-rated senior associates identified as having leadership potential. The focus was on individual career development and key to the programme was the role of a 'sponsor' – to make a partner responsible for coaching and mentoring a senior associate at this critical stage of his career. The plan was to force these coaching conversations, which the firm knew did not happen sufficiently often. On previous programmes for senior associates, the firm had found that over 30% hadn't discussed their performance or career throughout the year with their partner and that fewer than half had discussed what they were to get out of the three-day residential programme they were attending.

The firm knew that these differing levels of partner support made it an uneven playing field for potential partner candidates and even supportive partners needed to engage in more regular conversations. Each department or office was asked to nominate a partner to take responsibility for the development of their candidate(s) over the next period of their career. To reinforce the importance of the role, the chairman and global HR director launched the programme with a conference call attended by candidates alongside their sponsoring partner. They were told:

One of the most significant elements of this programme is the active involvement of sponsors. Each participant has their own sponsor and their role is to support you in your development, not only over the next few weeks before the residential programme but also over the next 12–18 months.

The sponsor role before and after the residential programme was mapped out and sponsors were issued with guidelines to:

- meet regularly with their candidates;
- be aware of their candidates' strengths and weaknesses;
- understand their candidates' development objectives; and
- have a clear plan, developed with their candidates, of how the candidates would fulfil their potential.

To assist with this, candidates completed a 'My Pathway' document comprising a self-review of current strengths and gaps in skills or experience, feedback gained from their sponsor and others during the residential programme and a personal development plan to implement on return.

The firm did not prescribe an exact process for each sponsor to follow, recognising that different offices and practices might need to do things their own way, but they were:

- asked to review the candidate's development plan after the two-day course and at least twice more – after six months and then after one year; and
- encouraged to meet more frequently than this to review progress.

Expectations were that sponsors, in addition to having coaching and mentoring conversations, would open doors for their candidates, create opportunities for them to raise their profile and participate in activities that would close any experience or skills gaps identified.

The role of the sponsor was recognised as particularly important for female candidates. They and their sponsors were invited to a special session during the residential programme to address their specific challenges and needs.

Forcing the conversations was successful. Of the total number of candidates, 95% had had a pre-course meeting (compared to 53% in February 2013 and 44% in October 2013). Only one candidate had not: "Unfortunately didn't happen; Partner said they were too busy to meet." The quality of conversations was considerably higher too, with 78% rating it as good or very good, whereas previously pre-course discussions for most had focused on how to manage the workload during their absence. This time the conversation had focused on the candidate's self-review in the 'My Pathway' document, which provided structure and forced them to be specific about development needs. Comments included:

- "My sponsor gave feedback on where he felt I was at each area and that was very helpful."
- "Internal communication: difficult but helpful!"
- "We know each other very well, so no problem to deliver key messages."
- "Self-appraisal = very good for mentoring."

Feedback on the post-course conversations revealed that 100% took place: 50% said they were very useful and 25% rated them as useful. These conversations focused on the candidate's own development plan. It is well known among the L&D community that getting candidates to write up a detailed development is difficult, with some firms relying on their L&D team to do the work for the participant. However, on this programme only one candidate didn't complete the plan (he is still keen to do so, but personal organisation is one of the key areas for him to work on!). The very fact that candidates had to discuss the plan with their sponsors appears to have made them more accountable for the follow-up. Of course, this is a high-performing group with the incentive of partnership ahead; however, we know from previous equivalent programmes that the follow-up did not happen to the same extent, or in some cases at all.

What made these conversations so valuable? Their comments demonstrate that they clarified planning:

It helped me to have a clearer view for the next steps of my career and discuss them with my referral [sponsor] in order to have a clear schedule in mind in respect of the partnership.

I found the conversations with managers/sponsors most useful as it gave me a clearer picture of where I am at on the track.

Candidates felt supported and invested:

I feel supported by those managers who have pushed for me to participate in the programme and have set aside time to discuss with me my career path.

At best, it could generate focused, follow-up activity by both parties:

I felt that the My Pathway discussion with my managers helped encourage them to start giving me more information about client planning, finances and to get me more involved in client BD at a higher level. This was always discussed previously, but there was never much traction.

This has been explored further in some interviews to identify what the best sponsors have been doing. One candidate said he has received frequent coaching and mentoring from his sponsor. Sometimes the sponsor initiates the conversation and sometimes the candidate. The action plan from the course "helped me to structure, to orient the discussion on specific points ... I was aware of the need to address them and wanted clarification". They now talk regularly about targets, business opportunities, internal figures, the re-modelling of the team – the general points that will make up his business case for partnership which he is about to write. Another candidate commented that the sponsor's mentoring approach was really valuable:

- in getting him to "focus on what I am doing, what are the next steps, how to get there";

- when things don't go quickly enough, being encouraging, saying "take your time, do things properly"; and
- by "bringing a bit of structure" to his plans.

These positive experiences demonstrate what can be achieved when coaching and mentoring conversations before and after a programme are encouraged.

1.6 Getting the coaching and mentoring conversation right

The skill in a post-course conversation is to keep it positive and focus the participant's enthusiasm into concrete action. The learner needs to be helped to apply the learning in a way that suits him and helps him to succeed. The partner needs to ask questions that help the learner to revisit what has been covered, think how to apply it in practice and to develop his own solutions. A partner who disregards what has been covered on a programme and who imposes his own approach risks undermining the participant's enthusiasm, confidence and initiative. A too-directive approach can be disempowering.

One modular programme run by a highly respected training company was abandoned after the first stage, because the practice leader did exactly this. Living up to her reputation as a control freak, she stepped in and dictated the way in which the learners should do their follow-up. The participants, who had been highly enthusiastic, were deflated, angry and convinced her approach would not work for them. She could have avoided this by using a coaching approach – by asking questions to help each of them to align what they wanted to do with what she needed the practice to deliver.

2. How to use coaching and mentoring to bridge the gap

This section provides some sample coaching and mentoring questions to assist the transfer of learning in six situations, from setting development objectives to reviewing what has been learned. However, these will need to be adapted to the needs and personality of the individual learner. Some learners need more support and others need more challenge.

2.1 Setting effective learning objectives and selecting the right course

Coaching and mentoring can help to turn vague development objectives into more specific statements of actions to be taken. Over the years I have seen many poor development objectives on appraisal forms where training is seen as a quick solution to an ill-defined problem, for example: "Attend time management training."

The coach or mentor could use questions to establish a clearer learning objective by identifying the specific skills that the lawyer will be able to demonstrate and knowledge that they will be able to apply in practice. Objectives focused on outcomes and context, with the use of active verbs which clarify the action needed, would help the lawyer to select the right course and be more focused when attending. In each of the examples below, many different learning objectives could be established so the following are illustrative:

Poor	Better
Attend time management training	Develop techniques for prioritising work and managing conflicting deadlines.
Go on a selling course	Develop the ability to build rapport with a potential client and use effective questions to identify needs for legal services.
Improve presentation skills	Learn to project voice in meetings and when making formal presentations so as to sound more authoritative.
Learn to take a stronger lead	Learn to plan transactions and run effective briefing and update meetings so that the deal team can work efficiently.

Setting clear learning objectives is particularly important where lawyers select their own courses, without the aid of their supervising partner or mentor. If objectives are vague and the lawyer lacks self-perception, then without a coaching conversation it would be too easy to select a course based on interest rather than need, or to rely on a formal training event when other development approaches might be more appropriate.

Here are some questions to set better learning objectives/select appropriate training:

- What specifically are you finding challenging/difficult in this area?
- Once you have attended a course, what do you want to be able to do that you can't do now?
- What behaviours do you need to change?
- In six months' time, what would it look like if you were doing this/knew how to do this?
- What will be the indicators of success?
- How else could you develop this expertise/skill?
- How will this affect your career?
- What will happen if you don't master this?

2.2 Coaching or mentoring questions before the lawyer attends a course

The aim here is to prime the learner for the event and clarify the partner's expectations that the learning should make a difference to the way he performs on return. For most learners, keep the tone supportive; but for anyone who lacks self-perception, provide more challenge:

- What are you expecting to get out of the course?
- What in this area of work do you find easy?
- What do you find difficult/challenging?

- How do you see this improving your day-to-day work?
- How will you prepare for the course?
- How will you manage your time and workload so you can focus while on the course?
- You've received feedback on or I've noticed you find difficult – so this is an area to focus on. What questions do you want to ask to help you address this?
- This is an area that is going to be important/where you have little experience so far – what challenges are you anticipating that the course can help you to address?
- How will this course stretch you/take you out of your comfort zone?
- What opportunities will there be for you after the course to apply what you have learned?

2.3 Coaching or mentoring after the event – on immediate return

As soon as learners return to work, the partner needs to tap into their enthusiasm and help them to identify what will be of most relevance to their day-to-day work or responsibilities. The conversation should reinforce the partner's expectation that action will be taken. This is also a great opportunity to share the partner's experience if the learner returns with concerns or perceived barriers to implementation. If a lawyer has found that they are already doing much of what is expected, then it is a good opportunity to reinforce this strong area of their performance and plan how to build on it.

- What was of most relevance?
- What did it confirm that you are doing well?
- What did you find you could improve?
- How will you do that? When? With whom? On what task?
- How can we create opportunities for you to practise that?
- What actions have you planned so far?
- When and how are we going to review how effective this action plan has been?
- What feedback afterwards will be helpful?
- What will be the consequences for you if you don't make these changes/achieve this plan?

2.4 Coaching or mentoring six weeks to three months after the training

At this stage the aim is to revisit the learning and see to what extent it is being embedded in normal practice and transferred to a wider range of situations:

- What do you think you have achieved since the training?
- How is this helping you?
- What have other people noticed?
- What feedback have you received?
- Looking back, how far do you think you have come since the course?
- At what stage are you with these skills: novice/intermediate level/master?
- How will you build on this?
- In what other situations will you be able to use this?

If no learning, action or desired change seems to have been taken, the conversation needs to identify what is happening and address any barriers or false assumptions that are getting in the way:

- I was expecting to see you doing [desired behaviours]. What is stopping you?
- I've noticed you [describe what the lawyer is or is not doing]. Your action plan was going to address that. What's happened? How could we address this?
- How committed to your original plan are you?
- What are you more committed to that is getting in the way?
- On what assumptions is this competing commitment based?[11]
- How valid are those assumptions?
- How could we test these assumptions out?

2.5 Coaching to support a follow-up project

If the lawyer has been asked to work on a follow-up project, then coaching can ensure that the project is aligned to what is needed not only for his development but for the benefit of the practice too.

Review the project plan together:

- How realistic is it?
- How worthwhile is it?
- To what extent will it test out the new skills?
- How will you make time for this/prioritise the work?
- How motivated do you feel to work on this?

Review progress at the mid-point:

- What has been achieved so far?
- What have been the benefits to you, the team, the firm?
- What has proved more difficult than you anticipated?
- What problems have you encountered so far and how could these be solved?
- If no progress: what has got in the way and how could this be addressed?

Review what has been achieved at the end:

- What have you achieved?
- How has the project helped you to enhance your skills?
- What feedback have you received?
- How will you build on this?
- In what other situations will you be able to use this?

11 For more help with coaching when there are competing commitments see Robert Kegan and Lisa Laskow Lahey, *Immunity to Change* (Harvard Business Review Press, 2009) or D Megginson & D. Clutterbuck, *Techniques for Coaching & Mentoring* (Elsevier, 2005).

2.6 Coaching or mentoring when your team member has received psychometric feedback

Some programmes include psychometric feedback to help lawyers understand their own preferred way of doing things, their strengths and their limitations. Usually such feedback is confidential, but if a partner has an open relationship with the lawyer, it should be easy to discuss the findings. The following questions can encourage the lawyer to be open and to process the feedback constructively:

- How accurate did you find the feedback?
- In what ways did your self-awareness increase?
- What changes will you make as a consequence of the feedback?
- What will you do more of/less of/stop doing/start doing?
- How did it change your perception of others with whom you work?
- How will that affect the way you work with them?

3. Conclusion

If these coaching and mentoring questions were asked of lawyers, it could transform the pace of development in law firms. Given the amount of time and money invested in formal training programmes, these quick conversations would help to hard-wire and extend the learning. This would benefit the lawyers, their teams and the firm, and also delight L&D managers throughout the legal profession who for years have been seeking ways of bridging the gap between formal training and on-the job application of learning: an issue known as the knotty question of 'training transfer'.

Planning and mentoring for successful onboarding of lateral hires

Marc Bartel
Heidrick & Struggles

1. Introduction

We all agree that success in our ever-changing economies, the pace of change of which accelerates exponentially on a global scale (even if some may feel that it always the same old, same old at home), requires prompt action, innovation and closer team unity. Companies, and therefore clients, are looking at their country, region or continent as their new field of action and growth, forcing law practices to integrate these facts and consider measures to keep following and serving their existing or new clients as they move, change or expand.

2. High expectations are placed on new lawyers joining

Economic pressures – be they downturns in some countries, as in Europe, or stagnation or growth, as in the BRICS countries – are creating a demand for new types of legal services in a given jurisdiction or sector, or simply causing a huge increase in demand for a certain type of existing service. This may still be under-developed, or may have been considered in the recent past as either a support to other practices or simply a low-fee type of work which does not align with the profitability expectations of some firms.

As an example, employment law in France has, in the recent past, offered a smaller market or a market with generally lower-than-average fees when compared to more mainstream practices such as corporate or commercial. As these so-called profitable mainstream practices struggle in line with the French economy, those active in the French market will have noticed that employment at companies is under tremendous pressure, causing unemployment to rise at many companies, whether French or international. This trend, unfortunate as it is for many families, is essentially due to the closure of factories and the relocation of production facilities to low-wage countries, or simply to the shutting down of operations which are not profitable enough, according to either the shareholders or the company strategy, or in line with the need for fresh capital to be invested in more productive sectors. All of this, combined with complex and rigid French labour laws and the pressure of a socialist president who cannot deliver on his election promise to preserve employment, has created a new and lucrative market for lawyers representing companies that are attempting to mitigate closure-related costs. There is also a new market for lawyers who represent the unfortunate employees who have lost their jobs and are looking to obtain fair compensation for suddenly being out of work and without any serious hope of finding work in a country where people are not mobile.

Suddenly, law firms of very different sizes see an opportunity to capitalise on the demand and on their existing clients' relationships. The immediate urgency becomes to build, develop or strengthen a labour law practice, as despite the low morale in France, even pessimistic economists expect the country to eventually return to growth, and consequently the employment law market relating to closure and ensuring legal and court battles to decline.

Thus, time is of the essence to become an actor in such a strong market – existing clients being unable to wait for a firm to slowly develop a practice or to naively rebrand one of its lawyers as an employment expert. Therefore, to enter in the market at short notice, the only option is to recruit the required talent from outside.

The pressure to strengthen client relationships similarly requires the firm to reshape its offering. Although not necessarily so acute in some countries, the fact that the world is changing, with loyalty disappearing, needs to be recognised. The hope that clients will stay no matter what is now gone. This is in part driven by their ever-changing needs to adapt to their own rapidly evolving strategies, but also by the wider offering available, which forces or tempts them to work with other quality lawyers. One way to protect and defend such core relationships and future sources of revenue is in some cases to add new talent. White-collar crime litigators – who can assist companies or individuals under heightened scrutiny and investigations by the regulators, which now need or wish to police their world to compensate for their leniencies or oversights of the recent past – are in greater demand. What better way to keep engaged with a client than when advising a CEO who is being investigated. Some may – sarcastically – say that CEOs can quickly move on as well and so it is not worth the effort. Whatever the case, once again the hiring of the required talent becomes an urgency.

The pressure to compensate for loss of revenue streams with new revenue streams has also brought about the need to hire new talent to strengthen other sectors or practices. The same applies to the need to optimise foreign offices or underperforming offices, whether it be domestically or internationally. Before the global economic crisis, many firms accepted that they had operations which were delivering well below expectations or simply losing money.

Having finally agreed, or discovered the hard way in some cases, that new talent is needed at least to protect the existing business or business opportunities, and that consequently others feeling the same pain or urge are targeting and eventually siphoning off their talent, firms faced increased challenges to retain their own talent. The main strategic aim on talent management should be to ensure that performing talent, even if recently acquired, remains at the firm to implement that firm's strategic plans.

Consequently, and for all of the above-mentioned reasons, firms have very high expectations for new joiners, which are seen as an immediate increase in direct and indirect income, branding, reputation or clients.

3. Poor success rate

The legal press, which is following these talent requirements and moves, regularly produces data showing how unsuccessful talent acquisition has proved within law firms. The data shows that more than half of lateral recruitments in larger firms lead to a departure of the recruited talent within a couple of years. It obviously does not account for those who do not meet the objectives but are kept on board for various reasons, including poor performance management procedures – a certain weakness from the (practice) management who will cover their poor recruitment process, which, as we will see below, must include a fair and performing onboarding programme.

This position is obviously not limited to larger law firms, as firms of any size always face the dilemma of adapting to the ever-changing market, and so face the question of whether to acquire talent. Even when the firm is in fact simply a cost-sharing organisation, there is always the hope that it will find a new partner who, besides sharing costs, will add value to the group as a whole. Although data may not be available, those experienced in the legal market as a whole will have heard all too often complaints about the lack of direct or indirect contribution or simply the lack of shared cultural values (also call egotism) by some.

Although it is not the focus of this chapter, firms should learn to recruit their partners. It seems that recruitment required for the above reasons is almost always reactive, defensive and opportunistic, done in some urgency and polarised on the portable book of business which, nine times out 10, is smaller or too often non-existent.

It is very important, therefore, not to assume that a proper onboarding will cure all the errors made during the recruitment process; but in all cases it will mitigate the damage and eventually bring a longer than expected success.

Similarly, it is obvious that the recruitment process and the management leading that process cannot be blamed for all failures. There are indeed many cases where the talent recruited and the welcoming firm looked like a match in heaven. So what went wrong when either party decides to terminate the relationship?

4. Proper onboarding – the need for a mentor and if possible an integration team

4.1. Mentoring and other supports

According to the latest studies about the cost of hiring failures, these are estimated to be between three and six times of annual salaries. However, we have evidence that the cost of hiring failures grows exponentially with the level of the position concerned. This means that while the cost related to a position remunerated at an annual salary of €300,000 will be around €1.2 million, the cost will be as high €2 million for a position compensated at €500,000.

Our experience, confirmed by the studies of other experts in the human resources sector, show eight main risk factors that affect the failure rate of recruitment. They are:

- the brand of the company (law firm);
- location;
- level of position;
- scope of the position;
- company's culture;

- sector strengths;
- the expectations of the position; and
- how one will be assessed.

Obviously, these risks factors do not apply or carry the same weight in all recruitment. However, they should all be considered when developing an onboarding programme for a newcomer.

In the same vein, the scope of the onboarding programme will vary with the size of the organisation and the resources available. The scope of the programme will also be dictated by the position level and the strategic value to the organisation. After all, the main purpose of a proper onboarding is to get both a quick and long-term return on the investment made by the firm, be it financially (recruitment costs, compensation paid) or as opportunity costs (billable time invested to recruit or one chosen over another).

Although there is no 'by the book' onboarding programme, there are elements that are essential if the objective is to integrate a person who should be helping the firm, and so the partnership, to meet a strategic purpose which will be directly or indirectly beneficial to all.

The first decision to be made is to identify a motivated mentor who will take ownership of the successful integration – a person who will think every day as he gets up that in the months ahead, the mentoring responsibility will be essential to the firm and and not simply a nice activity at the bottom of the priority list. So the firm must initially institutionalise that principle and recognise and value (as valuable time to the firm equal to billable time) all efforts required and made.

Depending on the resources available in the firm, a couple of colleagues should be playing an active and essential role. The first of these is the HR person, who must keep track of the process and ensure that meetings are held and documented, and decisions implemented. They must also check regularly with the mentee how the mentoring process is developing. If possible, a peer – someone with the same position who joined a few years previously – should also be involved as a support for day-to-day issues, or to pass on the tricks to overcome some of the integration challenges.

Who then should be the mentor? It has to be someone senior enough within the firm who is a good communicator, a people person, with some authority to move the process on and who has at least an indirect interest in the success of the recruitment.

Any new joiner is unlikely to know the culture of the firm, the various administrative procedures, the information technology used and the various key colleagues who will be spread throughout the various departments and practices.

Most of us understand that induction days should be organised, which should include basic information about administrative procedures and allow the newcomer to get acquainted with a few colleagues. Then, time being of value, everyone, including the joiner, will feel the urgency to start to work on billable matters. Such a logical attitude shared by everyone, connected to the anticipation of turning the page after a lengthy recruitment process and/or a stressful period faced during the departure and transition periods, may mean that the need for a proper onboarding or integration process is put aside.

A proper process should therefore include the following pillars and happen over time. Crunching everything into one week cannot be realistic or seriously useful:

- a review of the business plan and an agreement on the key steps with the required actions and resources, all of which must be written down and attributed a deadline;
- a true and fair description of the culture and a regular review of any misunderstandings, shortcomings or challenges;
- a mentor who will be responsible for keeping track of time and of the execution of actions, and for delivering on the firm side and reporting to management on a regular basis;
- regular meetings between the joiner and the mentor;
- a couple of meetings with the most senior management, such as the managing partner or a member of the executive committee, but preferably not from the same practice area as the mentor, to offer a more honest view; and
- a duration of 18 months.

4.2 Define objectives (both the essential and less important) together

At this point, we can assume that the person has been recruited and is joining the firm. It is now essential to implement an onboarding programme.

Best practice would in fact require an onboarding programme being in place and, before the person has joined, the agreed business plan and an oral feedback of the promises made to and by the new joiner during the recruitment process to have been received. It should be remembered that the recruitment process included a seduction phase, where both parties tended to oversell their skills and potential opportunities. To be practical, let us take an example. A firm is recruiting someone in London to develop an inbound Japanese clientele and outbound foreign clients, in cooperation with a Tokyo office. During the recruitment process, the firm's management sells that cooperative spirit and the will of everyone in London and Tokyo to work towards that aim. Furthermore, promises of opportunities and lead sharing are made and a key contact partner who can act as mentor in both London and Tokyo will be provided, obviously with the commitment to travel with the new joiner in the first weeks of his arrival to Japan in order to visit each other's existing clients.

Another more domestic example would be the recruitment in a small firm of another partner to become the expert in a given sector that the firm feels should be developed. The promise made by all is to introduce existing clients to the newly hired lawyer and to suggest new leads and opportunities.

One should not forget that in several instances the arrival of a new lawyer can be perceived, rightly or wrongly, as a threat towards one's business objective, future promotion or clientele.

As we all have experienced, seen or heard, suddenly everyone is very busy with current client work and so, despite the sometime genuine goodwill time passes and little is done, leading eventually to all parties being disappointed as the 2+2=5 plan turns out at best to be a 3. Furthermore, the unwritten rules which make up a fundamental pillar of the firm's culture are not integrated by the new joiner, who feels misunderstood, while the others find him an isolated or odd colleague.

So the very first step to be taken by the mentor in the onboarding process, which must also include the partner who led or sponsored the recruiting effort, should be to agree together both the essential and the less important objectives, and set a time for their implementation. None of that will work, though, unless someone is making sure that everyone sticks to their promises and to the deadlines. Such monitoring or even policing of tasks can be done only by senior management, someone who does not have a direct interest in the practice concerned. The mentor's responsibility is to help the mentee, but management must guarantee monitoring. Too often, because of the lack of authority of the monitoring partner, as one gets busy, the drive to properly onboard or support slowly disappears or everyone is left to their own devices, including mentor and mentee. It is even more unfortunate, then, when some firms do have a yearly review of past joiners; sometime the partner in charge will fudge the reasons for the poor success, blaming work or market conditions, or at worst will state that it is in line with their (poor) average standards. However, to be fair, the process may have been so poorly organised that there was little to monitor or drive through.

Obviously, the main objective should reflect the strategic purpose discussed by parties during the recruitment process. It can be the sole starting point, as anything short of that will be a recipe for disaster. It is sometimes avoided, as parties know that they will need to come back to reality and may wish to avoid such a scary fact. Such a reality check is essential and may reveal the promised portable clientele to be thinner than portrayed or that the cooperative spirit or strength of the welcoming practice may still need developing. In any case, it is better to re-focus the expectations and adapt the plan at the outset and possibly find out that there are still many other opportunities.

This initial discussion and planning should also be an opportunity to reassess the risk factors of the strategic project. Things may have changed in the firm between acceptance of the offer and joining: the firm may have recruited other lawyers or lost lawyers who were key to the practice; it may have opened offices, developed new clients or faced unexpected challenges. These risks, which should be re-evaluated, should include a realistic assessment of how long it will take for this new high performer to replicate past performance. Although the finance team and the practice may have crunched data during the recruitment process, this may often prove wrong – usually for the worst, but in a few cases for the better.

Harvard Business School, under the leadership of Professor Groysberg, has undertaken analytical studies in several client-driven industries in that field and concluded that it will likely take 18 months to three years for a new joiner, even a very high performer, to get back to past performance level, even in a very favourable environment. The conclusion may be that it may never happen if the environment is more challenging or not appropriate.

4.3 Culture

The most common reason why recruitment fails is linked to a lack of cultural integration. All firms have their own culture, which will have been briefly described or portrayed during the interviews held earlier in the process. There is no right or wrong culture; it is simply a strong value of the firm, which cannot and should not be fought, as the culture always wins. Learning this and buying into a new culture is far from easy. It requires guidance and spur of the moment explanation. Although those in the firm seem to know what the culture is about, it often proves difficult to phrase it and to make it easily understood. It is more a way of life, which can be fully understood only through experiences. However, in order to start the integration on the right foot, or at least to increase the rate of success of the strategic plan developed with and for the newcomer, it becomes critical to have a session about what the firm stands for with, for example, a list of dos and don'ts. On the occasion of the review meeting of the onboarding process, which should be held regularly to review implementation of the plan, it would be wise to discuss the culture experience. In fact, as not all members of the firm may have a clear or shared view of what the culture stands for, a discussion will be helpful to all parties. It may uncover reasons for inefficiencies in the firm or some who, by their actions, may not fully adhere to the culture, despite stating that they do. There again, the mentor and the peer will play a decisive role. The mentor will share the culture, but the peer will probably be able to live and share the culture on a daily and friendly basis. The peer will also be able to help the mentee contrast his perception of the new culture with his own past values. It is a longer journey, which must be embraced and understood at the outset of the process. The peer and mentor may also shine different lights on the key culture points of the firm.

4.4 Understanding the firm

Besides the culture, there is the need to help the newcomer understand the firm and how it functions. Firms tend to offer documentation, videos on their website and even a few meetings at the point of joining. It is often an onboarding tour and information crunch, when everything must be digested in a few days. Just as when learning new software, it very quickly becomes too much and irrelevant, as one has not yet been in the situation requiring the knowledge. It would be better to organise such an induction tour in different phases and, more importantly, make sure that relevant useful colleagues make a point of teaching the basics and regularly come back for refreshers and to go to the next level of learning. I can hear many readers claiming that lawyers have little or no patience for any unbillable, bureaucratic exercises, and that they often cancel internal meetings using the sacrosanct excuse that the client comes first – as if their clients would look in their diaries to make sure they call them just before an internal meeting. In that situation, the HR professional in charge of the process and/or the peer can really help and ensure a few rewinds or offer *ad hoc* suggestions and ensure that refresher courses are offered.

The mentor will be less involved, although he should be a role model. The mentee should learn by working with the mentor.

4.5 Define performance measurements together

When the strategic plan has been reviewed, revisited and agreed, with clear actions linked to a timeline, it become critical to discuss and agree with the mentor (and sponsoring partner or management) what the realistic performance measurements should be. The joiner has been voted or hired on the basis of a target revenue income, although costs income or investment costs are too often forgotten. However, successful integration is not simply about money, although that is often the sole driver of the earlier decision.

There are usually several other aspects to a successful mid-term integration, which – as in the example above – may be a joint visit to Tokyo to cross-sell clients, building the clientele of the firm, for which actions are easily measurable and quantifiable, such as number of meetings. It can also take the form of thought leadership prepared and shared with clients. Joint pitches lost are a factor showing integration and an effort to work as a team. It is not to say, though, that these should be used to hide weaker than expected income if indeed that is the case. In fact, even if the income generated is in line with the plan, there is much more to it. Reviewing how it has been achieved may show that it has been done outside the mainstream plan, alone without building internal or external relationships, through a new client which was not anticipated and which may offer cross-selling opportunities. In that case, it will show that the initial plan was not implemented and synergies not developed, and so, in the short to medium term, the added value of the new joiner may be lower than expected and the distance taken from the plan may put at risk the growth of the practice or of the clientele. In a year or two the joiner may suffer from the lack of integration and experience a dip in revenue or become an outcast, and everyone will be surprised without understanding why.

5. Assume

Assuming that some onboarding efforts to structure a process are being contemplated and put down on paper, it becomes essential to organise integration meetings with a structured agenda and assumed responsibilities.

The onboarding process – which should extend to 18 months, with regular reviews that may become less frequent after a few months – should be considered the responsibility of the mentor, who should have been involved in the recruitment process. Therefore, senior management should consider that proper planning, implementation and follow-up should become an element of the review of the performance of the mentor. In other words, if the mentor is underperforming on that topic, even though he did extremely well on other unrelated issues, he should be sanctioned for his lesser performance on the onboarding of the new joiner. After all, the recruitment was as strategic as the opening of an office or the promotion of a young partner, and its long-term impact should be optimal.

These regular meetings between the parties should be dominated by the WHY theme. If things are not going as well as expected, this is likely to be due to issues that can easily be corrected if they are identified in time and remedial measures are undertaken. It will often be discovered that the cause is simply connected to the lack of action by someone. The secondary benefit is that it will show how others in the firm behave and how supportive and committed they may be to the wellbeing of the firm and its partners.

Senior management should also prepare a standard onboarding process with a description of the expectations placed on all parties, including the mentor. One cannot invent oneself as a mentor if one has not been given at least a road map. The mentor should also be offered brief training and a presentation by an outside professional about what it means to help, drive and coach someone. There is more to the role than reading numbers and client lists. After all, it is a people business and management people are the key to success.

On-boarding and integration – 'accelerated transition'

According to latest studies about costs of a hiring failure, these are estimated at between three and six times annual salaries. However, there is evidence that the costs of a hiring failure grow exponentially with the level of the position concerned. This means that while the cost related to a position remunerated at an annual salary of €300,000 will be around €1.2 million, the cost will be as high €2 million for a position compensated at €500,000.

A previously unpublished study revealed eight risk factors affecting the failure rate when moving into another job.

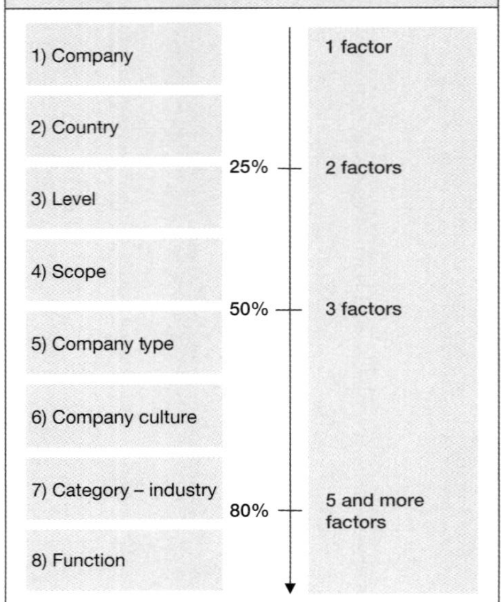

Accelerated transition supports the new executive efficiently with his emotional and intellectual integration into the new company and enables him to meet much faster the companies expectations regarding his performance.

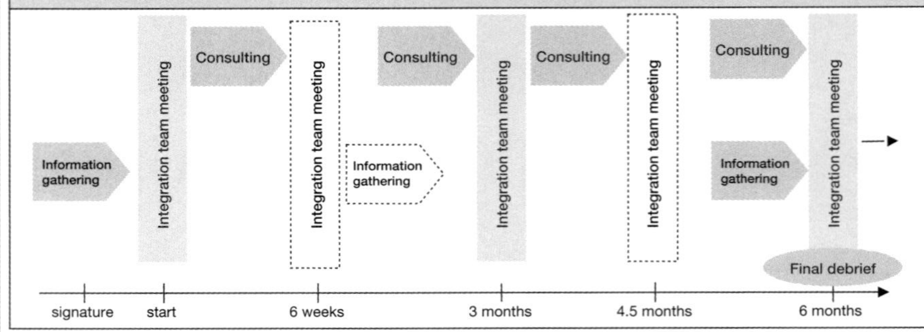

Return of investment:

	Without accelerated transition	With accelerated transition
Average salary	€300,000	€300,000
Costs of failure	€1.2 million	€1.2 million
Chance of failure	50%	15%
Costs of risk	€600,000	€180,000

Difference: €420,000

Investment €40,000

ROI approx: 1,000%

Mentoring and coaching across cultures

Philip Beddows
The Silk Road Partnership

1. Introduction

For people and businesses, the world continues to become more deeply interconnected – and more organisations that had been international are becoming global in nature – in more ways than simply being a reflection of the locations where they have offices or otherwise provide a service to their clients. This is no less true of law firms, whatever operating model they have adopted.

The talent of their partnerships, the fundamental value of firms, is becoming more culturally diverse around the world. This has implications if mentoring and coaching is to be effective and actively support the continued evolution and supportive fusion of global talent so that it can fully realise the promise of integrated, international practice and client service.

As yet, it is probably true that no commercial entity is truly culturally globalised. Many law firms are still influenced and fed by where their varied roots began and the predominant legal jurisdictions that influence their work. Cross-border mergers tend to create a matrix that provides the possibility of cultural fusion and diverse unity over time, if nurtured and developed with focus and patience. Today, most people on balance would probably agree with Philippe Rosinski, who said that he had "yet to find a truly intercultural society or company where members have embraced cultural differences and made the most of them. To my knowledge, such an entity is yet to be built".[1]

Mentoring and coaching has been active within the legal profession for many years, but the way in which it is purposely introduced to help a firm perform as an integrated yet diverse community of talent is not at all common. Mentoring and coaching tends to be more of a developmental exercise that is not thought of in day-to-day strategic terms. Rather, it is used tactically and too often (still) to fix a problem, or as an important element supporting talent and leadership development programmes, rather than being actively used as a boost to already winning talent, to enhance performance even more or as a way of working life in the community of the firm. A coaching culture may have begun to be created, but its open display in the way that people interact with and treat each other each day may not always be experienced.

Imagine if coaching and mentoring were not an intervention or organisational

1 P Rosinski, *Coaching across Cultures: New Tools for Leveraging National, Corporate and Professional Differences* (Nicholas Brealey Publishing, 2003).

initiative, but part of everyday communication and interaction between lawyers and those who work with them, without anyone involved being conscious that this was what they were practising. To achieve this would have huge positive implications about the development of potential and talent and the quality of human relationships across the firm internationally.

Every lawyer has the capacity to be a mentor and a coach, and each can benefit from being open to being mentored and coached by others, supported from within or from outside.

Mentoring is seen by many as an interaction between an older and, by implication, more experienced and wiser person and a younger colleague. However, and although in some countries there may be sensitivity to the idea, there is much merit in reversing this concept and providing younger mentors to older more senior lawyers, and even to do so across cultures. There is much that younger lawyers can do to mentor their more senior and older colleagues. Added to this, there is much that can be gained by deliberately setting up mentoring relationships across a firm's cultures, so that mutual cross-cultural learning can be accelerated, both corporately (particularly in the context of post-merger integration) and internationally across practice groups and different continents, thereby helping to cement the unity of a firm's international partnership.

There has been much debate and discussion about Generation Y, X, Z, Millennials and any other label one would choose, and the gulf of understanding and experience between them and older generations. Reverse mentoring can help to bridge this gap and cross-fertilise ideas and understanding. To take a very simple example of the effect – what older partner hasn't learned wisdom and truths from a teenage child or younger adult, or how to use their iPhone or social media such as Twitter?

As a firm becomes more international in structure, outlook and culture, its approach to how it enables the full flowering of the talent potential of its partners, as well as others, needs a fresh cultural perspective to make the most of the benefits that can arise from mentoring and coaching across cultures.

2. Awareness of the cross-cultural origins of coaching and mentoring

The first chapter in Philippe Rosinski's *Coaching across Cultures* is headed "The Recent Discipline of Coaching", after an introduction in which he writes that "Coaching as a profession is a relatively new phenomenon in organizations. It started just over a decade ago in the United States". Accepting that Rosinski writes of the modern profession of coaching, the truth is that coaching – like mentoring – has been with us, in all parts of the world, throughout time and didn't start as recently as the early 1990s in the United States.

Rebecca Normand-Hochman has already helpfully explored definitions around the terms 'coaching' and 'mentoring' in her introduction to this book. My own personal perspective is that coaching and mentoring are like two dancers who may perform singularly or in combination with each other. They may seem to emerge separately from two sides of the stage to engage the audience, but they are so closely related that at times, as they swirl together on the dance floor, one may not tell which is which, and the difference may not seem as important as some would believe.

I believe that it is much more important to know what 'coaching' and 'mentoring' do for people and organisations than to define their precise meaning.

While engaged in research on different cultural perspectives on coaching and mentoring, I spoke with a variety of people who were able to offer views from different parts of the world.

Bonnie Chan – one of the first professionally trained coaches in Asia, and a founder and past president of the Hong Kong International Coaching Community – offered me these words on the origin of mentoring:

I think its everywhere, but I am Chinese and if you ask me to name an example, it would be Confucius. But if I was from another place in the world, I could probably name an example from that country. Mentoring I think is a kind of nature of human beings.

When asked the same question on coaching she replied:

I believe the same as mentoring. I have had this same discussion with Hong Kong coaches. We always think that coaching originated from the West, whether Britain or America. I think well structured coaching is definitely from the West, where they knew how to put forward coaching as a service to help people to meet their needs. But in the old days, coaching was just a kind of human relationship. That's the reason why I, deep down in the bottom of my heart, think Chinese people really knew coaching in the old days and that's the reason why, if we go back to the old writings of Confucius, 'Kongzi' (as he was known to Chinese) had already started asking questions instead of telling – rather as we know Socrates asked questions. So I find asking questions is in the nature of human beings – if we don't know something we just start to ask questions. If we know how to ask questions to help another person learn, then that involves the evolution of human beings. That's fantastic and I think that is what Socrates was doing and did. To go back to the question of where coaching began, well-structured coaching that could become a service to meet with people's needs is Western. Where they put forward evidence-based, logical things in a very well-structured way like The IAC Coaching Masteries™ competences, The Inner Game, is fantastic because they're able to integrate knowledge to show people how important coaching is; but deep down, back to history, I think coaching is a form of human nature that started in all cultures.

Krishna Kumar, who founded India's first executive coaching school and one of the country's top tennis academies, commented that the word 'mentoring' originated in Greece. He noted that "the fundamental concept has been in existence since the beginning of time", that the word coaching drew its origin from sports, and that "all the ancient texts, myths, religions and philosophies have references to coaching and mentoring in practice". Vicki Zanini, president of the International Association of Coaching, headquartered in the United States, expressed the view that mentoring's origins may also be associated with the guru disciple relationship found in many religions. Zanini's view on coaching was that, as a profession, it became popular in the 1980s as an extension of sports coaching and business coaching, but actually originated from more than one place, with many coaches coming from the movement for the growth of human potential.

Krumar was correct about Greece. We find the first mention of the word 'mentor' in Homer's *Odyssey*, the story of Odysseus's 20-year adventure-filled journey back to Ithaca. As Odysseus set out to join the war against Troy, he handed his son

Telamachus into the care of his old friend 'Mentor', requesting him to "Tell him all you know." As Telamachus grew up into a man, he faced great challenges, having to assume responsibility in his father's absence. When the goddess Athena disguised herself as Mentor, encouraging, supporting and guiding Telamachus to come to important decisions and take action, mentoring was born. When referring to this story, Whitmore pointedly instructs the reader that when Odysseus says "Tell him all you know", he "thus unwittingly set some limits to mentoring" ("Coaching for Performance"). It's interesting to note that it was a goddess whose talents and commitment to a person made a mentor of Mentor.

The two oldest surviving pieces of western literature are Homer's *The Iliad* and its sequel *The Odyssey*, estimated to have been written almost 3,000 years ago c 720 BCE.

So mentoring is not new, and neither is coaching.

In his recent novel *Rise of the Sun Prince – Ramayana the Game of Life*,[2] Shubha Vilas tells a tale that is inspired by a rewoven presentation of the ancient Indian text of the Ramayana (c 500 to 400 BCE) to "provide food for contemporary thought drawn from an enduring masterpiece". His author's note includes a comment that speaks loudly to coaching and mentoring today:

In Rise of the Sun Prince, we are exposed to the struggles of an imperfect teacher, one who relentlessly fights his internal battles to rise above his shortcomings. And this, in a way, is the central hero of this book – Vishwamitta, the ever-angry sage. As the teacher mentors his pupils, Rama and Lakshmana, they too, mentor him to another sphere.

The reference to internal battles echoes Timothy Gallwey's book *The Inner Game of Tennis*[3] and the work of so many other writers and philosophers through the ages – the concept of a person's battle to master their inner self before they can face their real competitor. The other theme that I hope you will have spotted above is the reference to reverse-mentoring, where a person being mentored can themselves be mentoring their mentor! Definitely food for thought, which is tackled elsewhere in this chapter.

Moving further east, both Gallwey and Whitmore's definitions of 'coaching' chime well with a saying by Confucius about 2,500 years ago c 450 BCE, which also speak to us of the commonly accepted difference between mentoring and coaching:

Tell me, and I will forget.
Show me, and I may remember.
Involve me, and I will understand.

Socrates, one of the founders of Western philosophy, bequeathed us the 'Socratic method', which so many lawyers have come across during their time at law school. This has a direct connection with coaching methodology today and also pre-Socratic Indian philosophy concerning methods to help develop people.

The Socratic method involves a series of questions that encourages the person being questioned to think harder for themselves and gain insights that they would not learn if they were told. A coach and mentor may similarly utilise a series of questions to help the person they are working with better to clarify matters in

2 S Vilas, *Rise of the Sun Prince – Ramayana the Game of Life* (Jaico Publishing House, 2003).
3 T Gallwey, *The Inner Game of Tennis* (Pan, 1986).

their minds, at the same time arousing awareness about what they do not understand but need to learn. In his book *The Greek Philosophers*, W K C Guthrie wrote that Socrates:

was accustomed to say that he did not himself know anything, and that the only way in which he was wiser than other men was that he was conscious of his own ignorance, whilst they were not. The essence of the Socratic method is to convince the interlocuter that whereas he thought he knew something, in fact he does not.

In the busy world of international law today, as in all realms of business, minds are so overloaded with information and stimulation that they do not have sufficient time and space to simply think in quietness. A coach and mentor may provide such opportunities for a sounding board.

Dr Debashis Chatterjee, who taught leadership at Harvard and the Indian Institutes of Management in Calcutta, Lucknow and Kozhikode, recently published a remarkable book: *Timeless Leadership – 18 Leadership Sutras from The Bhagavad Gita.*[4] The *Gita* is part of the Hindu epic Mahabharata and is thought to have been composed between the fifth and fourth centuries BCE, which roughly corresponds to the same age as Confucius. Here is a short excerpt:

Vizualize a conversation on performance enhancement as a battle is about to begin. The two people involved are lead-archer Arjuna and his wise mentor and charioteer, Krishna. Arjuna's head is overloaded with information that he finds difficult to digest ... The busy mind, Krishna argues, is a mob of unprocessed thoughts and emotions. The only way to deal effectively with this mob is to create distance between the mob and the observer, who can now see the mob without being part of it.

Who could argue that today's commercial arena, wherever one is in the world, is a battleground of frenetic activity, competing demands, what appear to be insurmountable obstacles, changing political alliances, pressure, stress and deafening noise and distraction that prevent leaders from gaining clear perspective.

Two of the book's commentators provide insights that help us to think about cultural interconnectedness between people:

The practical wisdom evidenced is like no other book in modern management literature. Any leader – east or west, north or south – will gain a powerful perspective from seriously engaging with this book.

– Theodore Roosevelt Malloch, research professor, Yale University, and CEO, The Roosevelt Group

"Timeless Leadership is both timeless and borderless. It is timeless because the principles of leadership espoused thousands of years ago are contemporary.

– Jagdish Sheth, marketing guru and world renowned author

As Bonnie Chan identified, China's great philosopher and teacher, Confucius, could quite easily be seen as coach and mentor today. He may also be described as a guru, a definition of which the *Oxford Dictionary* gives as 'a revered mentor'. As you read this, can you think of anyone who has been your mentor or coached you, whether knowingly or not? While you're pondering this thought, if you do not have a mentor or a coach right now and yet face a set of objectives and goals that may

4 John Wiley & Sons, 2012.

make Roger Federer take a deep breath, read this excerpt from the dedications at the front of Vilas's book:

To my guru, Radhanath Swami, whose words of wisdom have inspired my heart, whose love and kindness have touched my soul.

To my guide, who has been a beacon of light of direction, a treasure house of wisdom and an unflagging source of encouragement.

Imagine if each lawyer in a firm had a mentor and/or coach of whom they could say such things. This is how great mentors and coaches can inspire and support people on a personal level and enable greater performance. Vilas's words remind us of the dedication and commitment required to mentor or coach someone, whether across cultures or not.

So, why am I sharing these insights from across the world in a chapter about mentoring and coaching across cultures? Some readers will already have 'got it'. The point is that coaching and mentoring are timeless arts and sciences that transcend cultures because they have been practised in their intrinsic and original form for thousands of years wherever humans have lived – in Africa, Asia, the Middle East, the Americas, Europe and Australasia. In fact, mentoring and coaching occurs every day in human interactions between people who have never heard the terms before or, if they have, do not have them or any constructs connected to them in their minds at that time.

The language and structure of mentoring and coaching may have been wrapped up in a more western form, as a modern profession with scientific structure and process; but if one appreciates the fundamental truths and learning about how people learn, grow, develop and perform with great success with the support and input of another person, then one can more easily manage to implement, deliver or receive mentoring and coaching across cultures.

3. What is culture'?

Before we delve any further into this, one inevitably needs first to attempt to define what is 'culture'. In attempting to do this, one immediately enters into a complex and inconclusive debate between experts that could fill many books, but I have a short chapter to encompass an even broader canvas, so will necessarily need to be succinct. Even so, in briefly defining the words, one also finds a serendipitous yet profound insight that connects definitions of the word 'culture' and the purpose of coaching and mentoring in a way that will enlighten and help us to understand them – for they are not mere words, but age-old concepts and practices that are rooted all across our cross-cultural and forever interrelated world.

Cultural considerations are inherent in valuing diversity and inclusion, topics of key importance to law firms. At a high level, UNESCO's Universal Declaration on Cultural Diversity states that:

culture should be regarded as the set of distinctive spiritual, material, intellectual and emotional features of society or a social group, and that it encompasses, in addition to art and literature, lifestyles, ways of living together, value systems, traditions and beliefs,

and that:

culture is at the heart of contemporary debates about identity, social cohesion, and the development of a knowledge-based economy.

The *Oxford English Dictionary* defines 'culture' as:

The arts and other manifestations of human intellectual achievement regarded collectively. – a refined understanding or appreciation of this,

and,

The customs, ideas, and social behaviour of a particular people or group.

The *Collins English Dictionary* describes the word in connection also with "the act or practice of tilling or cultivating the soil", since the word came to the English language from the French *'culture'* and Latin *'cultura'*, which relates to 'cultivation' and 'husbandry' of land, 'growing' and 'cultivation'. This links nicely with what mentoring and coaching can achieve for people and the growth and blossoming of their skills and lives.

3.1 Variety of cultures

Cultures exist in a complex and diverse range of contexts and at different levels. Most people tend to think of cultures in simple terms such as nationality, ethnicity or religion, but the variety of cultures that exist can be shaped by regional influences, linguistics, family, gender, sexuality, profession, academic *alma maters*, corporate norms, departmental differences, the rituals of fans of a particular football team and one's own personal culture and individuality. Sub-cultures exist in organisations, teams and even families.

Edgar Shein, former professor at MIT Sloan School of Management, describes categories of culture in his book *Organizational Culture and Leadership*:[5]

Exhibit I.1. Categories of culture

Culture	*Category*
Macrocultures	Nations, ethnic and religious groups, occupations that exist globally
Organisational cultures	Private, public, non-profit, governmental organisations
Subcultures	Occupational groups within organisations
Microcultures	Microsystems within or outside organisations

3.2 Corporate culture versus local culture and diversity

At the same time as international firms become more diverse in their people across the globe, potential tensions can arise when corporate culture and mindset meet cultural outlooks that can lose their value if subordinated and restricted by a potential corporate homogeneity.

When coaching and mentoring is introduced, the methodology and philosophy underpinning it may have originated in one part of the world, but not translate to all parts of a firm's global operations. For example, I have recently been involved in an element of a leadership development programme in China. An initiative that was begun and rolled out with success in North America and Europe was transferred and

5 John Wiley & Sons, 2010, Pt 1, p 2.

delivered in China, but with much less success, as it had not been culturally or linguistically adapted for better understanding. It was then re-run in a different way and with new language, also helping to make associations with Chinese cultural reference points so that the learning could occur more effectively.

There is a challenge in rolling out initiatives shaped in one part of the world to other locations before checking whether they are culturally transferable.

An extended corpus of research, writing, philosophy and methodology towards business practices has been developed in the West that has not been informed enough by alternative perspectives from the East. But fusion is underway and the more that leaders emerge within global entities from teams with a diverse educational, cultural and philosophical underpinning, the more that will be learned.

Coaching and mentoring philosophies and associated accreditation can also impact on culture – if, as suggested above, coaching in its structured modern form originates from the West, how then has the coaching profession surmounted this potential difficulty of 'translation'? The EMCC, being centred in Europe with its diverse set of nations, has created a good appreciation of cultural differences and ensures its materials and methodologies are appropriate across the region. Nigel Cumberland is of the view that "the EMCC seems to truly understand the nuances of different cultures, more so than some other coaching associations". Zanini reminded me that The IAC Coaching Masteries™ were specifically developed with the aim of producing clear standards and measures for what constitutes the highest level of coaching, and that can be understood in any culture around the world. This original intent was helpfully supported by a careful review conducted a few years ago by an international team of coaches.

3.3 Cultural identities

A shared culture can lead to shared identities that are seen and/or perceived as different. Members of the same profession may feel a bond that transcends the cultural differences between them. People from outside the legal profession may look at lawyers and talk of them as if they are collectively the same. Since the credit crunch in western economies, much newspaper print and conversations have referred to 'bankers' as if they are all a collective carbon copy of each other, instead of recognising that there are many types of bankers, let alone banks, and an even greater variety of types of people and professions working within them.

So are all lawyers the same, forming a collective singular culture? Of course not. Each legal jurisdiction around the world will inevitably produce different professional cultures. In the United Kingdom, we have the divide between barristers and solicitors, which has produced very different cultures in chambers and law firms.

Does attending Harvard, INSEAD or Cambridge produce a brand of alumnus for each *alma mater* that is different from other academic institutions? They are members of the same alumni community, but the student body has come from across the world, and so have the academic staff who teach them. They may all feel a close affinity and identify with one another, since they share a common bond in their respective institution, but are each uniquely different.

A nuclear family may have members with the same shared genetics and cultural underpinning, yet one of them may be more in tune with a person from another part of the world and have better chemistry and understanding with that person than they do with their own brother or sister. Different people may find it easier or more challenging to work with the two who are in tune but culturally diverse people, depending on their ability to tune into them and the degree to which they can be accepted by or accept the two.

3.4 Geographic sub-cultures

It is a quite amazing fact that in a world of over 7 billion people, no two are the same; even 'identical twins' aren't, despite looking the same on the outside.

Cumberland, one of my partners, has worked across the world and spent a particularly long period of time in Asia, based in Hong Kong, and is now living and working in the Gulf. During the past 14 years he has worked across all kinds of geographic cultures – many even within one ethnic group, (eg, Chinese, comprising Mainland Chinese, Hong Kong Chinese, Malaysian Chinese, Singaporean Chinese, Taiwanese Chinese, Indonesian Chinese). His observation is that:

> *One might think people from such Chinese groups might be quite similar, but no, they are not and there can be quite distinct differences. Similarly with the variety of Arabs from Morocco through to Iraq and Oman. It is often a surprise quite how distinct the cultural differences might be, eg, a Jordanian coachee/leader complaining how hard it is to be based in Cairo and/or to manage a team based in Morrocco.*

The origins, history, values, language, beliefs and roots of people and their cultures are important to appreciate if one seeks to help them to achieve their full potential. An American from Texas may have a very different sense of himself and way of looking at life from one from Massachusetts, just as a Bavarian may have a different cultural outlook from someone in Hamburg. India itself is like a rainforest in respect of the extraordinary rich set of cultures and people that lie within a single country, and China itself has a much greater variety of cultures and languages than many know about or appreciate.

A city such as London is an international melting pot – like a few others, it is a city where one literally meets the world, so anyone coaching or mentoring there will find it difficult not to find themselves doing so across cultures every day.

Another important dynamic in the international commercial world is that multiple layers of cultural connections are increasingly found in people whose heritage is a rich legacy of their parents and grandparents, so one can easily fail to appreciate who a person really is when coaching or mentoring them.

3.5 Assumptions and connections

It is easy when meeting individuals from within the same profession, and perhaps even attending the same academic institutions, to assume they are all on the same wavelength. They may have shared outlooks that have been learned along shared parts of their journeys, but differences still remain. This was highlighted by my colleague Cumberland, who confirmed:

> *My greatest challenge has been to coach leaders who act very global and western, but then one discovers that many of their thinking, behaviours and aspects of their mindset might*

be quite local, eg a Hong Kong Chinese born in Hong Kong but who might have worked for many years in London. I sense that such leaders have adapted to the cultures that they face, eg of being in Europe, in the City and with a particular law firm or bank's culture. But within or underneath their embracing of such cultures lies the traditional cultural dynamics of their childhood/family culture, eg tight knit loyal Confucian Chinese culture.

I asked him to compare this with his experience in the Gulf, and his answer was really quite interesting:

I have found it very easy to work within the Emirati culture in the United Arab Emirates. I have often wondered why and I think the answer might be a surprise when I suggest it relates to a combination of:

- *I was brought up in the countryside of Yorkshire where being with nature and the elements was important. This is similar in some ways to being an Emirati.*
- *Emiratis are also very pro-British, with many having studied there, and they like to work with the British.*

The cultural differences between the context the British and the Emiratis are brought up within appears to be quite different and yet my experience is that it has been easier for one to understand the other than one might have expected. Comparing this to the case of two cultures that are seemingly very similar, eg Malaysian Chinese versus Mainland Chinese culture – in this case, coming from a third culture I have noticed greater differences between them. The interesting thing is that they, being much closer to each other may fail to notice and appreciate the subtle differences between each other.

Zanini had another take on this:

Interestingly, my greatest challenge was with a client from a different part of my own country. The challenge was the difference in our communication styles. His language was very colorful and he spoke with fiery passion. I am soft spoken. I learned to match his tone energetically and we went on to successfully work together.

4. Language and understanding

Cross-border law involves great attention to the detail of what is actually meant and intended by the words used when translated into different languages, with all parties needing to be forensically clear about what is agreed in a contract.

Perhaps a key lesson in mentoring and coaching across cultures is that people speak different languages and when those languages are translated into another, it is possible that in the scientific exercise of translation, a lot of meaning can be lost. Across the world, English is increasingly used as a corporate business language by many organisations. This adds to the opportunities for misunderstanding, particularly if one speaker is using colloquial phrases or metaphors that do not have meaning for the listener. Interestingly, I have found that clients from around the world often have metaphors and stories that have the same essential meaning, but are expressed differently, and they like to use such things with explanations to express themselves with more meaning.

Cumberland shared that he has found that:

he biggest challenge has been when the individual that I coach may struggle to fully express themselves in English. This, combined with culturally unique styles of thinking and communication, can make for challenging coaching sessions.

He went on to share his solution:

I listen more, speak slower and sometimes in simpler English. I can be less challenging and understand that in some cultures the ideas of being very self-aware and introspective are not as strongly developed or expected compared to what one may expect from a British lawyer working in the City.

Mentors and coaches need to remember that just because two people are speaking the same language doesn't mean that they will entirely understand each other.

4.1 Communication beyond words

Words form only a fraction of the full extent of communication between two people. In their book *Nonverbal Communication in Human Interaction*, Mark Knapp, Judith Hall and Terrence Horgan[6] write encouragingly that:

It may come as no surprise to you that, in everyday life, you are an expert in non-verbal communication even though you have yet to read a page of this book.[7]

How we read a face, physically present ourselves in front of people, know what a baby's cry is saying or understand a hand signal is already programmed and learned without the need for any translation.

But we shouldn't let the writers encourage us too much, because while body language can sometimes be matched in meaning across the world, at other times the same posture or hand signal can have wildly different meanings and reactions. Respecting and knowing this is important for anyone coaching and mentoring across cultures.

4.2 A higher level of communication

The challenge of communication and language has already been touched upon. But what has also been mentioned is the similarity of approach to questioning when one person is working with intent to help the development of another and seeks to raise awareness and increase understanding.

Edgar Schein, whose categories of culture are summarised above, arrived at an understanding about a particular approach to communication that can help mentors and coaches across the world. In his book *Humble Inquiry: the Gentle Art of Asking Instead of Telling*,[8] he writes:

in an increasingly complex, interdependent, and culturally diverse world, we cannot hope to understand and work with people from different occupational, professional, and national cultures if we do not know how to ask questions and build relationships that are based on mutual respect and the recognition that others know things that we may need to know in order to get a job done.

He goes on to define 'humble inquiry' as "the fine art of drawing someone out, of asking questions to which you do not already know the answer, of building a relationship based on curiosity and interest in the other person".

Hopefully, having read this, you will have seen a thematic connection with

---

6 Mark Knapp, Judith Hall and Terrence Horgan, *Nonverbal Communication in Human Interaction*, 8th Edn (Wadsworth Publishing Co, 2012).

7 Knapp, Hall and Horgan, p 3.

8 Edgar Schein, *Humble Inquiry: the Gentle Art of Asking Instead of Telling* (Berrett-Koehler, 2013).

coaching and mentoring. It indicates why communication is one of the most important keys to success in mentoring and coaching, in whatever cultural or cross-cultural context. Thomas Leonard – one of the pioneers of coaching, who founded both the International Federation of Coaching and International Association of Coaching – spoke of coaching being an advanced way of communicating. Whitmore, whose leadership and thinking has been so instrumental in the development of coaching, has quite separately spoken of coaching being a higher form of communication.

5. Overcoming real or perceived cultural barriers in a mentoring and/or coaching relationship

5.1 The importance of culture as a consideration for a coach and/or mentor

Kumar takes the view that "an understanding of the coachee's cultural environment helps the coach to appreciate the reactions and thought processes of the coachee", and Zanini believes that "culture is essentially a filter with which we experience every aspect of our lives. It impacts how we interpret the world".

Cumberland's view supports this:

Culture is a key determinant of how a leader/coachee views the world, themselves in terms of their ethics, values, mindset, acceptable/unacceptable behaviours, etc. This has a key impact on how they approach the possibility of being coached and the subsequent process they may go through when being coached. My experience is that Arab coachees tend to use coaching more positively as a way to learn and be mentored. They are not embarrassed by being coached and are happy and even proud for colleagues to know. By comparison, I have found leaders from some other cultures, including Europeans, have been far less inclined to share with others that they are being coached, view it as a remedial intervention and are less comfortable with the idea that they could learn anything from working with a coach.

Chan expressed to me that:

Culture has some very interesting aspects in human beings. Particularly for someone moving out from their own culture – they start to see something different. For me, culture is awareness of differences. Its about a recognition of differences – from a coach's perspective, it's important to have an ability to be aware of differences, which is a kind of self-awareness, a way of knowing who I am. If you are enjoying the differences in another culture, then you find all sorts of new ways of doing things, but if you find yourself not enjoying the differences, you simply just notice the other person is different from you. In the business world, people have different ways to complete a project – handle them in a way that you have a bigger perspective, knowing the differences and better understanding oneself.

5.2 Take an interest and time to get to know the reality of the person you coach or mentor

It is a maxim in the world of coaching that a coach needs to be self-aware himself before coaching another person. It is also understood that one thing a coach-mentor can valuably do is help another person to know himself better, for from this greater self-knowledge comes awareness that can be directed towards his development. There was purpose and wisdom in the words ΓΝΩΘΙ ΣΕΑΥΤΟΝ – 'Know thyself' – said to have been written on a wall in the Temple of Apollo at Delphi, home of the famous Delphic Oracle. This is a timeless concept that is also echoed in many other cultures. In 2011, Indian academic and HR professional Dr V Ammineedu published a very thoughtful short book called *Know Thyself – The Gunas Framework of the Bhagavad-Gita*; and in doing so he was not recalling Delphi, but much older Indian philosophies that probably passed westwards along Hellenic connections opened up by Alexander the Great.

To coach or mentor someone, one really needs to be fully supportive and committed to that person, get to know who they are and appreciate their individuality. It is easy for external cultural wrapping, whether metaphorical or not, to distract one from seeing the real person and their potential that lies within them.

Even within the same culture, assumptions can be dangerous and also highly inappropriate. I remember being introduced as a potential coach for a senior female executive. The person briefing me added some personal feedback, suggesting perhaps I could encourage the individual to present more appropriately in their style of dress for the corporate environment they worked in, and wear less bangles. These comments were very instructive, revealing that the person briefing me hadn't fully grasped the extraordinary talents and potential of the executive in question, which I would immediately discover were remarkable. Their perspective had been clouded and their insight blinded by the self-distraction of what their eyes saw and the assumptions their mind was making. Quite what respect or attention they would have given Gandhi when wearing his dhoti and sandals can only be imagined – 'lawyer and statesman with a brilliant legal, intellectual brain' would clearly not have been a description that would have leapt to their mind!

It is a similar thing for coaches and mentors when faced with coachees or mentees from other cultures. It is important to appreciate who they are and the influences that have had a bearing on their development, thinking style, motivations and much more.

I was privileged to mentor a particularly fascinating person, from a distinct minority ethnic community in London, who had spent time living in, and continued to be involved with, a region with principally the same religion as themselves but with a quite different set of cultures. Their life story had been quite a journey of self-discovery and expression, and they took the time to explain all the cultural influences that had had a bearing on the person they were today, and why and how they had carved out their own personal and courageous cultural path. It was generous of them to be so open with me, as this helped me to appreciate their uniqueness, motivations and the cultural influences that were still shaping their development.

5.3 Additional insights for coaches and mentors

As part of research done around the topic of this chapter, I asked contributors a set of specific questions.

(a) What can most help a mentor or coach transcend cultural difference with their mentee/coachee?

Zanini's answer was:

Advanced listening skills, presence, letting go of agendas and biases, believing in the coachee/mentee, setting clear expectations for the relationship and, perhaps most importantly, developing a relationship of trust. I believe that when a coach who has truly mastered the art of coaching meets a client who is ready for coaching, in most cases they will transcend culture barriers. When this is not the case, a 'cultural' match will serve them both.

Cumberland offered a perspective informed by work across Asia and the MENA region:

High-level emotional intelligence, particularly awareness of how one's own styles and behaviours come across to others, and empathy – being able to put oneself in those from other cultures. Also, to be inquisitive, to explore and to seek to understand differences and people from different environments and geographies. I think it more important to match the experience of the coach with the challenges being faced by the leader. A successful coach can come from any culture as long as he can recognise when he is coaching someone from a different culture and adjust his style accordingly – by adjustment, I would suggest this means toning down those aspects of one's styles and behaviours that might be unique to your own culture, eg the Dutch being very frank and open.

Kumar's advice was that coaches/mentors need to:

Make an effort to learn, identify specific areas of mutual interest and expand on these areas to strengthen chemistry. Spend time in the initial stages learning about the culture by asking questions and being very non-judgmental.

Bonnie Chan's advice for coaches/mentors was that:

They need to receive coaching, for example on their wish to transcend cultural differences themselves as coach. They should get clarity on how they look at cultural issues and think about what kind of pitfalls they may find when coaching their clients. That will require learning through reading cultural-related books, interacting with people from different countries and also getting clarity about their own beliefs and values about a culture. It can be hard for someone to have a higher sense of other cultures – for example, a person who has been living in the same country for a very long time may think this or that is the norm and wonder why another person isn't doing it. Or if they go overseas for the first time, a person may think about how annoyed they are about what people from another culture may be doing; but this is all part of the learning process. It can take a long time to learn about and appreciate another person's culture. Once you know how to appreciate another culture then you are actually embracing a much richer knowledge and also a much richer way of doing things.

(b) What coaching or mentoring principle or approach best enables a coach/mentor to work with someone of another culture?

Zanini's response to this question was:

I would have to say presence. I believe that when you can be completely present with another person, you hear and see things you wouldn't otherwise. You tap into the

> *'unsaid' and you gain understanding and insights that you would have missed otherwise. Have confidence in yourself and your skills. Put the humanity of your coachee/mentee before their culture. Be authentic and real and do not try to be something you are not.*

Chan picked IAC Coaching Mastery No.4:

> *"Processing in the present – because if you are able to do this, you will be so focused on your client in the here and now, you will even forget to be conscious of your own nationality and maybe you'll be so connected and engaged with your client that they may have the opportunity to be so engaged in that space that they too may forget their nationality! Processing in the present, when two people can really engage with each other in creating a space to understanding some new possibilities, is the greatest thing we need to master in order to be a great coach."*

Cumberland's advice was:

> *Helping a leader through the process of self-discovery – using the process to understand what is making that leader 'tick', ie, what kinds of cultural nuances, beliefs and behaviours are they acting out and living.*

Jeannette Lichner, who has led an eventful international career at senior level in global financial institutions and is a trained coach, offered an additional view:

> *I believe that what is always critical is the ability to really listen, seek to understand where the person is coming from and how they perceive the challenges they are facing (why they appear as challenges), and being non-judgmental – putting one's own cultural (broadly defined) background aside.*

6. Conclusion

This chapter has aimed to offer some fresh perspectives to add to the existing literature on these topics. What I would like readers to take away from it is the insight that coaching and mentoring, in the broad senses of the words, are concepts and practices that have existed in different ways across most cultures throughout history, having emerged in response to the need to support the development of human potential, performance and fulfilment.

Although there are many significant cultural differences that one may encounter, the inner essence of most people is more similar than may at first appear. Humanity shares similar passions, motivations and needs – the original bits of our wiring are essentially the same, wrapped around by richly diverse cultural clothing, patterned by unique personal experiences.

Specific coaching challenges for lawyers

Sarah Martin
Saïd Business School; Coombs Martin

He is our star performer but ....
She is an outstanding lawyer but ...
He is very competent at client work and at business development, but ...

What is it that tends to follow when a law firm's senior partner or HR director makes a request for the help of an executive coach?

Coaching has become sought after across a wide range of business sectors because of the contribution it can make to building lasting and positive change for individuals and organisations. The strong focus on helping clients to identify the nub of their challenge and discover their own bespoke, actionable and practical solutions can help to create both individual and firm-wide benefits with long-term impact.

At the heart of the coaching approach is the premise that the solution lies within the individual. As we shall see, that is part of its increasing appeal and success with lawyers.

1. What is different about lawyers and law firms?

In 2011 *The American Lawyer* ran an article entitled "A Breed Apart"[1] and there is now an increasing body of leadership and management research and literature focused on the legal sector and what makes it unique. As David Maister wrote:

> *I'm now ready to make a concession: Law firms are different. The ways of thinking and behaving that help lawyers excel in their profession may be the very things that limit what they can achieve as firms. Management challenges occur not in spite of lawyers' intelligence and training, but because of it.*

Lawyers have been trained as experts and selected by their firms, at least to some extent, because of their expertise and intelligence. In an increasingly competitive and commercial marketplace, lawyers also need to harness a range of other skills and abilities. Some of these tend to be more natural to lawyers than others. To progress within many firms today requires talents more akin to those of managers and leaders in the corporate world. From my experience of working in and with law firms over the past 25 years, I have seen a number of specific themes developing in the reasons behind requests for coaching lawyers.

1 Larry Richard and Lisa Rohrer, "A Breed Apart? How personality characteristics influence who becomes a lawyer – and how far they rise" *The American Lawyer*, July 1 2011.

The coaching challenge is often grounded in how to increase their effectiveness in the more relationship-driven aspects of their roles.

In this chapter I explore three particular recurrent challenges for lawyers and how coaching can be useful in finding positive solutions. These are areas where lawyers tend to find difficulty in the journey from expert to leader in their field or firm:

- collaboration and teamwork;
- developing others and delegation; and
- difficult conversations/holding people accountable.

2. Are lawyers different? What does the evidence show?

Before we look at these specific coaching challenges, let's consider the results of some recent research focused on the personalities of lawyers. These studies give us an overview of certain common personality traits, preferences and motivations that are often at play in law firms, and certain behavioural tendencies when lawyers are under pressure or stress. It is no surprise that the latter is particularly important given the pace at which most lawyers work today.

A recent sizeable study sheds some light on the typical psychological make-up of the legal profession and is based on the Caliper personality assessment tool administered to some 3,000 lawyers in the United States.[2] Of the 18 personality traits measured, lawyers' scores were significantly different from the population norm on six. The researchers contend that no other professional group has generated a profile that is "systematically such an outlier from the norm". The results are summarised in the table below.

Personality trait	Population	Lawyers' average
Scepticism	50% (by definition)	90th%-ile
Autonomy	50%	89th%
Abstract reasoning	50%	78th%
Urgency	50%	71st%
Resilience	50%	30th%
Sociability	50%	7th% (12th% including rainmakers)

As the study points out, if you are a client looking for a lawyer, these are probably traits you are seeking. But in terms of being part of a firm, being led, managing

2 Dr Larry Richard, "Growth is Dead" (Adam Smith Esq, October 2012).

others, delegating, collaborating or adapting to a changing and difficult legal market with all the challenges of 'more for less',[3] it's a different story.

3. How can coaching help?

Through the coaching case studies we will look at examples of how these traits, and those revealed by other studies, manifest themselves in practice and how coaching can help to improve interpersonal dynamics. These studies seem to paint a rather negative psychological landscape for lawyers. But it is not all gloom and doom. A recent study[4] using the Hogan Personality Instrument (HPI) confirmed that a strong personality trait (69th percentile) for lawyers is their love of learning and intellectual challenge. To my mind, this is one of the major contributing factors to the success of the coaching approach with lawyers. Presented with psychometric results, 360 data and research-based evidence (including from neuroscience) of how detracting behaviours can be changed, lawyers are keen to understand and learn. The coaching relationship provides a confidential space for learning and development of self-awareness.

This creates a safe opportunity for development that could otherwise be inhibited by a generally low appetite for risk. The non-directive coaching approach respects the autonomy of the individual, something that is very precious to most lawyers and allows them to set the agenda.

A coaching approach also respects the strengths of the client and explores what it is about them that is unique and makes them stand out from the crowd. In that positive context it is possible to find the motivation and resilience to work on some of the more tricky development areas.

All names and certain details have been changed in the case studies to preserve anonymity. They are, however, all based on real solicitors.

4. Case study: collaboration and team work

Appreciation is a wonderful thing: it makes what is excellent in others belong to us as well.
Voltaire

4.1 The challenge

The senior partner of Joanne's firm was keen to build a collaborative environment to capitalise on the combined expertise and skills of the partners. He explained one of the major challenges he was facing. The firm needed people to behave in a constructive and supportive manner in order to arrive at solutions. It had plenty of people who could spot problems, but it really wanted people who would take responsibility for working through problems collaboratively and generating solutions.

As recent studies show,[5] there are significant benefits for firms and lawyers who collaborate effectively. Collaboration helps to create a better understanding of clients

---

3 Richard Susskind, *Tomorrow's Lawyers: An Introduction to Your Future* (Oxford University Press 2013).

4 Jeff Foster, Larry Richard, Lisa Rohrer and Mark Sirkin, *'Understanding Lawyers: Why We Do the Things We Do' – Results from the Hogan Assessment Project of Lawyer Personality* (Hildebrandt Baker Robbins and Hogan Assessments Inc, 2010).

5 Heidi K Gardner, "Effective Teamwork and Collaboration" in Rebecca Norman-Hochman (ed), *Managing Talent for Success: Talent Development in Law Firms* (Globe Law and Business, 2013).

through different touch points and can lead to higher-value, more innovative and sophisticated work. This is of significant competitive advantage in a world where many of the more traditional streams of legal work have become commoditised.

Like many lawyers, Joanne did not find collaboration easy. The senior partner described her approach as "just wanting to win the argument" and how she excelled at that. He reported how this skill stood her in good stead in a court environment, but was highly destructive in a team environment where it's not about winning and losing, but about finding a way forward as a team.

These challenges in relation to collaboration and teamwork come up time and again for lawyers and law firms. Why is this so tricky for the legal sector? If we look at the psychometrics again, we can see some of the contributing factors. For those who tend to have such low sociability (7th percentile) and such high autonomy (89th percentile), teamwork and collaboration are not going to be the most natural bedfellows. High abstract reasoning (78th percentile) leads to a tendency challenge and find holes in most things, including the suggestions of colleagues. The low resilience score (30th percentile) feeds into low risk taking; teamwork involves taking some risks because you will inevitably be ceding some of your control. High urgency (71st percentile) creates pressure on oneself and can lead to impatience with others. Extremely high scepticism scores (93rd percentile) come as no surprise. Lawyers are professional sceptics; they are selected, trained and hired to be sceptical and spot flaws. This serves the client well, but the problem is that they tend to carry their scepticism into their dealings with each other and it contributes to low trust environments.

Trust is the foundation for all teamwork, as demonstrated in Patrick Lencioni's five dysfunctions of a team,[6] the highly respected research-based model on team-building and collaboration.

4.2 The five dysfunctions of a team

Without trust, all the other dysfunctions of teams start to flow. Fear of conflict making it difficult to have challenging discussions. Lack of commitment because you are not sure whether others will commit and whether it will be worth it. Avoiding accountability for what is happening and becoming busy as individual agents rather than focusing on the collaborative or team result. There is plenty of discussion about the top part of this pyramid, but not about the bottom part – possibly because it is too uncomfortable. However, it is the foundation that you need in order to challenge people and hold them to account. This is a theme we see again later.

Returning to Joanne, she is a star at her firm. She has a powerful reputation for her skills and clients. Many law firms still operate on a 'star-based' model (often reinforced by remuneration structures) that does not tend to sit comfortably with encouraging collaboration.

So how could coaching help Joanne to develop her ability to collaborate? We will see how Joanne and her firm benefited by working through the simple, yet powerful, GROW model based in the non-directive coaching approach. After the important preliminaries of establishing her wish to try some coaching, getting to know her a

---

6 *The Five Dysfunctions of a Team: A Leadership Fable* (Jossey-Bass, 2002).

little and confirming the confidentiality of the coaching discussions, the first step was her goal setting for the coaching work. In this way you work to the client's agenda. Many lawyers have such a strong sense of autonomy and innate dislike of being told what to do that for them, the non-directive approach of identifying and working through their challenge or blockage and finding their own solution has even greater and longer-lasting impact. Much of the power of the coaching relationship and process arises from asking open questions, giving the client time to think and listening with full attention to the answers.

4.3 Goal setting

What were Joanne's goals and what would be a successful outcome for her? Joanne had experienced some difficult and fractious interactions with her colleagues and as a result was seeking to reduce the need for any collaboration. She found it too challenging and frustrating. We explored what might motivate Joanne to change her approach to colleagues. She was keen to be given an opportunity to lead certain firm initiatives and was seen as very capable of doing so. These initiatives would inevitably require her to collaborate with others. Joanne's goal was to lead these projects for the firm and her coaching goal was to channel more energy into working with and alongside her colleagues in exchange for the new challenge of leading the firm's initiative.

4.4 Reality – what is happening here?

We started by exploring Joanne's strengths to set a positive context for the coaching work and to see how we might engage those strengths in enhancing her ability to collaborate. Her head of department was very quick to describe her many skills and how she had so much to offer the business: she was highly innovative, sees new opportunities, had high aspirations and was very goal focused.

We then reviewed Joanne's psychometrics and the patterns largely followed those in the studies based on larger lawyers. These included higher scores on autonomy and scepticism and lower scores on trust. They also included a tendency to withdraw in times of conflict and stress. We explored what that meant in practice for her professional relationships: that she tended to focus on the task at hand rather than getting to know people; that she expected hidden agendas and so was unlikely to rely on support from others. While she was effective at seeing the drawbacks to others' proposals, she could come across as critical and discouraging. Withdrawing under pressure could be interpreted as being aloof or lacking commitment.

4.5 Options – what could she do to change things?

Coaching makes the client work hard at considering possible solutions, ranking them and deciding which to test out. This continues to build ownership by the client of the problem and has chosen solution or solutions. I asked her: "What might you do? What have you tried already? What have you considered but not yet tried? What else could you try? How will you judge the options?"

Rather than bringing a natural scepticism to each relationship, we discussed how to experiment with an opposite presumption – that everyone is a potential ally. If appropriate, after a full discussion of the options a coaching client has generated I may, with permission, make some additional suggestions. In this case, I introduced Joanne to a model that has at its heart an interest in discovering opportunities for reciprocity.

Cohen-Bradford model of 'influence without authority'[7]

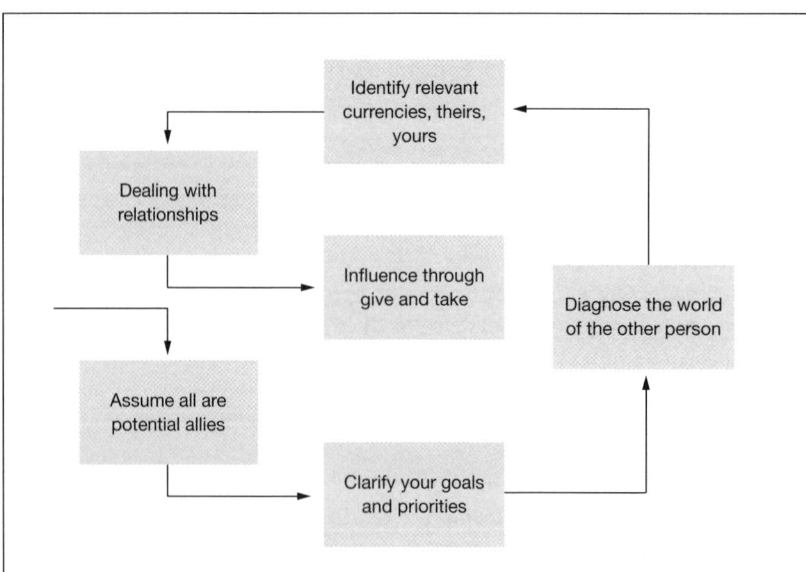

7 Allan R Cohen and David L Bradford, *Influence without Authority* 2nd Edn (John Wiley & Sons, 2005).

We looked at ways to develop common understanding and empathy through listening skills, becoming more open to what others have to say and, where appropriate, adopting more of their suggestions. We explored the differences between competing and collaborative behaviour, and how it may not always be advantageous to win all the discussions. We looked at the past triggers for her frustrations and her retreat into a non-collaborative stance, and at ways in which she could try to respond differently. We discussed how she could develop rapport by mentoring others in adopting a more innovative and exploratory approach to legal challenges.

4.6 Will – what is her will to take action?

Finally, it is essential to create a commitment to action and accountability for the outcomes. Coaching is about action and it usually helps to get down to a granular level of practicality. I asked her: "So, what's the first step? How will you do that? When will you take it? How do you rate your motivation to do this on a scale of 1 to 10?" As my coach once told me, if the rating is below 7, it probably isn't going to happen, so you have to go back and examine how to get more traction.

Joanne's action plan was granular and specific. She generated all the ideas for action through discussion and responses to questions in the coaching sessions, reading and reflection. She started with some simple steps in terms of setting up meetings with a number of people to develop a better understanding of their aspirations, challenges and strengths. These were the first steps to building better relationships and trust, the foundations of collaboration. She experimented with rebalancing the feedback and comments she gave to her colleagues, giving recognition and appreciation of any positive contributions, good ideas and extra effort before challenging constructively and debating. She mentored junior members of the team.

4.7 Outcome

The overall outcome included a strong team approach on the new firm initiative and a much more positive, enjoyable and productive set of working relationships.

5. Case study: delegation and developing junior lawyers

The best executive is the one who has sense enough to pick good men to do what he wants done, and self-restraint enough to keep from meddling with them while they do it.
– Theodore Roosevelt

5.1 The challenge

Jonathan is the head of a department and a brilliant lawyer. He is typical of many lawyers who struggle with the challenges of developing their junior colleagues and delegating effectively. The senior partner put his finger on Jonathan's Achilles heel: "Delegation and time management!" He described his partner's instinct for doing everything himself and how he becomes a natural blockage because he is not prepared to let go. His time management then becomes another issue because he is trying to cope with more than he should.

This is a common challenge for lawyers. Again, we can gain some clues as to what is underlying this from the psychometric research. The Motives Values and

Preferences Inventory (MVPI) is a psychometric that measures core values related to work preferences, interests and job satisfaction: what a person wants, needs, values and finds of interest. A summary of the results from study of 1,800 lawyers[8] is set out in the table.

Extracted from MVPI lawyers' average results

MVPI scale name	Description of what is valued	Lawyers' average percentile results
Aesthetic	Quality, product look and feel, attractive surroundings	63rd
Commercial	Business opportunities, commercial gain	43rd
Recognition	Fame, visibility, publicity	43rd
Altruistic	Helping others	41st

We can see that lawyers' highest average scores were for aesthetics, indicating a tendency to place high value on quality. In certain circumstances this can be overplayed to perfectionism. Combined with tendencies (shown in the personality studies) to high levels of autonomy, low levels of trust, very low appetite for risk and a role that places a high premium on accuracy and 'getting it right', we can see why lawyers may not find that delegation comes naturally. We also see that they have relatively low average scores for altruism, suggesting that some lawyers may place more value on their own work than in developing or helping others.

The Hogan Personality Instrument (HPI), illustrated opposite, describes the 'bright side' of personality, aspects that tend to lead to successful performance.[9]

In the HPI scale the lowest average score for the lawyers was on interpersonal sensitivity, indicating that on average, "Lawyers are more task-orientated and tend to speak their minds, but may also come across as cold, critical and argumentative." In contrast to the comparative data set of executives in the research study, the lawyers had the profiles of individual contributors rather than managers. Indeed, many lawyers are somewhat reluctant leaders or managers. Their expert success has led to promotion to manager, removing them from the expertise they know and love. If we look at models such as 'The Seven Transformations of Leadership',[10] lawyers tend to

---

8 Jeff Foster, Larry Richard, Lisa Rohrer and Mark Sirkin, *'Understanding Lawyers: Why We Do the Things We Do' – Results from the Hogan Assessment Project of Lawyer Personality* (Hildebrandt Baker Robbins and Hogan Assessments Inc, 2010).

9 Jeff Foster, Larry Richard, Lisa Rohrer and Mark Sirkin, *'Understanding Lawyers: Why We Do the Things We Do' – Results from the Hogan Assessment Project of Lawyer Personality* (Hildebrandt Baker Robbins and Hogan Assessments Inc, 2010).

HPI scale name	Definition	Lawyers' average percentile score
Learning approach	Enjoys academic activities, values learning as an end in itself	69th
Ambition	Leader-like, status-seeking, achievement orientated	52nd
Adjustment	Degree to which are steady under pressure or conversely moody and self-critical	44th
Interpersonal sensitivity	Degree to which socially sensitive, tactful and perceptive	40th

be at the expert level, which is only the third of the seven levels. The characteristics of an expert in this model are that they rule by logic and expertise, they are good individual contributors, but as managers, "they can be problematic because they are so completely sure that they are right". The authors suggest that for experts to move to the next leadership level of achievers they can benefit from training or coaching on emotional intelligence, delegation, teamwork and becoming more aware of the differences between their assumptions and others.

5.2 Goal setting

The first step was for Jonathan to decide whether he wanted to be a leader of his department or preferred to remain exclusively in his expert role. Once Jonathan had clarified this, his goal was to be able to delegate more consistently and effectively and so reduce his workload. He would measure his success by the 'bounce in his feet' once his load was reduced.

5.3 Reality – what is happening here?

Jonathan described being overloaded and exhausted. He recognised that he was not a very organised person or systematic in his approach. He saw this primarily as a product of the tussle he felt between client work and managing the department. In 360 feedback there was extensive praise for a wide range of leadership attributes, personal qualities and legal skills. There were also some very clear messages about his challenges with delegation and ability to develop the next generation.

His colleagues thought that to be more effective, Jonathan needed to build better trust in the people beneath him. He came across as over-protective and always wishing to keep control. He would often take pieces of work back from colleagues. His natural approach was to keep everything; his strong instinct was to do it himself.

10 David Rooke and William R Torbert, "The Seven Transformations Of Leadership", *Harvard Business Review*, April 2005.

5.4 Options – what could he do to change things?

For Jonathan, the turning point came in his approach when he realised the impact that his lack of delegation was having on his team. "I realise that some people suffer more than I realised – it needs sorting out." He began to appreciate how his approach meant that they in turn found it difficult to be organised. He absolutely did not wish them to see his lack of delegation as a lack of faith in their abilities.

He generated some options in response to the specific feedback:

- developing a style that started with listening and indicating that the person may be right and exploring their point of view: "Can he develop his touchy feely side? He doesn't find it easy to give praise";
- developing a degree of pragmatism in areas where there is some latitude to do so: "I think he worries about what will happen if he releases control"; and
- recognising the achievement and pleasure in developing someone else to do what you do and be as good as you: "He feels he is the only person who can do certain things".

5.5 Will – what is his will to take action?

Bolstered by the appreciation of his strengths, Jonathan had a strong commitment to tackling his obstacles to effective delegation. He developed a plan of action that involved introducing more structure to his department and enlisting the help of his PA to:

- manage his diary more effectively;
- set up regular meetings and aim not to cancel or move them;
- ensure that the majority of action points from meetings were not his;
- give clearer instructions and balance feedback; and
- have a clearer office and files so others could then access.

5.6 Outcome

Jonathan's department became visibly more organised and effective. He regained the bounce in his step and created more time to contribute to the strategic thinking of the firm, to develop his client relationships and to develop other partners into management roles.

6. Case study: difficult conversations/holding people accountable

A person may cause evil to others not only by his actions but by his inaction, and in either case he is justly accountable to them for the injury.

– John Stuart Mill

6.1 The challenge

"He protects his under-performers, which creates problems for me and for him. He doesn't want to face up to people who cause problems for him." The senior partner of a major UK law firm asked me to meet one of his firm's senior lawyers. Henry is a head of a significant and very successful department in the firm with many lawyers reporting to him. He has won many awards for his work and is a well-recognised expert in his field. The senior partner was clear that Henry's contribution to the firm was very significant and highly valued. "He is by far my star performer." The main reason for exploring coaching was heartfelt and clearly articulated: an important leader in the firm was having severe difficulties in holding under-performing partners to account.

This is a theme that crops up time and time again with lawyers. If we look at the psychological research, we gain a few insights as to why that may be so.

The Hogan Development Survey (HDS) is a highly respected, well-researched and widely used psychometric instrument. It measures, on a self-report basis, behavioural tendencies that can negatively affect our performance. It looks at our risks of adopting certain derailing behaviour in stressful situations such as when we are over-tired, ill or time pressured. It focuses on our reputation; how others may experience us or perceive us in those circumstances. While the HPI measures the 'bright side' of our personality, the results from the HDS are often described as showing the 'dark side' of our personality. The higher our score is, the greater the chance that this behaviour could hamper our success.

Research in 2010,[11] looking at nearly 2,000 lawyers, showed that lawyers have the highest (most problematic) scores in the areas set out in the table below.

HDS highest average results

HDS scale name	Definition	Strategy for coping with stress	Lawyers' average percentile score
Excitable	Becoming tense and over-critical	Moving away	68th
Cautious	Being reluctant to take risks and make decision	Moving away	68th
Leisurely	Tendency to resist authority	Moving away	68th
Reserved	Distancing themselves, becoming uncommunicative	Moving away	65th
Sceptical	Tendency to be lacking in trust	Moving away	62nd

11 Jeff Foster, Larry Richard, Lisa Rohrer and Mark Sirkin, *'Understanding Lawyers: Why We Do the Things We Do' – Results from the Hogan Assessment Project of Lawyer Personality* (Hildebrandt Baker Robbins and Hogan Assessments Inc, 2010).

The HDS scales are grouped into three strategies for dealing with stress. If we take the analogy of the stressful situation of an unexpected encounter with a lion, they represent the three options: running like hell, getting out the spear or getting out a juicy piece of steak! In other words, a flight response ('moving away'), a fight response ('moving against') and a negotiated or compromise response ('moving towards').

The interesting thing here is that all of the areas in which lawyers tend to score most highly represent the 'moving away' response. We have a strong tendency to distance ourselves from the source of stress. One senior partner describes a typical response from one of his top lawyers: " When his stress levels rise he starts sending anti-establishment missives, he goes to ground, he disappears."

That source of stress is most often another person. The research showed the contrast with other managers and other professionals, who tended to favour 'moving against' strategies and push back at the source of stress.

6.2 Goal-setting

So how can coaching help lawyers with this challenge? Let's return to Henry. After the important preliminaries of establishing his wish to try some coaching, getting to know him a little and confirming the confidentiality of the coaching discussions, the first step was his goal setting for the coaching work.

I asked him: what made this so important for him now, and what made it so important for his firm. For Henry, it had become important because he was taking so much of the flak for the under-performance of other people. He was carrying them and it was a heavy burden. His financial targets and his wellbeing were on a downward spiral. Both were having an adverse impact, on his department and the firm financially and on overall morale.

I asked him what his desired outcome would look like. He wanted to be able to hold frank and constructive conversations with certain identified colleagues about how they could improve their performance and remove some of his load.

6.3 Reality – what is happening here?

Raising Henry's awareness was fundamental to enabling the enduring change in his behaviour. 360 interviews with the firm's leadership, his colleagues and direct reports provided direct and rich data that was difficult for him to move away from or ignore.

These are just a couple of examples that helped him to see the nature of the problem and the impact it was having on him and others.

"He doesn't want to confront people. It's hard for him to get the process started of being frank."

" He has high standards but is tolerant of weakness, which means he takes on more and more. He will work round weaknesses rather than dealing with them – everything lands back on his plate."

6.4 Options – what could he do to change things?

We then went on to explore what he could and wanted to do about this challenge. Henry chose to set up some conversations with some of his partners. He saw the benefits to himself and his partners of inviting them to take responsibility for their own actions. On several occasions he made the analogy of the parental role and the need to relax the control and allow his colleagues to learn from their mistakes and omissions.

He built his resolve by reflecting on and itemising his answer to the question: what are the benefits of having the difficult conversation with that partner? He enhanced that resolve still further by first considering his answer to the question: what is stopping you having it? He then worked through strategies to meet each of those blockages.

6.5 Will – what is his will to take action?

For Henry, it was useful to run through the practicalities of how to set up the conversation and then to do a role-play. Once he had decided whom he needed to speak with, why and when, we set up some very clear and specific questions for him to consider. Once we got to this focused stage, these questions were much more specific and tailored to his chosen action plan than the open coaching questions we started out with. For example: are you clear about what you want out of the conversation? When would be the right time to have it? Have your prepared the physical setting? Have you had time to prepare? What will the impact of your words be on the listener? Can you position this to create a positive outcome? Can you listen without resistance? What insights can you generate? At this stage, it always helps to have a concrete and reasonably granular action plan.

6.6 Outcome

Henry had three of these conversations with significant impact on his partners' performance over the following months. In turn, this freed him up to focus on his own challenges.

7. Conclusion

Like many coaching outcomes, these examples are not instant fixes or a linear path to change. It is usually an iterative process and often a bumpy journey. The power of coaching in meeting these challenges is that it draws the solutions out from within the person who has the most to gain and has the most knowledge about the problem and all that surrounds it. Those solutions are far more likely to be enduring than any advice, however wise or well targeted. But coaching is not a panacea and may form part of a solution that might also require organisational change, or the support of sponsors from within the firm or mentors such as provided through the International Bar Association Law Firm Mentoring Programme.

For lawyers, the major hurdle with coaching is often the high degree of scepticism they bring to the process. If they already have an appetite for change, can be convinced by hard data or can see quick wins, then the greater the chances of real engagement and success as these case studies show.

How mentoring and coaching can help with life balance issues

Rachel Brushfield
EnergiseLegal

1. Introduction

Work-life balance is a strategic, structural, global and multi-dimensional issue.

Achieving a balance between home life and work life is increasingly becoming a priority for many. Growing numbers of people are endorsing a lifestyle career anchor, which implies that their primary career objective is to balance and integrate the demands of their career, their family and their own needs.

A healthy work-life balance increases the likelihood of a life free from mental health-related problems such as stress, depression and anxiety. The term 'work-life balance' was coined in 1986 and companies and firms began to offer work-life balance in the 1980s/1990s. Originally, women's needs were the focus, but now it is becoming gender neutral.

People are the highest expense in a company and therefore more hours from fewer people is a vital lever, as is encouraging additional hours from discretionary effort. This can be achieved by the carrot or the stick, and most law firms have focused on implicit sticks and few carrots, except financial reward.

The credit crunch and its aftermath have made people rethink what is important and, for many, work-life balance is important. The sacrifice of relationships, health, hobbies and marriage at the expense of work is a great one. The often-quoted "Few people when they get to their death bed wish they had spent more time in the office" still holds true, and even more so now that the rewards for the majority of lawyers are lessening for the effort expended.

2. Definition of 'work-life balance'

Work-life balance is the combination of achievement and enjoyment through both work and life outside work, and is an individual and subjective matter. Work-life balance is having enough time for work and enough to have a life. An individual's life varies considerably in respect of number of dependents, health, interests, financial pressures, responsibilities, career and personal ambition, personalities, needs, wants, values and motivations. This mix is constantly changing, with employees going through different life stages. External factors such as marriage, divorce, death and birth can also change an individual's perception of his own work and life. Employers need to invest time and thought in the employee proposition, the psychological contract, and segment and target different employee groups as part of the talent management strategy.

3. Factors affecting work-life balance of lawyers in the legal profession

Many factors affect the work-life balance of lawyers in the legal profession. These include:

- the competitive nature of law, internally and externally, magnified by reduced equity and the associate surplus;
- uncertainty of time commitment;
- the lawyer personality;
- a presenteeism culture;
- flexible/part-time working unfairly perceived as a lack of commitment and career ambition;
- left brain focus on hard measures and a dismissive attitude to less tangible measures such as happiness and career fulfilment and motivation;
- up or out, churn and pyramid law firm models which disguise the negative impact of lawyers' work-life balance and disengagement; and
- transparent explicit publication, measurement and tracking of individual performance and fee earning.

4. Insights from neuroscience and the physical, mental and emotional impact of stress and tiredness resulting from poor work-life balance

Self-awareness enabled by having a coach and self-coaching helps lawyers to manage their own responses and to increase their resilience. Stress, fear and tiredness all inhibit clarity of thought and attention to detail is essential to provide accurate advice. Put simply, the growing area of neuroscience helps the understanding of performance and of how to manage and maximise our own brains and bodies. Lawyers can learn techniques to disassociate from challenging feelings and situations, so that they can concentrate better, despite external factors.

Emotion has a powerful influence on learning and memory. Learning and memory involve multiple brain systems which are engaged in different stages of information processing.

The exponential development of neuroscience will provide scientific data to support the effects of poor work-life balance and high and sustained levels of stress and tiredness, as well as the effects of sleep and mindfulness practice on the brain, memory, concentration and emotions, decision making and accuracy.

5. Impact of poor work-life balance on lawyers; stress, addictions, mistakes

Symptoms of a poor work-life balance are numerous: some are very visible (eg, absence), and some less visible (eg, mental health issues building over time).

A poor work-life balance causes stress, and stress has a big impact on productivity.

Forty one percent of employees lose 15 to 30 minutes' productivity a day; 36% lose more than one hour a day; 23% report that their productivity is not affected by stress.

Forty six percent come to work too stressed to be effective on one to four days a year; for 30% it is five or more days. One quarter say that stress does not influence their effectiveness.[1]

'Learned helplessness'[2] is a growing phenomenon. It is a 'giving up' mindset in weary lawyers fed up with working more for less rewards. Its symptoms include;

- burnout;
- complacency;
- defensiveness, irritability;
- over-sensitivity;
- diminished creativity when more is needed; and
- reactivity rather than proactivity with business development.

It can be a precursor to depression in a profession already experiencing higher levels of alcohol abuse, suicide and drug addiction than other professions.

6. Impact of poor work-life balance on law firms' reputation, talent attraction and retention

Increasing work-life balance options benefits law firms. They help to retain talent, reduce costs associated with attrition and recruitment, provide better use of office space with 'hot-desking' and teleworking, increase diversity with better problem-solving and promote increased productivity by reducing stress.

Work-life balance is "somewhat important" to 44.7% of HR managers in multinationals and 49.2% think it is "very important". The belief that a work-life balance policy could have a positive effect on reducing absenteeism was held by 97.7%. In over 70% of the companies surveyed, work-life balance is an important component of the company's policy for reducing absenteeism. Less than 30%, however, have implemented work-life balance policies with the involvement of employees or their representatives.[3]

Beliefs about presenteeism and that employees who work part time lack job/career dedication can stop lawyers from taking up work-life balance options. Law firms that embrace work-life balance policies can use them to their advantage, attracting the best talent as well as having alumni who positively promote the firm when networking and online, as well as return themselves when needed. Generation Y and the Millennials actively seek a healthy work-life balance and with a shortage of them in the population, law firms need to ensure that they engage and attract them away from their competitors. Work-life balance-friendly policies need to be an integral part of an employer's brand and play a pivotal role in a positive psychological contract. Negative PR on websites such as Legal Cheek and Roll on Friday, while tongue in cheek, can damage a firm's reputation.

---

1 The HR Specialist, "The effects of stress on workplace performance" (December 20 2012) (ComPsych Stress Pulse Survey, October 2012). available at www.businessmanagementdaily.com/34123/the-effects-of-stress-on-workplace-performance#.

2 Dr Larry Richard, "We need a chief resilience officer" (August 21 2013), available at www.lawyerbrainblog.com/2013/08/we-need-a-chief-resilience-officer/.

3 International Bar Association Global Employment Institute, The IBA GEI 'Balancing report' *Strategic trends in National Law and Multinational policies on work-life balance and the implications for Human Resources Law* (March 2012), available at: www.google.co.uk/url?sa=t&rct=j&q=&esrc=s&source=web&cd=1&ved=0CC4QFjAA&url=http%3A%2F%2Fwww.ibanet.org%2FDocument%2FDefault.aspx%3FDocumentUid%3D90E4EA4F-C5A1-4088-A619-8E4D42B91153&ei=i0M5U63KFsSshQf254HADA&usg=AFQjCNFyIBATa5ApXFXVChvh_cUvqSMr9Q&bvm=bv.63808443,d.ZG4

7. Impact of poor work-life balance and resulting stress on law firms' financial performance and productivity

Poor work-life balance and its impact affect all sectors. For example, it is estimated that burnout at work costs Canadian businesses C$12 billion a year in health claims, lost productivity and absenteeism, according to the Conference Board of Canada.[4]

Research shows that employees who experience increased stress due to work-life conflict and hold the perception of having less control over demands at work and at home are less productive and more likely to be absent or leave the organisation.[5] Only 6.1% of multinationals consider that work-life balance is not important at all for the hiring of staff.[6]

Stress has a big effect on attendance, with 55% of employees missing one or two days a year due to stress, 29% missing three to six days and 16% missing more than six days a year.[7]

8. What benefits does coaching bring to enable work-life balance for lawyers?

Pure coaching – that is, non-directive coaching – helps lawyers to come up with their own answers rather than being told what to do by someone who is not them. Its approach is personalised, with the coach's job being to see the specific situation through the coachee's eyes. The combination of time and space in the diary ring-fenced for focus, being asked incisive questions, reflection and tools and exercises provides useful and time-efficient and effective solutions. Different personality types (eg, introverts and extroverts) and differing 'dominant senses' (ie, visual (seeing), auditory (hearing) and kinaesthetic (feeling)), will find specific aspects of being coached more or less useful. Some coachees think and get clarity by expressing themselves, so being asked questions and expressing answers will help them. Other coachees will gain insight from reflection and writing after the coaching session itself, following time to process thoughts and feelings. For others, simply having a deadline for action is beneficial.

Coaching has many benefits, which help lawyers to increase their self-awareness of factors affecting their work-life balance and what they can influence:

- a witness to expression and intention;
- commitment to change;
- writing down specific actions;
- the surfacing of feelings and thoughts supported by hearing them reflected back by the coach;
- clarity and new perspectives on specific factors;
- actions and accountability to support change;
- defining SMART goals;
- support, time and space to think about important, but not urgent issues;

---

4 Isherwood and Cajic, 1998

5 Adams 1976; Boles & Babin, Netemeyer *et al* 1996; Boles, Howard and Donofrio 2001; Frye & Breaugh 2004.

6 IBA GEI Balancing Report (at fn 3 above).

7 "The Effects of stress on workplace performance" (at fn 1 above).

- awareness of conscious and unconscious habits and behaviours, raised different perspectives and new perspectives, problem solving; and
- brainstorming ideas and hearing examples to shed new light on old issues and utilise strengths to support change.

Poor work-life balance and tiredness can inhibit clarity and creativity and sometimes the last thing the coachee needs or wants is a question. A carefully crafted coaching contract for a coaching programme from the outset and clear defined outcomes from an individual session or intervention will ensure that the coachee gets what he wants and needs. Coaching helps lawyers to think about and action stress management techniques and make proactive decisions which will improve work-life balance over time, given attention. These include time management, mindfulness (covered later in this chapter), 'big win' business development, smart working such as delegation, and setting goals that motivate lawyers to carve out time for themselves, such as for a favourite sport or hobby.

9. What benefits does mentoring bring to enable work-life balance for lawyers?

Individual or group mentoring from a lawyer or professional who has experience of the issues and challenges faced by the mentee is useful in helping to focus on improving work-life balance and providing a different type of help to coaching. It normalises any challenges, reducing self-consciousness of not coping or feeling stressed. Lawyers respect lawyers and the master and apprenticeship nature of the legal profession makes lawyers receptive to being mentored when some may resist coaching, perceiving it as remedial or a sign of weakness.

People get so close to issues or themselves, they can find it hard to see the wood for the trees. For lawyers under pressure to earn fees, this is magnified. Hearing ideas and experiences from a mentor who has been down the path they are on is therefore sometimes essential, because respect for experience is present with tangible evidence of what does or doesn't work to improve work-life balance. Mentoring enables the sharing of ideas and experience, so it can spark off insight, provide new solutions, useful resources or fresh perspectives on challenges.

10. The importance of chemistry and respect in the coach/coachee and mentor/mentee relationship

Coaching is, in part, a journey of change from vulnerability to greater self-awareness. This is especially true for issues associated with work-life balance – for example, stress, anxiety and under-performance – which can make the coachee feel vulnerable, exposed or weak. A compatible coaching chemistry/bond and respect is essential for coaching to work and for the coachee to be open to change and support. Chemistry creates trust and is a combination of personality, values and skills such as empathy, and the ability to build rapport and stay present helps its creation. Self-awareness is a prerequisite of a good coach, and a skilled coach will naturally adapt his style to that of the coachee.

Different coachees will respond to different styles and types of coach and the approach of the coach will create/affect the chemistry. Coaching styles include directive, reflective, structured, conceptual, facilitative, supportive, action oriented, fluid and practical.

A similar style between coach and coachee may result in immediate chemistry as communication style and perspectives are similar, whereas a different style may present a greater opportunity to learn from challenge with a very different perspective.

Confidentiality is the bedrock that enables trust to blossom. Coaching is still perceived by some lawyers as remedial and there may be cynicism or scepticism that it is a 'ploy' to create evidence to get rid of them from the firm, so they withhold effort and commitment, leading to the failure of the coaching.

What creates chemistry and respect is an individual thing. Chemistry and trust tend to be rooted in a feeling that is either present or absent. Respect from lawyers often comes from the accomplishments of the coach; his track record of tangible results, relevant experience and case studies of the issues that are the coachee's goals, and credibility from client testimonials, training and qualifications and the calibre of the firms with which he has worked. Both chemistry and trust are intrinsic in the delivery of results – both return on expectation and return on investment. A contrasting personality type can be useful to provide new perspectives, but may inhibit the chemistry essential to enable personal change. Coaches who were originally lawyers with a proven track record of success may have the edge with lawyer coachees, as they understand what it is like for the coachee in a way that a coach without a professional services background cannot. In the changing legal market, the opposite may be useful too.

11. The impact of different personality types

Coaching can help lawyers to develop their own effective resilience-building strategies, mainly cognitive ones.

Most researchers believe that there are five broad categories of personality traits:

- extraversion;
- agreeableness;
- conscientiousness;
- neuroticism; and
- openness.

Work-life balance is a mix of enjoyment and achievement.

Extraversion and neuroticism are traits that can impact on balance. High neuroticism, which is associated with emotional instability,[8] can lead to an unstable work-life balance.[9] Individuals high on extraversion are more likely to experience greater work-life balance than those with high introversion scores.[10]

---

8 Ewen *et al*, 2003.

9 Kinnunen *et al*, 2004.

10 A Victor Devadoss and J Befija Minnie, "A study of personality influence in building work life balance using fuzzy relation mapping (FRM)" Indo-Bhutan International Conference on Gross National Happiness (Chennai, India) (Vol 2, October 2013) 211–216.

Research into the reasons for female lawyers entering law school and their later career satisfaction has shown that those who went to law school to develop existing talents or fulfil personal, realistic or materialistic goals were happier as lawyers than those who were interested in the actual outcomes of lawyering or who were seeking intellectual stimulation.[11]

Daicoff also found that the lawyers who were people oriented were more likely to drop out of law school or be dissatisfied as attorneys.

Personality type has a big impact on work-life balance. The Myers-Briggs Type indicator, a personality instrument based on the work of Carl Jung (1923), is about how we take in information (sensing = S, intuition = N), how we make decisions (thinking = T, feeling = F), whether we derive our energy from the external or internal world (extraversion = E, introversion = I) and how we organise our lives (judging = J, perceiving = P). The combination makes up 16 different personality types. The majority of lawyers are six out of the 16 Myers Briggs types; ISTJ, ESTJ, INTJ, ENTP, INTP and ENTJ. The S/N and T/F pairs are closely correlated with job satisfaction. NT as a type like work that has an impersonal and analytic approach to ideas, information and people. Myers Brigg types that do not fit the norm in the law may work harder to try to fit in and overcompensate, resulting in poor work-life balance and burnout.

12. Major life stages and their impact on work-life balance

Work-life balance varies at different life stages, with some life stages especially challenging, particularly for those with dependants. The belief that it is important to achieve a balance between paid work and personal life and that this enables them to work better is held by 90% of people. Most agree that it is a joint responsibility of employers and employees; 55.2% would like to work more flexibly and want knowledge, clarity, fairness, autonomy and trust at work.

The growth in international clients and the law firms that serve them can have an impact on work-life balance if frequent flying around the world between offices/to clients is involved and they have jet lag to contend with. A secondment to another office for three to six months as part of training can be an enjoyable career interlude that doesn't necessarily cause a poor work-life balance, just a different regime; so it depends on the individual's attitude to change and personal circumstances.

13. Role of self-coaching and reflection

Self-coaching is the practice of a lawyer asking himself a series of open, incisive questions and making time to think in a conducive environment to create insights, new clarity and actions, enabling change and an improved work-life balance. Self-coaching is coaching without a coach and a very useful follow-on to having a coach. A key part of a coach's role for lawyers is helping coachees to self-coach, extending

11 Susan Daicoff, "Lawyer, know thyself: a review of empirical research on attorney attributes bearing on professionalism" 46 Am U L Rev 5 1997 available at: www.wcl.american.edu/journal/lawrev/46/daictxt.html.

the benefits and value that coaching brings. A simple three-question self-coaching structure such as, 'What do I want?' 'What will that do for me?' and 'How will I know I have got it?', for example, can create useful insights and actions to improve work-life balance fast.

The act of reflection can feel like wasting valuable fee-earning time or doing nothing, which lacks tangibility. A skilled coach can help lawyers to create structure and focus for purposeful reflection so it is more task-like, with clear and actionable outcomes. A series of open, incisive questions, providing a framework to address key factors affecting work-life balance such as the use of time or impact of stress, combined with support to create a regular habit to review at a specific time of day, week or month, can positively impact on work-life balance when focusing on what factors can be influenced.

14. Cultures of individual firms

A work-life balance ethos helps lawyers who want to have greater involvement in public life and the community. Work-life balance, especially in the legal profession, is largely down to the attitudes of the supervising partner.

Policies that support work-life balance help; but without a healthy psychological culture that supports work-life balance and leaders who encourage it, policies are mere words on a page. HR needs to pay as much attention to the psychological contract of employees as to the employment contract. Making sure that employees feel motivated, respected, cared for and valued is important. Work-life balance and the hours that lawyers spend at work affects this. For example, the firm paying for a taxi home for a corporate/commercial lawyer during a stressful case is a small, low-cost gesture that speaks volumes and helps work-life balance.

Often lawyers are reluctant to use options by their firms that support work-life balance, such as flexible working or part-time/job-share roles. There needs to be an active, heartfelt promotion of a culture with healthy work-life balance supported and practices used by senior management.

Of HR managers in multinationals, 63% do not have a policy on work-life balance. However, a strong majority think it is a somewhat or very important issue, and link it to health and safety policies; while 93.9% believe that work-life balance plays a role in the hiring and retention of talent. Work-life balance is thought to be 'somewhat important' by 44.7% of HR managers in multinationals, and 49.2% think it is 'very important'.[12]

15. Healthy habits and behaviours for good work-life balance

Small changes can make a big difference to work-life balance and wellbeing. New habits take approximately 30 days to be embedded and new neural pathways to be created. A coach creating accountability and providing support or a 30-day chart to record and track new habits to support improvements in work-life balance is effective and ties in with the lawyer routine of measuring fees and utilisation. What gets measured gets done and what isn't measured is often forgotten.

---

12 IBA GEI Balancing Report (at fn 3 above).

Healthy habits such as going to bed 30 minutes earlier and setting a mobile phone reminder, or spending 30 minutes at the end of the week reflecting on what factors have affected stress levels and work-life balance and what can be done (eg, saying no), are cumulatively effective over time. Coaching creates a structure to examine them and make them a priority, ring-fencing time for important non-urgent tasks that are counter-intuitive to the short-term culture of law firm partnerships and fee earning.

Behaviour is driven by beliefs. A coach helps a coachee to examine his beliefs and behaviours, to analyse, unpick and change them – shedding new light and gaining fresh perspectives on what is done and why. Conscious beliefs such as 'fee-earning hours each day mean everything to my career success as a lawyer' and unconscious beliefs such as 'fear of failure' or 'I am not good enough' can drive unhealthy behaviours, such as perfectionism, working long hours and presenteeism rather than working smarter (ie, more efficiently and effectively). Part of a coach's role is to hold up a mirror and help coachees to see what they are too close to or too busy to spot themselves.

16. Mindfulness and switching off as a preventative strategy

Lawyering is a very cerebral profession and intelligent lawyers, who are primarily thinking rather than feeling personality types, can find it hard to switch off and be rather than do or think. Energy and time can be expended in worrying about past decisions or future ones, rather than focusing on the present.

Mindfulness is a practical technique that helps lawyers to switch off and be present, helping to reduce stress and increase productivity. It is easy in theory but harder in practice to be present, but the benefits of doing so provide motivation from practice and experience of the rewards. It increases wellbeing and efficacy in a lawyer's private and professional life and increases the likelihood of the causes of poor work-life balance being noticed and changed, if they can be influenced.

Practically, mindfulness gets an individual to get out of his mind/thinking and connects him with his senses, to be conscious of what is happening in the here and now, putting their attention on being present in the moment. Objectively pausing, noticing breathing, observing thoughts and feelings gives awareness of how the individual is reacting to a situation or problem. It provides fresh perspectives, and the opportunity to moderate reactions quickly, review the facts and responses, and adapt and respond thoughtfully and mindfully. Mindfulness is intelligent and purposeful reflection and putting attention on our senses, instead of letting the mind rule and dictate. Other benefits include better creativity and problem solving, deeper and more curious listening, dealing better with unexpected events, reduced anger because of insights about the cause, listening with all their senses and so being more genuine and responsive in interactions with others (both colleagues and clients), greater focus and calmness, more compassion, enhanced focus on output rather than input and how to best achieve it, and a heightened enjoyment of being alive rather than automatic responses.

Mindfulness is time efficient, effective and costs nothing. Just five to 10 minutes of sitting quietly in a chair with a good posture, listening to his own breathing and external sounds, connecting with his senses of smell, sound, touch, taste and how he is feeling, rather than staying caught up with internal thoughts and wrestling with the monkey mind, enables a lawyer to regroup and relax. Programmes in mindfulness are now being taught at law schools in the United States, such as example the University of Miami School of Law. Mindfulness is starting to be integrated into classes on negotiation, professional responsibility and relationships.

17. Conclusion

The law firm model and lawyer personality do not naturally facilitate work-life balance. External interventions with coaches and mentors are therefore very useful to counter this. This is especially so given that the importance placed on work-life balance is typically not backed up in reality by the implementation of policies on the issue.

New developments in neuroscience and hard data and measures on the correlation between the brain, environment and performance will give scientific credibility to the importance of a healthy work-life balance, low stress and their correlation to high performance and good productivity. Talent drain and its measurement and the problem that it causes firms, client relationships and employer brand and reputation will also put the spotlight on lawyers' work-life balance and how significant it is. The unwillingness of Generation Y and the Millennials to tolerate the excessive hours and negative impact on life that they have witnessed in their parents will encourage law firms to embrace work-life balance and the role that coaching and mentoring has in its creation and maintenance positively, rather than reluctantly. This can only be good for the individual lawyer, the firm and its clients.

Coaching for retirement

Bill Knight

Retirement is a 'life event' in the same class as marriage, moving home, divorce, bankruptcy and a spell in prison. It can have a major effect on the person retiring. There are some who object to the word 'retirement', pointing out that with increases in life expectancy, leaving the occupation in which you have made your career is just a stage in life's journey. But retirement is a useful term and most of us know what it means.

Retirement marks the end of something. It also marks the beginning of the third stage of life, with its connotations of mortality. It invites reflection and poses a serious challenge – what to do in the time we have left? Most of us fail to prepare for this at all, keeping busy until the moment comes. We do not discuss it seriously with anyone, even with our partners. We realise that there will be time for travel and enjoyment, but somehow we put off serious consideration of our future lives. And with any luck they will be long – perhaps 30 years.

On retirement, we lose status, power and the structure that has ordered our lives. We are thrown back on ourselves. Thus far, we have been institutionalised, first in our families, then in education, then in employment. Now we are on our own and, unless we are lucky enough to have some overriding desire to do something different, we are left fit, active and redundant. This ought to be a happy time, with leisure for all those things we wanted to do – but what, exactly, were they?

Our families may not be much help. Our partners have lives of their own, made while we were at the office, and our children are grown and busy. One problem that affects us in the United Kingdom is that our profession has increasingly become executors of transactions and litigation rather than strategic advisers. Those of us advising business lose touch with our clients as they become more senior in their companies and we find it hard to get board appointments after retirement because we are thought of as people who carry out transactions rather than as those who decide on them. Also, we are not as popular with business as we might be. Rightly or wrongly, too many of us have reputations as expensive advisers who are not prepared to share the risks – and that does not make us welcome in the boardroom after retirement.

So what to do? Ideally, the way ahead has been planned in advance, but retirement may come unexpectedly and most of us are no good at this sort of planning because we can't imagine what it will be like until we do it. A coach can help, especially if he or she has been through the experience. A long talk with a skilled, sympathetic but disinterested interlocutor can start to disentangle the skein and plan the way ahead. And the good news is that we adapt. After a year or so, with luck, we will be happy. Coaching will shorten that journey.

The case study below touches on these themes and some other issues. It is a study of an English lawyer, but I hope the issues are sufficiently universal to make it interesting to those from all jurisdictions.

1. Mary Wingate – a case study

Mary Wingate, an English employment lawyer in her late 50s and a partner in a large London firm, was asked one sunny morning in June to go to see her senior partner. Mary liked her senior partner and remembers admiring his crisp white shirt as his secretary showed her into his office. He offered her coffee and they sat down. Without much further preamble he asked her when she was thinking of retiring. He praised her contribution to the firm over many years, he was appreciative of her hours and her billing, but he explained that the firm needed to promote younger partners and it was time for her to call it a day. Mary said she would think about it and her senior partner stood and opened the door for her when she left.

Mary did indeed think about it. She returned to her office feeling slightly sick and surprisingly angry, although her head told her that, short of legal action – the idea of which she dismissed almost at once – there was nothing much to be done. She found she could not concentrate on her work and for the first time ever she left early and went home. The meeting with the senior partner had not altogether been a surprise; she had known that it would happen eventually and many colleagues of her age had already gone. But she had not faced up to it before. Now she had to confront it and she felt angry, confused and rather lost.

That evening she talked it over with her husband Richard, a businessman with a few years to go before retirement, and he suggested that she should just take it easy – they had enough money, after all. Mary's reaction to this suggestion was immediately negative. Certainly there had been times, more often recently, when she had thought how nice it would be not to go into the office, but she was in excellent health and she felt full of energy. Her children had grown, her hobbies, mainly painting and walking, were just that – hobbies – and life, quite a lot of life with a bit of luck, stretched before her. She had friends, of course, but as a full-time working woman she wasn't equipped with the networks which would fill her time, and anyway the thought of book groups and charity lunches left her cold. What was she to do?

The next day Mary told her senior partner the truth about how she was feeling. He was firm about retirement, and suggested a date three months away, with a reasonable financial package, but he was also sympathetic and offered Mary coaching at the firm's expense. He recommended two coaches the firm had used previously and suggested she see both of them before making up her mind.

2. The chemistry session

Coaching was something new for Mary. She had heard about it, but she only had a hazy idea of what it involved. In a spirit of try anything once, particularly if someone else is paying, she called the first name on the list – John. He invited her to come to his office for what he called a 'chemistry session'. He told her to allow an hour.

Two weeks later they met in John's functional office and sat opposite each other across the table. Mary noticed the clock and the box of tissues. John, who Mary thought was about 60, said that the only thing he knew about her was that she was a lawyer about to retire. He offered to talk first. He asked her if she had ever been coached before. When Mary said that she hadn't, John said he had better explain one or two things. The first was that, although her firm was paying, the sessions would be entirely confidential between him and Mary. There were only two exceptions to this. The first was that John was supervised as a coach and might wish to tell his supervisor some of the issues that could come up in Mary's coaching. John explained that his supervisor could be trusted to keep those issues to herself and Mary would just be known as 'Mary' in supervision. He said that they had tried pseudonyms but they didn't work, as the real name always slipped out sooner or later. John also said, apologetically, that if at any time he thought that Mary might do harm to herself or others he might have to do something about it. Mary was rather impressed by this and thought that the coaching probably would be entirely confidential.

John said that he thought he should try to explain the difference between coaching and mentoring. He said that he saw them at different ends of a spectrum. Pure coaching was non-directive. The coach did not give advice. His sole duty was to understand the issues facing the coachee. If he could do this, the coachee would then understand the issues too, probably for the first time, and the way ahead would be clear. At the other end of the spectrum the mentor gave advice to the mentee, possibly quite firmly. John said that, if he was allowed a little pedantry, he hated the word mentee. Mentor was not a verb, he was the tutor of Telemachus. However, it would be a little strange to call the client Telemachus so 'mentee' it had to be.

In practice, said John, most coaching has an element of mentoring in it. Even at the non-directional end, the experience of the coach tells him or her which questions to ask and guides the discussion. In the case of coaching for retirement, or 'transition' as some coaches like to call it, mentoring was particularly important because the coachee was entering a new world with no experience to guide them. The critical points were not to be judgemental, to let the coachee take the decisions and not to be remotely put out if the coach's suggestions were disregarded.

By this time Mary was wondering where this was going. John helped her out. "Frankly," he said, "it is easier if we just do it. Shall we give it a go? This is what we call a chemistry session and at the end we should both know whether it's going to work." Mary nodded her assent and John asked her what she wanted to talk about. Mary said, with a hint of asperity, that it was pretty obvious they ought to talk about her retirement.

"OK," said John, "anything in particular?"

"Well," said Mary, "I don't know what I am going to do."

John asked her why she wanted to do anything and Mary said that she thought she would be pretty bored if she didn't. John said he had assumed that she was in good shape financially, and Mary nodded. John then asked her what she thought she was going to miss about work. Mary was silent for a moment. "I think it's really the intellectual challenge," she said. John wrote that down on his pad.

"What else?" he said.

Mary added companionship. John challenged her on that. Did she have any really good friends at the firm? Mary had to agree that she did not. There were many people there she liked, but she couldn't imagine spending much time with them socially, apart from a set-piece lunch or dinner. The thing about work, she thought, was that your relationships were based on getting things done and you were expected to maintain the civilities at all times, while the friendships you made at school, university or other shared experience were based on being in the same boat, rubbing along together and finding out whose company you preferred. She had never thought about that before. But she would still miss the day-to-day contact with her team and her clients. John wrote that down.

Under John's gentle prodding she admitted she would miss the extra money. Her investments were fine, but she would see a drop in income. John asked her if she would miss the status of being a partner in a large London firm. Mary denied that.

"I've never been one for status," she said.

John challenged her again and warned her that she might be surprised. He told her that Anthony Trollope said that dignity is accorded to those who bear a share of the world's burdens, and that she would find that to be true. There was also a question of her sense of self-worth, but John did not pursue that.

"What else?" he said.

Mary added routine and structure to the list.

"What else?" said John.

Mary couldn't think.

"If there was one other thing," John said, "what would it be?"

Mary thought long and hard. John said nothing.

Eventually Mary said, a little diffidently, "I think it's about power."

"Say more," said John.

"Well," said Mary, " I was thinking. When I was told I had to go, I realised there was nothing I could do about it. I am an employment lawyer, and I suppose I could have got something on its feet for age discrimination, but really I can't go on in the firm if they don't want me; it's just unrealistic. So any claim would just be about money, and they're being quite generous about that. And then, for the first time I thought, I'm getting old, and this is what happens to the old. They lose power."

John looked at her. "We need to talk more about that," he said, "but we don't have time now. There are only 10 minutes to go and I want to talk about some practical things and give you some advice.

"If you decide that you want to be coached by me, the firm has said they will pay for six sessions. I don't want to see you again for six weeks, and then the remaining five sessions should be after you have left the firm, because you will be still caught up in it all until you actually go. I think we can agree that the objective of the coaching should be to decide what you are going to do?"

Mary nodded.

"Good," said John, " if you decide you want to go ahead then let me know and I will write to you confirming that and setting out our commitment to confidentiality and some stuff about data protection. Now I am going to put Mentor's hat firmly on my head and give you some advice. You don't need to take it, but frankly, it's worth the price of admission."

3. Some practical advice

"First, retirement is a big step and it will take you at least a year to get used to it. I wish someone had told me that when I retired. It's as big a life event as divorce or bereavement. You need time to reset your mental map after such a change. If you feel miserable after six months, don't worry too much – you will get used to it and cheer up. This is not a matter of business, it's an emotional journey.

"Second, do a budget. Most people don't do that while they are working. Get out your credit card and bank statements for the last year and work out, category by category and month by month, where the money went. Then do a budget for next year against your retirement income and fill in the actual figures month by month. You can download useful templates from the web. Just Google 'household budgeting'. You will find it an interesting thing to do. The point of the exercise is not only financial. Most people worry when they realise that, for the first time, their income is more or less fixed. Budgeting will give you a sense of control.

"Last, and most difficult, you will have to work out what makes you happy. I doubt that anyone has asked you that before and it is not an easy question to answer, particularly as it takes a year to get used to retirement, so you won't know for a bit.

"I think we have discussed enough for you to think about. If we go ahead then next time I shall ask you to tell me the story of your life, so be prepared. And one more thing. Are you going to have a retirement party?"

Mary said that she hadn't thought about it.

"You should," said John. "We are going to be discussing your new life and before we do that you should celebrate the old one, and mark its closing."

4. Back into the past

Mary found that she had enjoyed the chemistry meeting with John. A purposeful talk all about Mary with someone who took notes was cheering in itself. Nevertheless, before telling John that she was going to go ahead, she called the other coach the firm had suggested, and arranged a chemistry meeting with him. But two days before the meeting, the coach called her and asked her if she was married to Richard Wingate. When she said she was the coach said that, although he had never met Mary, he knew Richard well and played golf with him regularly. He was sorry but he didn't really think it was appropriate for him to coach Mary. He didn't go into detail with his reasons, but when she thought about it Mary saw that his friendship with Richard would mean that one side of her life would effectively be off limits for discussion, and she respected his decision.

She told John she would go ahead and, as promised, he wrote her a formal letter confirming the arrangement. The firm paid the fee for the six sessions upfront – a surprisingly large amount. For the next six weeks Mary occupied herself with winding up her affairs at the firm, handing over her files and clients. Everyone was very nice to her. The clients were very understanding – perhaps a little too understanding, Mary thought. Everyone asked her what she was going to do with herself and Mary simply said that she was going to take time to think about that. At the end of the six weeks Mary found herself quite suddenly with nothing to do and another month to serve. She decided to take the rest of her holiday and come back for her leaving party. The firm had been very generous about that and was prepared to do the right thing.

Before she went on holiday, she had her next appointment with John. As he had said, he asked her to tell him the story of her life. For nearly an hour, prompted by his detailed questioning, she did so. A conventional middle-class upbringing. Only child. Father a solicitor in the Midlands. Showed promise at school. Scholarship to Lady Margaret Hall to read law. Articles in the family firm. Marriage to Richard. Move to London. Assistant solicitor at a West End firm. Started to specialise in the new field of employment law. Career briefly interrupted by children. Moved to her present firm 20 years ago, where she effectively founded the employment law practice and built it up. Some attempts to participate in the management of the firm, but it wasn't for her – she stuck to fee-earning. Interests outside the law apart from her family – painting, walking, opera and theatre.

After three-quarters of an hour Mary stopped. "Do you mind if I ask you a question?" she said.

"Of course not," John replied.

"Why are we doing this?" she asked.

"Why do you think?" said John.

Mary said she supposed that John was looking for interests that could be translated for something for her to do in retirement.

"Not really," said John, although he admitted that might be useful. What this was really about, he told her, was getting her to focus on herself and see her life in context. All her life, until now, she had been in an institution. First her family, then school, then university and then one law firm after another. All her life she had been expected to conform to the rules of an institution and in return it had looked after her, found her things to do, and educated or paid her, or both. Now she was on her own. She had to come to terms with herself as an individual.

"Do you remember," said John, "in our last session you said that you were losing power?"

Mary said she did. Indeed she had felt that even more keenly as she handed over her files.

"But don't you see," said John " that the power you are losing is power within an institution – power only in accordance with its rules. What do you think you are gaining?"

Mary thought for quite a long time. "Freedom?" she asked.

"I think so," said John. " You are the author of your life. You are holding the pen. You decide what to write. You are gaining power, not losing it."

"That's all very well," said Mary, "But I don't know what to do with myself."

"We'll talk about that next time," said John, "And in the meantime I am going to send you a poem, and when we next meet I shall want to know what you make of it."

Mary was a little alarmed at the idea of a poem. Nobody had sent her a poem for years and the last time anyone had wanted to know what she thought about a poem, she had been at school.

John was as good as his word. This is the poem he sent her.

The Song of Wandering Aengus
I went out to the hazel wood,
Because a fire was in my head,
And cut and peeled a hazel wand,
And hooked a berry to a thread;
And when white moths were on the wing,
And moth-like stars were flickering out,
I cast the berry in the stream,
And caught a little silver trout.

When as I laid it on the floor
I went to blow the fire aflame,
But something rustled on the floor,
And some one called me by my name:
It had become a glimmering girl
With apple blossom in her hair
Who called me by my name and ran
And faded in the brightening air.

Though I am old with wandering
Through hollow lands and hilly lands,
I will find out where she has gone,
And kiss her lips, and take her hands;
And walk among tall dappled grass,
And pluck,till time and times be done
The silver apples of the moon
The golden apples of the sun.

– W B Yeats

6. Finding the way

John and Mary met again a month later, two weeks after she had left the firm. As usual, John started by asking Mary what she wanted to talk about.

"Getting me something to do," she said, "but do you want to talk about the poem?"

"We can leave that until later," said John. "How are you getting on?"

Mary told John that her leaving party had been a success. The senior partner had done his stuff with a handsome tribute and she had felt a real sense of pleasure and accomplishment. There was no denying, however, that it had been a slightly out-of-body experience as she realised that this was really the end of her time with the firm.

"And since then?"

Mary said that her time had been fully occupied. Her daughter was expecting a baby and seemed to be lining Mary up for the duties of an unpaid nanny. "She even asked me to mow her lawn!"

"Let's get down to business," said John. "What do you want to get out of our session today?"

"Well," said Mary, "we have an hour together. We won't solve all my problems in that time, but we might get one or two leads."

"I love coaching lawyers," said John. "You can think straight. Was it Edmund Burke who said that the legal education sharpens the mind by narrowing it? – Sorry," he added, as he caught a look in Mary's eye which indicated that she had not come here to talk about Edmund Burke.

For the next half hour they ran through the possibilities. Top of the list was a judicial appointment with a tribunal, then the possibility of training as a mediator or applying for an academic or teaching appointment. They talked about jobs outside of the law. Would Mary consider a role as a non-executive director? Women on boards was the flavour of the year, after all. Mary was not keen on that. "I've never been good on committees," she said. "I never enjoyed it at the firm and my spell on the Law Society's Employment Law Committee was not a great success. I just wanted to do it all myself."

Mary's reluctance to join a committee ruled out work as a charitable trustee and most public appointments that would otherwise have been suitable. They talked about her hobbies. Could she take up painting seriously? Could she go back to university?

7. A question of mortality

At the end of the half hour, the energy in the room was low. "Let's stand up and change places," said John. When they had done so, and swapped their glasses of water, he said, "Now ask me something."

"OK," said Mary, "Does everybody think about time?"

"You had better say more about that," said John.

"Well," said Mary "I am 58. I have, say, 20 more years of active life, and at least 10 in which I could work if I wanted to, at least part time. But I have never thought like this before – looking forward I mean. One of my partners used to have a sign on his wall that said, 'How come I'm over the hill when I never got to the top?' I used to think it was just a joke but now I'm not so sure."

"Yes," said John. "I think that after a certain point in their life most people change their attitude to time; that is to say that they become conscious of it. I think the remark about the hill is a good one. We spend most of our working lives trudging up the hill, seeing only the ground in front of us and then, one day, we reach the top and see the view, which is the rest of our lives, stretching out before us. That day is not normally the day we reach the pinnacle of our careers; it may be sooner or later and that, I suppose, is the point of the joke and why 'over the hill' has real meaning as an expression.

"Anyway, once you have seen the view, it stays with you. It does make you a bit more serious. After all, it's about mortality. Emily Dickinson says, about depression,

'When it comes, the landscape listens –
Shadows – hold their breath –
When it goes, 'tis like the Distance
On the look of death –"

"Not another poem," said Mary.

"Difficult to get away from them. Poets think about this sort of thing. Anyway, there is one consolation. I don't think anyone can be said to be wise who has not seen the view from the top of the hill. And why did you ask about time?"

"Because it's part of my thinking about what I am to do in retirement. I seem to be in a hurry. The unforgiving minute and all that."

"Now it's your turn to quote poetry. Some people call what you are experiencing 'the pull of the future' – the idea that something which is expected or dreaded in the future has an effect on us now. In this case, of course, it is old age and death. I think that is a very interesting idea. As usual, it helps if you are aware of what's going on. So tell me, what did you think about the Yeats?"

Mary said that she wasn't sure. It was obviously about a quest. But who, or what, was the glimmering girl? John said that he didn't know either, but he thought the man with a fire in his head might be seeking his own identity, his true self, and that if he found it he would be content.

"Does he find her?" said Mary.

"It's ambiguous, isn't it, but I think it's optimistic. Anyway, it's good stuff. Plenty of spin on the ball, as P G Wodehouse might say.

"I suppose I think that there are many things that make for a good life. Family, friends, nature, art; but most of us, while we have the energy, are happiest if we are pursuing something that really absorbs us. We can find that in family, friends, nature or art, or we can find it in work or sport or something else; but whatever it is, it is a vital part of us – the glimmering girl, if you like.

"Let's change places again."

When they had done so, John summed up. "You said that you might consider a judicial appointment, becoming a mediator, seeking an academic appointment, taking a further degree or taking painting seriously. Which of those is the most interesting? Not the most worthy or the most lucrative, but the most interesting."

"The judicial appointment."

"OK, for next time I want you to look seriously into that and come prepared to tell me whether it's a possibility. Anything else?"

"Well I came here looking for a job and I seem to have ended up discussing the Meaning of Life."

"That's coaching for you," said John cheerily. "See you next time."

8. The breakthrough

Over the next month Mary tried to get used to not going to the office. She visited the dentist, cooked a little more elaborately than usual and cleaned out her wardrobe. She saw a lot of her pregnant daughter and tried to parry the subtle and not so subtle hints that now she had time on her hands, baby care would be just the thing. She checked into the possibility of a judicial appointment, but the more she thought about it, the less appealing it seemed – all that note-taking, and she was used to taking sides. When she thought about the other possibilities she had discussed with John, she just felt depressed. The coaching was enjoyable, but it didn't seem to be going anywhere.

Mary had always slept well, but now she found herself waking at four in the morning and unable to go back to sleep. Not that she thought constructively; she just lay there next to her sleeping husband, unable to imagine how to fill her days. It was ironic, she thought, that all her working life she had solved her clients' problems with calm, logical thought, but now she was casting about in search of her own future. It began to seem pointless.

When she came to the next appointment with John, her depression and impatience were evident. She told him that although a judicial appointment seemed a possibility, she really didn't want it, so they were back to square one.

John and Mary spent the next 20 minutes going over all the other alternatives. Mary tried her best to be positive, but there was no disguising the fact that her heart wasn't in it.

At length, the conversation faltered into silence. John looked at Mary, lost in thought.

"Looking back over the past year," he said, "can you remember a day when you lay in bed in the early morning thinking, 'This is going to be a good day'?"

Mary said that the first day like that which came to mind was a day when she knew she was going to settle a major case and get everything she and the client wanted.

John took out his pad and drew a large cross on it, with the number 0 at the centre and the number 10 at the end of each axis. Against the axes he wrote, in turn, 'meaning', 'enjoyment', 'learning' and 'performance'.

"Now," he said, "I want you to score your job as an employment lawyer out of ten on each of these axes."

"What does 'meaning' mean?" asked Mary.

"You decide," said John.

Mary scored each axis as nine, except for learning, which she scored as seven. John looked at the pad.

"This is the score of a lawyer at the height of her powers," he said, almost to himself. "The fact that you scored seven for learning at your stage in your career is particularly significant. When learning falls, performance will fall sooner or later."

There was a long silence, finally broken as John heard himself saying, "You should start your own firm."

"I can't do that," cried Mary.

"Why not, is there some legal reason?"

"Well, no. I joined the firm 20 years ago to start their employment practice and brought my clients with me. I refused to sign any covenants or restrictions in case it didn't work out. But that's not the point. I am retired!"

"There are no rules," said John.

And slowly all the lights went on.

They both sat for a moment in silence. "You mean I really could?" said Mary.

"Well you tell me, but it's pretty obvious that is what floats your boat."

Mary sat thinking. Then she stood up, very excited. "You mustn't tell the firm."

"Of course I won't. This is completely confidential. I even wrote to you about that."

"Oh I am sorry, I forgot." Mary was flushed with excitement. "I can't do any more today. I need to think about this." And she leant over the table and kissed John on the cheek. "Thank you," she said, and rushed out, forgetting her coat.

9. What happened in the coaching?

And there we will leave Mary and John. After a pause, they completed the course of six coaching sessions. By then, Mary had joined a firm in which the partners shared central overheads, but kept their own practices and fees. She was essentially a sole practitioner and could control her time in a way she had never been able to before. She used the remaining sessions with John to discuss the establishment and promotion of her practice, which did well. Husband Richard's reaction to his wife's new lease of life shortly before his own retirement is not recorded here, but it can be said that Mary's daughter did not take at all kindly to the loss of babysitting services.

So what was going on in the coaching from John's point of view? At the beginning of the chemistry session, he knew nothing of Mary and if the firm had offered to tell him about her, he might well have refused, preferring to form his own opinion. He used the chemistry session to get to know her a little, by finding out what she would miss in retiring from her practice, and formed the hypothesis that she was intellectual, quite driven, obviously good at her work and not given to easy friendship. He also thought that, although she denied it, she would miss the status that went with her job.

The advice he gave her was good advice, particularly the suggestion that it would take her a year to get used to leaving practice. We live our lives by maps rather than by the actual terrain. When we go into our bathroom at night, we reach automatically for the light switch. We do not expect anyone to have moved it. Similarly, when we reach the kerb in England, we look right for the oncoming traffic. I know of an American who, staying at the Savoy Hotel, went jogging down the Embankment early one morning and looked left to a clear road. He was killed as he stepped in the path of an oncoming car. His map did not correspond to the terrain. So it is when our daily lives change in a major way. It takes time for the maps to be redrawn. If we try to keep the old maps, reality will eventually come bursting through in a very painful way – this is sometimes called a nervous breakdown.[1]

John followed best practice by writing to confirm the overall objective of the coaching – the 'meta-agenda', as it is sometimes called. He also used the letter to cover himself in data protection terms if he wanted to keep notes about Mary on a computer and to remind her to give him plenty of notice if she wanted to cancel a session. John qualified his obligation of confidentiality to allow him to discuss Mary in supervision when John himself was coached about his practice. Supervisors often bring insights to bear, particularly when it is the coach's own prejudices which are affecting the coaching.

The first session about Mary's life served the purpose that John had explained. When coaching retirees, it is important to understand the progress from institutionalisation to what Jung called 'individuation', as the coachee is unlikely to understand it quickly without a little help. The session also enabled John to know

---

1 For more on maps, see R Skynner and J Cleese, *Life and How to Survive it* (Cedar Books, 1996).

Mary better. Mary never really spotted that she knew nothing at all about John, except what was on his website. In the jargon of the trade, John 'contained his story'.

The second session, although apparently inconclusive, tells us quite a lot about coaching. John believes in inner game theory as explained by W Timothy Gallwey in *The Inner Game of Tennis*[2] and applied to coaching by Myles Downey's *Effective Coaching*.[3] Inner game theory holds that our potential is limited by the interference that we ourselves inject into the game. After years in her firm, Mary's horizons were limited by her own mind (interference) and John was trying to make her see that the possibilities were pretty limitless. John used the GROW technique. First, he established the Goal for the session, and congratulated Mary on seeing immediately what could be accomplished in an hour. It sometimes takes most of a session to establish a sensible goal! They then discussed the Reality of her situation and her Options. These proved to be not very stimulating for Mary and, on instinct, John changed roles and got Mary to ask him a question, which leads to the discussion on mortality and the pull of the future. This is the sort of discussion it is difficult to have with anyone but a coach and it enhanced Mary's self-awareness, which is one of the principal objectives of coaching. Finally, John switched back and they agreed the Way forward, which was for Mary to research the possibility of a judicial appointment.

The third session gives us the breakthrough. Inner game theory says that when all interference is removed, we enter a state that Gallwey calls Self 2 (Self 1 being our normal day-to-day self, as it were). Here it was John rather than Mary who entered Self 2, as he removed the dark glass through which we viewed Mary as a former lawyer and revealed her as she was, a woman in the prime of life, at the height of her career, who had been ejected from her firm for reasons only of chronology. The rest is easy.

Readers may say that I have cheated by picking a lawyer who returned to practice rather than retiring to pursue a different career, or none. But although the eventual outcome may be obvious now, and indeed may have been obvious to the reader, it was not obvious to Mary and John, blinkered as they were by the verdict of 'retirement'. Mary's new practice as an individual was very different from her former big firm existence and could be considered as a new start, requiring her to reinvent herself. Over the years, she would be able to decide how much or how little to take on.

It is important to make the point that there are no rules and that is one of the reasons I chose an outcome that was unexpected, at least to the players. I should say, however, that as in acting, there are no rules, but it is important to know them. The questions of individuation, limitless possibility and the chance to pursue the 'glimmering girl' apply whether the retiring lawyer goes on to consultancy, sports administration, teaching, non-executive directorships, a further degree, garden design, writing books, painting, music-making or, like me, to become a professional photographer. In Mary's case the glimmering girl was the practice of law, and why

---

2 Pan, 1986.
3 Texere Publishing, 2003.

should she not pursue her? She might have to go through the retirement process again in a few years' time, but that applies to anyone who stays active after leaving the law, and it will be easier the second time. Given the age profile of our profession, English lawyers who do nothing at all after leaving practice are few and far between. But they exist, and there are no rules, so good luck to them.

Retirement is an important and difficult process. Most of us work it out for ourselves in the end, but a coach can be a present help in time of trouble. It is good to have a hand to hold as you step into the light.

Where next in coaching and mentoring?

David Clutterbuck
European Mentoring and Coaching Council
Lis Merrick
Coach Mentoring Limited

Although mentoring has been practised informally for thousands of years and coaching for perhaps 150 years, formalised (ie, structured or supported) coaching and mentoring have relatively short histories. In the context of employment and community applications, both date from the early 1980s. It comes as no surprise, then, that they exhibit the growing pains and uncertainties of an adolescent discipline. In this chapter, we briefly review the recent history of both, before exploring current and emerging trends and attempting to predict how these may evolve in the next decade.

1. A historical perspective

Supported mentoring, sometimes referred to as mentoring programmes or formal/structured mentoring, first emerged in the United States in the early 1980s. It quickly spread to Europe, where it adapted into a different model. From these two bases, supported mentoring spread across the rest of the world. Examples of both models and hybrids of them now appear in at least 80 countries. More formal structured mentoring is actually an organisational attempt to imitate some of the great informal mentoring relationships that exist, by providing opportunities to individuals who may be unable to broker such relationships themselves.

At first, the existence of two models was seen as more of a problem than a benefit. The US-generated model (which emphasised sponsorship, use of the mentor's power and influence and a generally hands-on, relatively directive, one-way learning approach) and the European-generated developmental model (which emphasised helping mentees with the quality of their thinking and doing things for themselves) seemed incompatible, especially within multi-country programmes, when participants had different expectations of the relationship. In many talent programmes in the European corporate world, there is now a hybrid model of structured mentoring that has developed, with some of the more subtle aspects of sponsorship incorporated into development mentoring. One example of this is the mentoring programme that Irwin Mitchell LLP has just introduced in the United Kingdom, where the mentor is discouraged from being a true sponsor, but has role modelling, supporting the mentee around understanding and managing internal politics and how to raise his exposure and visibility are encouraged as relevant mentor behaviours.

There was also (and to some extent remains) some confusion with coaching, where the emergence of new, non-directive, client-centred approaches produced an overlap with developmental mentoring. The concept of coaching began to appear in literature in the 19th century, but it was really the publication of Tim Gallwey's book *The Inner Game of Tennis* in 1974[1] that heralded the advent of business coaching. This concept of an inner game brings an insight into the psychology of human performance, which was echoed in 1988 in Sir John Whitmore's book *Coaching for Performance*,[2] where the lynchpin of coaching is attributed to goal focus and performance – interestingly, not the principles that Gallwey was using in his philosophy of 'relaxed concentration' and helping individuals to discover their true potential.

Attempts to establish clear water between developmental coaching and developmental mentoring are by and large notable for their lack of success – partly because people have come to the world of coaching and mentoring from many different disciplines and perspectives, and partly because practitioners anxious to protect commercial interests have sometimes ascribed positive qualities (most notably the avoidance of jumping into advice giving) to their own approaches and negative qualities to approaches they see as competing for the same space. A more objective perspective sees these two powerful disciplines as having more in common than they have apart, and as highly compatible ways of supporting a client's personal development. Table 1 offers one analysis of the similarities and differences.

It appears unlikely that there will ever be consensus as to the meaning of coaching and mentoring globally. However, it is critical that, within the context of structured coaching and mentoring that organisations/individuals are working within, some common understanding is achieved, even if it is on a very localised basis and purely around purpose, scope and application.

Both coaching and mentoring have undergone rapid expansion in the workplace in the last 30 years, which can be understood in four dimensions.

1.1 Geographical

Executive coaches and life coaches can be found in almost every country of the world, with some national professional associations having thousands of members. Although this has predominantly been a north and west expansion, the south and east are rapidly catching up. However, there can still be challenges finding a coach in some parts of the world that organisations are comfortable working with – for example, in China and the Pacific – and some western coaches will work virtually with clients in less developed parts of the globe. Mentoring programmes are common in most developed nations and have spread to developing countries largely through the activities of multinational corporations. The sophistication and volume of organised mentoring globally still lag behind the main hubs of activity in the United States, Europe and Australasia.

---

1 W Timothy Gallwey, *The Inner Game of Tennis* (Random House, 1974).
2 Sir John Whitmore, *Coaching for Performance* (Nicholas Brealey Publishing, 1988).

Table 1: Developmental mentoring and developmental coaching compared[3]

Similarities	Differences
• Focus on the quality of the learner's thinking. • Coach/mentor uses experience to craft powerful questions. • Advice giving is permissible, but not as a first resort and only in specific circumstances. (A common complaint about ineffective coaches is their over-rigid adherence to never giving advice). • Much of the learning occurs in the reflections of the coachee/mentee between or long after sessions. • Coach and mentor both have a duty of care towards the coachee/mentee.	• Mentors more likely to make introductions, help develop networks. • Mentors more likely to help explain politics of a particular organisation or profession. • Mentors tend to be role models in many relationships. • There is a high degree of acceptance and confirmation generated by a more senior mentor, which does not occur in coaching. • Coaches (in the workplace context of line manager to direct report) more likely to give feedback. • Coaching tends to be a short or medium-term assignment or activity focused on performance in a defined field or role. • Mentoring tends to be a medium to long-term relationship focused on career or on more holistic, less well-defined issues. • Mentoring is often a professional friendship which can continue for many years. • There is more emphasis on training and supervision in coaching than mentoring. • Coaching is more often a paid arrangement – or not, depending on context.

1.2 Range of applications

The main expansion of coaching has been from sport into business and life coaching. Emerging applications include maternity coaching (derived largely from maternity mentoring and one of the cases where the coaching role demands more subject expertise than the mentoring role) and team coaching, of which more later. In our experience, executive coaching has become widespread in the legal profession, with many senior partners viewing this as coming with the territory, although below partner level it is commonly used for more short-term performance development activities. Increasingly, law firms are looking to educate lawyers with coaching skills themselves, particularly to support their team development and year-end processes. This is not always straightforward, as, with the complicated reporting structures and hierarchies in some firms, partners can be left with onerous workloads with regard to

3 Reprinted with some additions, by permission of the author from David Clutterbuck, *Everyone needs a mentor*, 5th edn (CIPD, Wimbledon, 2014).

interim and year-end appraisal processes. Mentoring has seen a much wider expansion of applications, including supporting HIV-positive refugees into work, diversity management, small business development, rehabilitation of ex-prisoners and any kind of career transition. Within the legal profession, mentoring is used primarily as a means of developing talent and supporting through and after the partner process, for both new partners and those who have been unsuccessful. In some firms where there is gender imbalance at partner level, mentoring has been used to positively discriminate on behalf of women, with a sponsor senior partner being designated to support the female lawyer through the promotion process. To give an example of how internal mentoring can be used in different ways within one organisation, Nabarro LLP uses mentoring to support participants on its talent development programme for the firm's potential future partners, as well as in business development groups. The latter are run by partners to support associates in developing relationships with clients new and old, as well as marketing activities such as thought leadership and sector focus.

1.3 Range of models and methodologies

Coaching has borrowed (and continues to do so) from psychology, counselling, psychotherapy and pseudo-disciplines such as neuro-linguistic programming. Mentoring has taken more theory and concepts from career counselling and management science. However, there is a tremendous overlap depending on the experience and background of the coach or mentor and, within organisational mentoring, the amount of upskilling and development that the organisation is providing to its mentors. Current new ideas and disciplines filtering through into coaching and mentoring include positive psychology, neuroscience and various mindfulness practices. The competence and confidence of the coach or mentor tend to reflect in the number of different disciplines they may borrow from in their regular practice.

1.4 Evidence base

An analysis of academic and other research in coaching and mentoring shows distinctly different emphases. Coaching is very much developing evidence-based theories and as it grows as a profession will develop more of a research base. In the same way that psychology originally borrowed from philosophy, coaching has borrowed from psychology until it establishes itself over time. Mentoring has lagged behind a little in this evidenced-based development and has leant heavily on management theories and, increasingly, some of the coaching literature in order to move forward with credibility. This is due more to less interest in mentoring, as the increasing commercialism of paid coaching has overtaken it in the last decade.

2. Emerging themes for coaching and mentoring

In this section, we attempt to review a variety of emerging themes, concentrating on those for which there is already an observable trend, which we can project into the future.

2.1 Professionalisation

A plethora of bodies have sprung up around the world to help establish coaching as a profession. The largest of these are the International Coach Federation (IFC) and the European Mentoring and Coaching Council (EMCC), but there are also other bodies with international reach, such as the Association for Coaching (AfC) and World Association of Business Coaches, as well as national bodies such as South Africa's COMENSA. The ICF and EMCC have led the drive to accredit training and to establish competencies and standards, both for coaches and more recently for coach supervisors. Standards for team coaches are already under discussion. The inclusion of the AfC in the Global Coaching and Mentoring Alliance is a significant step in consolidating standards across the whole coaching profession, at least in the context of executive coaching.

Mentoring is far less organised at an international level, perhaps because there has been less commercial incentive for professionalisation (most mentors being volunteers and unpaid). The EMCC derives originally from the European Mentoring Centre. It is now active in 22 countries within and around Europe, including Morocco, and has affiliates in other, more distant countries. The International Mentoring Association (IMA), until recently largely unknown outside of North America, is also making its presence felt more widely, with professionalisation of mentoring schemes a strategic priority. The IMA has recently produced mentoring programme standards for educational and community programmes, with an emphasis on sponsorship mentoring approaches. These complement the International Standards for Mentoring Programmes in Employment (ISMPE), which are developmental mentoring based.

The concept of the professional mentor is recent, but already taking hold in some countries. The rationale is straightforward – senior executives coming up to retirement want to continue to be useful and to work. They don't want to become coaches or consultants. They do want to be able to draw on their experience, but not in a directive way. Professional mentoring academies are now appearing in the United Kingdom, Brazil, Poland, Denmark and elsewhere.

There is also a small but growing movement to professionalise the role of mentoring programme manager, with the IMA and EMCC both exploring the practicalities. To design, launch and sustain a successful mentoring programme takes considerable skills of mentoring subject knowledge, project management, facilitation, creativity, internal organisational knowledge and people skills. Although some organisations are keen to upskill their own HR teams to incorporate this role, there is also an increase in outsourcing to virtual programme managers or creating self-service mentoring hubs for all to access.

2.2 Questioning of assumptions

It's not surprising, in a developing profession, that a lot of received wisdom is not supported by empirical evidence. A major step forward has been the growth in collaborative studies between academics and practitioners, which has led some of the most common assumptions to be tested, both in terms of observation and through gathering data on what experienced coaches and mentors actually do and on outcomes from different kinds and styles of intervention. There is a great deal more work to do here, but some of the evidence we already have includes the following:

- The assumption that coaches don't need relevant knowledge of the client's world is both inaccurate and, potentially unethical and unsafe. Appropriate knowledge is frequently required to structure powerful questions and avoid steering the client into danger.
- Much the same appears to be the case with giving advice. While effective coaches and mentors refrain from jumping into advising, they retain the option to do so when it is in the client's interests and the client has exhausted his own thinking resources. The more experienced coaches and mentors become, the more comfortable they become with crossing this boundary – and the more sensitive to whether and how to do so.
- SMART goals are core to coaching and mentoring. Evidence from a number of studies shows that this is a simplistic assumption, more about the coach or mentor's need to control than the needs of the client. In fact, goals in coaching and mentoring relationships are more often emergent and evolving – or even the end product of the coaching/mentoring process.

2.3 Mindfulness

Increasing attention is being paid in coaching and mentoring research to a range of related phenomena including mindfulness, presence and intuition. To some extent, this is a reflection of the influence of schools of psychology such as Gestalt, and Eastern practices such as meditation; but ontology has also greatly influenced approaches in South America and Australia – to the extent that there is a growing literature on ontological coaching. Ontological coaching is about generating shifts in a coachee's 'way of being'. A human's way of being is not a fixed state, but one of continual change, and the role of the ontological coach is to work with clients to design a way of being that the coachee assesses serves him.

Mindfulness coach training is now very popular and many coaches are using mindfulness techniques themselves as well as sharing them in a transparent way with their clients. It is also playing a part in our understanding of attentiveness – how we listen, how we raise awareness of our internal and external environments, how we practise acceptance and non-judgement and so on.

2.4 Neuroscience and coaching

There has been a real revolution in understanding how the brain works in the past 10 years and how this affects behaviour. Some coaches are now using neurobehavioural modelling as a way of putting neuroscience into use in their coaching. It may be that psychology as a discipline begins to disappear as neurobiology takes over as providing the rationale for human behaviour. Executive coaching is a form of attachment and coaches are beginning to appreciate that brain-based coaching, utilising intelligent emotions and simulation are where coaching is moving towards.

(a) ***Coach maturity***

The concept of coach maturity is again a recent development. It takes into account two primary developmental directions: from inexperience to mastery and from early stages of socio-emotional and cognitive development to later stages.

Table 2: Stages of coach maturity

Coaching approach	Style	Critical questions
Models based	Control	How do I take the client where I think he needs to go? How do I adapt my technique or model to this circumstance?
Process based	Contain	How do I give enough control to the client and still retain a purposeful conversation? What's the best way to apply my process in this instance?
Philosophy based	Facilitate	What can I do to help the client do this for himself? How do I contextualise the client's issue within the perspective of my philosophy or discipline?
Systemic eclectic	Enable	Are we both relaxed enough to allow the issue and the solution to emerge in whatever way they will? Do I need to apply any techniques or processes? If I do, what does the client context tell me about how to select from the wide choice available to me?

3. How we can expect it to evolve?

3.1 Team coaching

The level of similarity between coaching in the worlds of sport and work is surprisingly low – which perhaps explains why it has taken a relatively long time for employers to engage with this powerful tool for improving collective performance. Team coaching differs from facilitation and team building. One sign that team coaching is joining the mainstream is the arrival of professional development programmes to help experienced one-to-one coaches step up into this considerably more complex and arguably more demanding arena. Team coaches need to have a good understanding not just of coaching basics, but of team dynamics and team psychology, collective decision making, systems theory and a variety of other topics not needed in one-to-one coaching. Another sign is discussion within the European Mentoring and Coaching Council and elsewhere of the requirements to be an effective supervisor for team coaches. A set of competences can be expected for this role before too long.

It is also predictable that companies, which have so far mainly just talked about adding team coaching skills to the portfolio of their professional and lay internal coaches, will take the plunge and invest in relevant training and support. When this happens, team coaching will become much more widely used across those organisations.

3.2 International mentoring

Multinational companies are faced with the dilemma of needing to have consistency of mentoring – especially for programmes that pair people across national or divisional boundaries – yet being able to respond to local needs. Many multinational mentoring programmes have failed because of perceived cultural imperialism on the part of the international headquarters.

Good practice appears to involve:

- designing the programme(s) or the corporate approach to mentoring with input from a wide range of sources, and particularly from local HR and line managers;
- recognising that in countries that speak the same language, the context of mentoring may be very different (trying to impose a US approach on the United Kingdom, or vice versa, is likely to meet resistance);
- openly acknowledging the impact of culture on the style of mentoring and including relevant cultural awareness elements in any training and supporting information resources;
- designing training content and support materials with a core of common elements (definitions, skills, emphasis on learning dialogue) and a more flexible approach to case studies, role plays/real plays, links with local mythology and social mores;
- educating local HR professionals so that they can become champions for mentoring and identify opportunities to support regional/international programmes and to launch local programmes aimed at specific, local issues;
- clarifying other important contextual factors – for example, the qualities associated with effective leadership are not universal and there are significant differences between cultures, which may need to be taken into account; and
- wherever possible, rooting the mentoring story in the mythology or religious beliefs of the country. Islam, Buddhism, Christianity and other religions all exemplify learning dialogue, as do many of the stories told to children in East Africa, and in Asia-Pacific cultures.

3.3 Second-wave mentoring

This is the name given to the reinvention and reinvigoration of both corporate and community mentoring programmes in the light of experience.

One driver of this movement has been the desire by organisations which have been relatively early adopters of supported mentoring to learn from their own and other people's experiences. At a recent conference in London, more than two-thirds of HR professionals responsible for mentoring programmes indicated that they were to a greater or lesser extent dissatisfied with either the management of their mentoring programme or the outcomes from it.

What has gained the description 'second-wave mentoring' has a number of other drivers. Among these are:

- the desire to make mentoring available to much wider audiences. This in turn puts pressure on programme managers to find lower-cost solutions, without sacrificing quality. However, many attempts to do mentoring on the cheap – especially by using off-the-peg online solutions – have failed to deliver the quality required. In particular, they have tended to push mentoring towards shallow, transactional skills and knowledge transfer, rather than longer-term deep personal change;
- the need to link mentoring more closely with talent management and succession planning;
- more critical questioning by enterprise leaders as to the outcomes of mentoring for participants and for the organisation, leading to a need for more effective measurement processes;
- increased frustration in developmental mentoring programmes, when mentors relapse into sponsoring behaviours;
- rejection of formal programmes (as currently practised) by some minority groups;
- disparity between programmes in terms of failure rates, leading to re-examination of matching and re-matching processes; and
- the impact of the International Standards for Mentoring Programmes in Employment, which have begun to set expectations of what a good practice mentoring programme looks like.

3.4 Coaching as a leadership style

Many organisations are now incorporating into their leadership development a coaching style approach to tackle issues, problems and individual and team development.

3.5 Less emphasis on using goals in coaching and mentoring

The use of goals in coaching and mentoring is increasingly being questioned, but there is growing evidence that SMART goals are not always appropriate in the rapidly changing world we live in. The implications of this are significant for coaches and mentors, as well as those who organise programmes within organisations.

3.6 Increase in supervision for coaches and mentors

The degree to which different countries and schools of coaching accept the need for supervision varies, with Europe being very pro and the United States more reluctant. This may relate to the higher proportion of life coaches in the United States and a lesser emphasis on professionalism.

3.7 Group mentoring

Where there are not enough mentors to go round, some programmes resort to group mentoring or a combination of group and individual mentoring. There is very divided opinion on whether group mentoring is the same as action learning. There is almost no literature on the topic of group mentoring – so far!

3.8 A systemic approach to using coaching and mentoring

For organisational coaching and mentoring to be truly effective, it must follow a systemic approach to enable a holistic approach to support individual, team and organisational learning. Systemic coaching and mentoring should be seamlessly woven through the core values, leadership behaviours, talent approach, theories-in-use and reward systems of the organisation.

Many programmes are introduced as quick-fix interventions, which offer only short-term relief. Organisations themselves are complex interrelated systems, so a short-term linear approach to introducing coaching and mentoring is too naïve and simplistic for it to be effective. Without a systemic approach, the underlying forces within the organisation will create an unconscious negative counterbalance to the more positive outcomes emulating from the coaching and mentoring interventions. Irwin Mitchell LLP is one law firm in the United Kingdom which is taking a systemic approach to its organisational mentoring.

3.9 The utilisation of internal coaches

The Ridler Report (2013) says that 79% of organisations are planning an increase in the amount of internal coaching they want to use. Internal coaches are a cost-effective and practical way of providing more coaching within organisations and companies are appearing to use more internal and less external coaches following the recession.

4. A look to the future

Some of the themes we have extrapolated from a wide variety of organisations, both within and outside the legal profession, are:

- greater integration between different mentoring programmes in the same organisation;
- clarification of the different interpretations of mentoring within the same organisation;
- greater consideration of the differences in expectations of mentoring from diverse cultures; and
- greater use of social media to change how mentoring is delivered.

A key issue now emerging for many companies is the extent to which employees (and particularly talented employees) can be supported in developing dynamic networks of mentors. In these networks, there may be one or two close mentoring relationships focused on medium to long-term career development, several medium-term relationships focused on development of specific (leadership) competencies, and *ad hoc* short-term relationships focused on transfer of skills or knowledge.

Intrinsic in these mentor networks is that the traditional senior to junior hierarchy of relationships is often irrelevant – it is the learning exchange that is important and peer and reverse mentoring will play an increased role.

5. A research agenda

Research in mentoring has emphasised quantitative studies of behaviour. Many (mostly US) studies examine efficacy of mentoring from different perspectives, relying on the concept of 'mentoring functions' (a mish-mash of roles, behaviours and relationship factors) and assuming that the more functions exhibited, the more effective the mentoring. Unfortunately, this assumption itself has not been proven. Many studies also make the errors of conflating different contexts (eg, line manager/direct report relationships and relationships between people not connected hierarchically) or failing to ensure that participants' understanding of a mentoring relationship is consistent across the sample. By far the majority of research has been from the perspective of sponsorship mentoring, with relatively little from a developmental mentoring perspective, although the two approaches have been proven to be different social constructs.

Potential themes for mentoring research in the legal sector might include:

- where coaching and mentoring are complementary and how;
- the impact of mentoring on career planning, especially at key transition points, such as graduate entry and becoming a partner;
- the impact of mentoring on team dynamics;
- the role of mentoring in succession planning;
- how to persuade busy partners and senior partners to invest time in mentoring;
- the role of managing partners in creating the climate for sustainable mentoring;
- the impact of mentoring on retention;
- the impact of mentoring on knowledge transfer; and
- the impact of mentoring on diversity at senior levels.

The fact that it is easy to create a list of research topics tells us how little sector-specific evidence we have. There is no doubt that mentoring can be a highly effective and cost-effective intervention. However, in order to make it even more effective, we need good-quality research studies and case studies. Now that the sector has its own Mentoring Institute, we will hopefully see a significant increase in the evidence base.

About the authors

Marc Bartel
France managing partner, Heidrick & Struggles
mbartel@heidrick.com

Marc Bartel is France managing partner at Heidrick & Struggles and heads the functional practices in Europe and the Middle East. In addition, he leads the global legal, risk and compliance practice in Europe.

Mr Bartel focuses on the legal sector in both industry and private practice. He specialises in classic legal in-house positions and partner searches. Before joining Heidrick & Struggles, he held various senior management positions (including chief operating officer, Asia regional managing partner and deputy chief executive officer) within leading international law firms such as Lovells, Linklaters and Jeantet.

Mr Bartel obtained a business law degree and a master's in comparative law from Lyon University and a master's in comparative jurisprudence from New York University, and is a member of the New York Bar. He also obtained an MBA from the MIT Sloan School of Management.

Mr Bartel is fluent in French and English and has a working knowledge of German.

Philip Beddows
Founding partner, The Silk Road Partnership
philip@silkroadpartnership.com

Philip Beddows is a founding partner of The Silk Road Partnership, operating in Europe, the Gulf, India, Southeast Asia and Greater China. He has been working in the coaching and mentoring arena for 23 years, is a leading exponent in his field and was trained by one of the preeminent Inner Game coaches. He has particular expertise working in the international financial and professional services fields, especially the law.

Mr Beddows has helped to create and build and been co-owner of a number of coaching, board mentoring and training businesses. He has richly varied life experience, including leadership roles in military, political, educational and charitable spheres.

He is a founding fellow of the Institute of Coaching Professional Association (a Harvard Medical School affiliate), a non-executive director of the Institute of Mentoring, and a member of the European Mentoring and Coaching Council and the International Association of Coaching, serving on its Professional Development and Research Committee.

Christopher Bockmann
Executive coaching and organisational consulting
cbockmann@icloud.com

Christopher Bockmann has an international career in organisational and personal development. He advises professional service firms on leadership development and coaches partners and executives along the whole leadership life cycle. Mr Bockmann also supports his clients during periods of strategic or organisational change through group coaching.

He started his career working for the European Commission in Central Europe. In 2000 he joined Clifford Chance to participate in building its corporate university. His last role before creating his own practice was European director of learning and knowledge at Linklaters.

Mr Bockmann is currently running a leadership programme for lawyers at Sciences-Po Business School, Paris. He runs a regular study on partners' careers within professional service firms.

He is a French and Norwegian national and graduated from INSEAD Business School in organisational psychology and Cambridge University in political sciences.

Rachel Brushfield
Director, EnergiseLegal
rachel@energiselegal.com

Rachel Brushfield is a career, talent, learning and development strategist and coach and the founder of EnergiseLegal, Energise LLClub and Energise – The Talent Liberation Company. She has more than 27 years' experience in helping the legal profession embrace change. Ms Brushfield is a published author on talent management, professional development and gender balance, and has written more than 18 articles for legal magazines including *Managing Partner* on topics such as emotional intelligence, talent drain and female career success.

Helping women to 'blow their own trumpet' for career success is a specialism and she has written more than 10 articles for The Association of Women Solicitors. Her events include 'Portfolio careers' for The Law Society and 'Personal branding' and 'Liberating your talent' for the Association of Women Solicitors. Ms Brushfield writes practice notes and templates for LexisNexis, career guides for *The Telegraph* and content for cost-effective professional development for law firms. She was a panellist on Generation Y at the 2014 International Bar Association Women Lawyers' Conference in Paris.

David Clutterbuck
Special ambassador, European Mentoring and Coaching Council
david@davidclutterbuckpartnership.com

David Clutterbuck is one of the pioneers of coaching and mentoring. He brought the concept of structured mentoring to Europe more than 30 years ago. Visiting professor at Sheffield Hallam, Oxford Brookes and York St John Universities, he is regularly listed among the United Kingdom's most influential HR professionals. Author or co-author of around 60 books, he is a co-founder of the European Mentoring and Coaching Council and practice lead for Coaching and Mentoring International, a global network of specialist trainers and consultants.

Professor Clutterbuck's current research interests include team coaching, international mentoring programmes, ethical mentoring and systemic talent management.

Heidi K Gardner
Distinguished fellow, Harvard Law School Programme on the Legal Profession
hgardner@law.harvard.edu

Heidi K Gardner (PhD) is a distinguished fellow at Harvard Law School's Programme on the Legal Profession and a Harvard Law lecturer. Her research focuses on leadership, collaboration and management in knowledge-based organisations, particularly professional service firms. She is currently writing a book on the topic. Previously, she served on the Organisational Behavior Faculty of Harvard Business School, and her research was awarded the Academy of Management's Prize for Outstanding Practical Implications for Management. She has published articles in the *Academy of Management Journal, Administrative Science Quarterly*, the *Journal of Organizational Behavior* and *Harvard Business Review*, as well as numerous book chapters and practitioner-focused articles. She has lived and worked on four continents, including as a management consultant for McKinsey & Co and a Fulbright fellow. She earned a BA in Japanese studies from the University of Pennsylvania, a master's from the London School of Economics and a doctorate from the London Business School.

Bill Knight

williamjlknight@btinternet.com

Bill Knight was senior partner of Simmons & Simmons until his retirement in 2001. Since leaving the firm he has served deputy chairman of council at Lloyd's of London, a gambling commissioner, chairman of the Financial Reporting Review Panel and a director of the Financial Reporting Council. He was a specialist adviser to the Treasury Select Committee in relation to the Financial Services Authority's report into the failure of Royal Bank of Scotland. In 2012 he was awarded the OBE for services to financial regulation.

Mr Knight is one of the founders of BCKR, a company which exists to encourage lawyers to obtain board appointments. He is a qualified coach and a professional photographer (www.knightsight.co.uk).

Sarah Martin

Programme director and leadership coach,
Saïd Business School; Coombs Martin
sarah@coombsmartin.com

Sarah Martin is a programme director and leadership coach at Saïd Business School. Ms Martin originally trained as a lawyer. She worked in mergers and acquisitions at Allen & Overy, and was senior counsel in the chairman's office of BP PLC. She has more than 20 years' business, legal and corporate governance practice at board level, combined with advanced training and experience as a business coach.

Ms Martin is also a founding partner in Coombs Martin, an executive coaching consultancy in London. She has been coaching professionals and executives since 2007. Her focus is on leadership in professional services firms. She is author of *Creating Effective Relationships in Law Firms* and *Effective Decision-Making in Law Firms*.

She holds an LLB from Manchester University and an MSc in management as a Sloan fellow at London Business School. She is an accredited business coach and special adviser to the International Bar Association Law Firm Mentoring Programme. She sits on the advisory boards of the Institute of Mentoring and of Human Rights Watch's Children's Division.

Lis Merrick

Managing director, Coach Mentoring Ltd
lismerrick@coachmentoring.co.uk

Lis Merrick is managing director of Coach Mentoring Ltd., a director of the Professional Mentor Academy Ltd, on the board and an accredited assessor for the International Standards for Mentoring Programmes in Employment and a visiting fellow of the Coaching and Mentoring Research Unit at Sheffield Business School.

Ms Merrick works as an executive coach and consultant in coaching and mentoring on a global basis, and has more than 25 years' experience of working in cross-cultural environments, including senior HR experience with the Thomas Cook Group and Merrill Lynch. Her experience in mentoring programme design and development is now nationally acclaimed in the United Kingdom, with over 60 mentoring programmes to her name. Her expertise and research is predominantly in the field of mentoring and coaching with regard to talent management, mentoring senior women and supervision in mentoring.

John E Montgomery

Executive director, National Legal Mentoring Consortium
jemontgo@law.sc.edu

John E Montgomery is executive director of the National Legal Mentoring Consortium, a national organisation with representation from all parts of the legal profession in the United States. The consortium promotes mentoring best practices. He also is dean emeritus of the University of South Carolina School of Law. He has participated in the design and evaluation of several bar mentoring programmes, and speaks and writes on mentoring in the legal profession.

Rebecca Normand-Hochman
Founder and director, Mentoring Collegium Limited, Institute of Mentoring
rebecca.normand-hochman@instituteofmentoring.org

Rebecca Normand-Hochman is the founder and director of the Institute of Mentoring, which provides insight, research and advice to advance mentoring best practices in the legal profession.

As a French-British former lawyer, Ms Normand-Hochman practised international finance law in London and in Paris. Her experiences as a lawyer with Allen & Overy in Paris laid the foundation for her present work in talent management.

She has carried out extensive research on law firm talent management, and her work draws on best practices and collaboration with leading experts in leadership, change management, coaching and mentoring.

Through her current work with the Institute of Mentoring and the involvement of a number of law firm partners, talent management experts, coaches and professors, Ms Normand-Hochman focuses on the subject of mentoring. She is pursuing research and providing advice to adapt best practices to the specificities and challenges that relate to the practice of law.

Since 2012, she has been leading the main talent management initiatives of the International Bar Association Law Firm Management Committee. These include the coordination of this book and *Managing Talent For Success* (2013), and leading the International Bar Association Law Firm Mentoring Programme. She is an officer and advisory board member of the Law Firm Management Committee.

Sally Sanderson
Director, Profex Consulting
sallysanderson@profexconsulting.com

Sally Sanderson is a multi-award winning consultant to law firms and has been working in the professional services sector for more than 25 years. She provides bespoke leadership development programmes for a range of law firms from magic circle to niche practices, and works in the United Kingdom and internationally.

Her awards include two from the UK Legal Education and Training Group: Best Training Provider 2011 for a programme which could demonstrate quantifiable improvements, and Trainer of the Year 2003 for her "professionalism, enthusiasm and credibility, understanding of the legal market and ability to ensure programmes are relevant and tailored".

Ms Sanderson has a degree in English from Oxford, and managed learning and development departments at Arthur Andersen and Theodore Goddard before setting up Profex Consulting in 2001. She is a fellow of the Chartered Institute of Personnel and Development.

Robert Sharpe
Psychologist
rs@robertsharpe.com

Robert Sharpe is a chartered psychologist with a clinical and mentoring consultancy in London W1. He holds a PhD in psychology and specialises in relationship development, resilience building and mentoring of law firm partners and partner-track associates. He is director of mentoring psychology at the Institute of Mentoring.

Dr Sharpe is an accomplished seminar leader and workshop facilitator who regularly advises senior management of law firms, ranging in size from major internationals to single-office, local firms. He has extensive experience in cross-cultural cooperation in the workplace, having consulted within more than 20 law firm offices in Europe, Asia, Australia and the United States.

The author of three popular applied psychology books, Dr Sharpe also carries out legal reporting, advises on strategy and facilitates the on-boarding of lateral hires. Responsive, available and collegial, he is equally at home advising on high-level strategy or practical specifics. His passions are one-on-one mentoring and development of individual excellence.

Nigel Spencer
Global director of learning and development, Reed Smith LLP
nspencer@reedsmith.com

Nigel Spencer is currently at international law firm Reed Smith LLP, where he is responsible for designing and implementing the firm's talent development strategy globally. An accredited executive coach (Meyler Campbell Business Coach), Dr Spencer has embedded coaching in experiential leadership development programmes for staff and clients and also created internal coaching faculties.

Dr Spencer co-chairs the national body of legal education professionals (the Legal Education Training Group), working with international business schools to conduct research into coaching, leadership development and strategy. He is also a member of the Saïd Business School Coaching Community in Oxford and coaches for its executive programmes.

Previously, Dr Spencer created the first graduate full-time MBA in the legal sector, worked at PricewaterhouseCoopers, and before that in academia, directing international interdisciplinary research projects, latterly as a senior research fellow at Worcester College, Oxford. His research and publications have focused on group dynamics, hierarchy, power, agency and cultural change.

Jon Stokes
Director, Stokes & Jolly Ltd; Saïd Business School, Oxford University
js@stokesjolly.com

Jon Stokes is a director of leadership and management development firm Stokes & Jolly Ltd (www.stokesjolly.com). He is a business psychologist and leadership coach who consults and advises at board and senior levels on senior leadership development, leadership transitions and the in-depth assessment and selection of senior executives. Mr Stokes trained and worked as a psychologist and psychotherapist at the Tavistock Clinic and Institute in London, where he became director of the Adult Psychotherapy Department and then the founder-director of the Tavistock's Organisational Consultancy Service. Mr Stokes is an associate fellow of Oxford University's Said Business School, where he teaches on leadership, an associate faculty member of Henley Business School, where he works on the Advanced Personal Leadership Programme, and an associate at the Institute for Government.

Sally Woodward
Founding principal, Sherwood PSF Consulting
sally.woodward@sherwoodpsfconsulting.com

Sally Woodward has 30 years' experience working as a leadership coach and consultant specialising in supporting clients through organisational and personal change. She also teaches coaching skills to leaders as an associate faculty member at Meyler Campbell, the leading trainer of business coaches. Her existing client base includes senior lawyers and other professionals in both international law firms and in-house departments. Ms Woodward began her career as a law academic at Cambridge University, then practised as a solicitor before doing an MBA at London Business School and holding a senior management role in the leading firm of Freshfields during that firm's rapid growth from 1985 to 1997. Ms Woodward is co-director of the Law Management Programme at *Instituto Empresa* in Madrid, having previously, with Stephen Mayson, developed and taught for 10 years on the groundbreaking MBA in legal practice management at Nottingham Law School.